Brave New Pitch

Samir Chopra is professor of philosophy at Brooklyn College of the City University of New York. He blogs at The Pitch on ESPNcricinfo and at samirchopra.com. He can be found on Twitter as @EyeOnThePitch. He is the co-author of *The India–Pakistan Air War of 1965* (Manohar Publishers, 2005); *Decoding Liberation: The Promise of Free and Open Source Software* (Routledge, 2007) and *A Legal Theory for Autonomous Artificial Agents* (University of Michigan Press, 2011). He is currently working on a book on the 1971 India–Pakistan Air War (HarperCollins, 2013).

Brave New Pitch

The Evolution of Modern Cricket

SAMIR CHOPRA

Harper
Sport

First published in 2012 in Harper Sport
An imprint of HarperCollins *Publishers* India
a joint venture with
The India Today Group

Copyright © Samir Chopra 2012

ISBN: 978-93-5029-371-3

2 4 6 8 10 9 7 5 3 1

Samir Chopra asserts the moral right to be identified
as the author of this work.

HarperCollins *Publishers*
A-53, Sector 57, Noida, Uttar Pradesh 201301, India
77-85 Fulham Palace Road, London W6 8JB, United Kingdom
Hazelton Lanes, 55 Avenue Road, Suite 2900, Toronto, Ontario M5R 3L2
and 1995 Markham Road, Scarborough, Ontario M1B 5M8, Canada
25 Ryde Road, Pymble, Sydney, NSW 2073, Australia
31 View Road, Glenfield, Auckland 10, New Zealand
10 East 53rd Street, New York NY 10022, USA

Typeset in Calisto MT 10/13
InoSoft Systems Noida

Printed and bound at
Thomson Press (India) Ltd.

Dedicated to Papa and Mukesh Mama, for making cricket romantic, always

Contents

CHAPTER 1

Brave New Pitch

In July 2008, Mahendra Singh Dhoni, Indian wicketkeeper and future captain, opted out of a Test series in Sri Lanka claiming overwork and fatigue.[1] Dhoni had just finished playing in the inaugural season of the Indian Premier League (IPL) and in two one-day international tournaments—the Kitply and Asia Cups. In April 2010, during the IPL's third season, after playing a crucial match-winning innings for the Chennai Super Kings, Dhoni, by then a highly successful and well-regarded captain of the national cricket team, disarmingly and candidly remarked, 'Your franchise pays you so much money, you should at least make the semi-finals.'[2] Dhoni's remarks sparked controversy among those who remembered his declining Test duty for the nation, but all he had done was draw attention to the truth that there were new paymasters in town, likely to skew priorities in a manner already visible to all.

Change, supposedly, is the only invariant. This quasi-adage rings especially true in cricket which, while often termed a charming bastion of conservatism, has morphed over the years as colourfully as a chameleon and as bewilderingly as the shapeshifters of ancient mythologies. Modern cricket bears as much resemblance to the village green game of the nineteenth-century as the jet airliner bears to the horse-drawn buggies that clattered down roads in the years gone by. Predictions and prognostications in cricket are thus a perilous business.

Still, cricket shows in its continuing evolution and current dynamics, the possible outlines of its future configurations; where cricket might proceed in the years to come may be revealed by an examination of its tumultuous present and its recent most important changes. Cricket's form, whether the action on the field, or the machinations off it, will change; given the incessant flux of the sporting world's political economy, and indeed, cricket's own history, it would be foolish to imagine a perennially static game. The most important drivers of this transformation are likely to be a familiar combination: the fans, the administrators, the players, and the broader social-economic-technical home the 'external' world provides; the game will continue to act as a lens, prism and mirror for these embeddings.

A variety of forces have shaped cricket's recent dynamic evolution: political, via the arena it provides for the clash of nationalist aspirations; technical, via the radical changes the media has wrought, starting from Kerry Packer's televised revolution and continuing on to today's utter dependency on television rights deals, the cricket channels on YouTube, the effervescent community of cricket bloggers that provides the best writing on the game, the Twitter feeds that led to the sinking of Lalit Modi's fortunes as IPL commissioner, and continue to embarrass any player foolish enough to fire off one hundred and forty intemperate characters; and economic, via the change in labour relationships made possible by Kerry Packer's World Series of Cricket (WSC), the Indian Cricket League (ICL) and the IPL, as well as contemporary work patterns that make the shorter game, the day-night Test, the impatience with the loss of time in a Test, realities that drive the game into ever-new directions.

Cricket's current state of ferment often signals encounters of thesis and antithesis, in the contemporary clashes between Twenty20 tournaments and Test and first-class cricket, between the 'Anglo-Australian axis' of Old Cricket Power and the Board of Control for Cricket in India (BCCI), encounters that require the constant engineering of syntheses satisfactory to those interested in cricket's ultimate welfare. Some of cricket's future is justly feared; some envisaged changes promise to transform the game into a generic accompaniment to the mass-produced entertainments of our times. Cricket has maintained a steadfast heterogeneity from the world of sport, sometimes risking marginalization, sometimes risking classification as not-modern; the loss of this distinctness, this cricketing culture, deserves a better coda, if one is necessary, than an undignified, rushed, showing of the door.

But cricket's future form could also confound the Cassandras, in being genuinely rich and exciting in a way that caters to the changing tastes of the world's fans and players, that appropriately utilizes the avenues opened up by a new media world, that sees its limited-overs versions not as parasites but as genuinely productive and enriching symbionts. This future does not require one format's prosperity to cost the demise of another; rather it requires an ecological balancing, a mix of appropriate prioritization, scheduling and incentivizing by administrators, players, and media rights holders alike. This non-competitive future for cricket's different formats requires all concerned to bring both pragmatism and idealism to their deliberations and machinations for cricket's next steps.

Cricket's longevity is a function of its commanding a loyal following that has produced a rich, complex set of traditions. These are not to be overturned lightly. In particular, Test cricket, a marvellous exception to most things sporting, in its refusal to embrace modernity, its embrace of ambiguity in its results, and the prime underwriter of the rich fount of fan fantasy crucial to cricket's construction of legends, deserves respectful care to shepherd it through the rough seas it is currently navigating. Test cricket needs not just public avowals of respect and support, but concrete safeguards; not a constant public berating for failing to 'entertain' but rather, an acknowledgement of its hard-won pleasures, much as one might defend the tome-like novel against the comic book. To do so is not to denigrate the comic book; it is merely to point out the novel's distinct pleasures.

Thus, cricket's possibly-rich future needs an infusion of a judicious blend of conservative and revolutionary visions; in this book, I will often take turns at adopting their perspectives. The conservative is sceptical of poorly managed, destructive experiments; the latter welcomes the experiment, even if destructive. A classic statement of the conservative position is, 'More money in cricket is a good thing provided...professionalization is responsibly managed. That means making changes conservatively and, crucially, resisting the impulse to trade in the integrity of the game for revenue.'[3] The revolutionary position appears implicitly in fervid hopes that the IPL—and leagues like it—grows in leaps and bounds, displacing international Test cricket as variants of the IPL squat squarely over the cricketing landscape.

Such calls for moderation, for tightrope walking of the highest order, are justified because no other game in the world seems to face a crisis, even if possibly creative, quite like the one cricket does today; no other game's community is engrossed in a debate about the possible overturning of centuries' long tradition in favour of a new format and organization that bring a new understanding of its most basic notions. No other game appears to have its fortunes tied so closely to the economic and sporting health of one participant; no sport is bankrolled to quite the same extent by one entity. That dependency has already dramatically skewed modern cricketing conversations; like all dependencies, it breeds charges of arrogance, cultivates resentment and demands responsibility; it will continue to be the most important factor in all discourse about cricket for the foreseeable future.

It is contemporary common wisdom to describe world cricket through the prism of the rise to sporting and economic power of Indian cricket, the Indian cricket team, the BCCI, and the IPL. These entities are not identical; their conflation can be both edifying and problematic. But one or the other will persist in remaining front and centre in any discussion on cricket today. Most particularly, thanks to the IPL, to attempt a description of cricket at this juncture of the game's history while ignoring the possible move from nation-based Test and one-day international cricket to global franchise-based Twenty20 cricket is to feign not having noticed the proverbial eight-hundred pound gorilla. The changes that franchise-based cricket promises are 'radical' in a way that does justice to the etymology of the word, for they go to the very roots of the game as its fans know it; both the initial indictments of, and the hosannas paid to, the IPL revealed the deepest fears and the most extravagant promises of franchise-based cricket. The Twenty20 league represents the logical culmination of a drive always present in cricket: the eager, bustling, commercial sensibility that has jostled for space on cricket's stage with its other, more staid, actors. But former jostlers were content to share the limelight; this new upstart threatens to buy the theatre company as well.

The Twenty20 league has forced a conversation about the relevance of Test cricket in the modern world, about fans' and administrators' understanding of players as professionals—and not quasi-bonded labour paying steady, unquestioned homage to the nation—and about the relationship of entertainment and business to sport. Thus, in responding to the IPL, and to the potential for revolutionary change that it embodies, it has become possible to speak of a great deal more in various registers. Speaking of the IPL might even provide moments of personal archaeology. What drew us to the game? What is it the cricketing conservative seeks to preserve? What does the cricketing revolutionary seek to overthrow? What does the revolutionary intend as replacement?

If all the changes promised by the IPL and its brethren are not to be embraced, that will not be because the world of cricket needs no remedy; the IPL found the place it did because of genuine problems and expressed needs. Addressing these provides an opportunity for the game to reconfigure itself; cricket might still find a way to return to its older, hopefully suitably modified, methods, to ensure a richer future without delving into all that was found problematic in the IPL and its associated franchise model.

Which path cricket takes will ultimately be determined, hopefully, by conversations amongst its fans, players and administration; this book hopes to be a part of it, by providing a fan's perspective, one steeped in 'dreaming, realism and history'[4] in equal measure, one struggling to find cricket's place in the modern world, one not yet sure of his own role in cricket's imagined future.

The India Complication

If India looms large in these pages, it is because the future of the game appears so dependent on the Indian fan, the Indian player, the Indian consumer, not just in India, but around the world as well. To not be India-centric when writing on modern cricket seems merely feigned cosmopolitanism. For cricket has made a passage from Anglo-Australian export to sporting centrepiece of a new economy, embedded in a new culture. The balance sheets of the BCCI and the IPL, the size of Indian television audiences, which often give modern television rights deals their impressive heft and drive the salaries of players worldwide, the editorship of the world's biggest cricket website, India's victory in the 2011 World Cup, the dependence of the International Cricket Council's (ICC) decision-making on the BCCI's concurrence—have meant that India has come to occupy a central position in cricket.

This imagery has resulted in considerable dissonance, resulting too often in debates about the IPL and the modern administration of cricket degenerating into accusations and counter-accusations of bad faith, colonial hang-ups, oversensitivity and a little too much sneering than might be deemed healthy for all concerned. Thus, sincere worries about the perversion of the game's ethos by a vulgar entertainment culture or overzealous, myopic commercialization, are often complicated by the taint of an apparent lack of tolerance for a change in the identity of the helmsmen of cricket. Conversely, the promising injection of dynamic entrepreneurship into the sometimes hidebound global management of cricket is too often borne along on a cloud of myopic contempt for any attempt to retain tradition or promote temperance.

Concerns about cricket's future in modern debates can, all too often, seem like fears of the rise of Indian cricket, of the take-over of a garden party by the nouveau riche, and of the displacement of the cultural, national character of the game, as evidenced by the anguished cries of Anglo-Australian administration, media and fans, which greet most moves made by the BCCI or the Indian cricket team. Nothing would explain the anxiety expressed by this Anglo-Australian axis better than deep-rooted fears of not just the nature of the game but its associated symbolic culture changing. Apprehension about this culture's displacement might explain some of the angst so visibly on display in recent times. It cannot be the mere presence of moneyed influence; professionalism and its new priorities were introduced into cricket well before the BCCI's balance sheets made their appearance. It cannot be the vulgarity of coloured clothes, white balls, music on a cricket field or the garish televised spectacle; those were introduced to world cricket well before Lalit Modi sold the rights for a DLF Moment of Success. The identity of the agent of change thus appears as a complicating

factor in discussions about modern cricket. Its recurrence in the pages
to follow is unavoidable.

The IPL: Jaldi and Tamasha

In his *History of Indian Cricket,* Mihir Bose introduces the reader to two
words familiar to every Indian—if not in Hindustani, then in their
vernacular equivalents: jaldi, the exhortation to hurry up, and tamasha,
an entertainment, or more perspicuously, a show. The peculiarity of a
supposedly laid-back culture giving rise to the decidedly unmellow rush
for the exits on the Delhi Metro, the relentless cajoling for a hurry-up
on the street, the tea stall, the shop counter, the board room, is not
lost on any visitor to India. Thus in a country that would appear to
be eminently suited to the longer form of the game, where the whiling
away of mornings with endless cups of tea and the late-night dinner
were cultural ideals that produced Test cricket's most dedicated fans,
it was ironically unsurprising and perhaps inevitable that it would play
home to the hurried-up tamasha of the IPL and turn it into the grinning
Cheshire cat of the cricket world, contemplating the next saucerful of
tradition and entrenched power-relations to be demolished.

The IPL's initial seasons provoked a welter of emotions, and
responses both condemnatory and adulatory. In the former dimension
were worries about its influence on Test cricket, aesthetic discomfort
at the crass commercialization on display, including perhaps the
prominence the television cameras afforded the grinning visage of Lalit
Modi, and concern about its ability to upend the motivational structures
of domestic and international cricket in a wholly destructive fashion.
In the latter, there was admiration, and not just emanating from India,
for its delivery of an exciting multinational assemblage of players, its
broadening of the appeal of cricket, its elevation of player salaries to
levels that promised genuine post-career security, its provision of an
entertainment package neatly wrapped for the post-work hours, its
promise, via the franchise system, of a chance for cricket to join the
modern sporting world, earn the prestige associated with a premier
international sports league, develop a worldwide labour market for
cricketing professionals, and truly enjoy a global expansion.

The clash between those that feared and despised the IPL and those that paid obeisance to it, or at the least, were enamoured of its revolutionary potential, was thus laid out along clearly marked and fiercely defended battle lines. Reactions to the IPL have changed over the years, and no analysis of the IPL's influence can discount the changes in its fortunes and leadership, and the roller coaster ride it has undergone from its triumphant opening night in Bangalore on 18 April 2008, garlanded by Brendon McCullum's furious 158, to Lalit Modi's maudlin, rambling, Bhagavad Gita-invoking farewell speech at the close of the third IPL, to the staggering paydays enjoyed by Indian players at the fourth and fifth season's auctions, and the drop in its television ratings following India's victory in the 2011 World Cup. This last event introduced a further wrinkle in speculation about the IPL's influence, as it boosted nation-based cricket and its supposedly moribund fifty-over version; the decline in television ratings also made it apparent that the Indian fan's supposedly limitless appetite for cricket did in fact have a saturation point.

ENFANT TERRIBLE

The initial negative reactions to the IPL were of a piece with the cricket world's opening responses to Twenty20 cricket: dismay at the sheer vulgarity of games dressed up like charity events put on by celebrities, where the cricket seemed disjointed and over-accelerated, where the batting—with its boundary-rope-clearing emphasis—was one-dimensional, and bowlers were reduced to glorified extras, one step away from being replaced by costumed bowling machines. This spectacle was set off by strobe lights, loud music, cheerleaders, fireworks, and disc jockeys' exhortations. Never before had the game's managers so underestimated the attention span of a cricket fan as they did during an IPL game. The presence of Bollywood and its representatives, whether as team owners, fans, or template suppliers for the choreographed dance number that the typical IPL match appeared to be dressed up as, rounded out the picture of excess and crassness. Cricket, as we knew it, appeared to be missing. As Mukul Kesavan, the IPL's most pungent and acerbic critic, noted, 'As a cricket match, it was awful…somewhere along the way, Lalit Modi…mislaid the cricket.'[5]

These aesthetic worries were followed by apprehension about the IPL's effect on Test cricket, which seemed destined for supplanting by the rich, crowd-pleasing, telegenic new entrant that promised that Holy Grail of all employment deals: more money for less work. Test cricket appeared headed for the status of quaint relic, and first-class cricket, that nursery of the longer versions of the game, seemed curiously irrelevant. The sheer size of IPL player salaries threatened to trample any aspirations a cricket player might have for the national, longer form, especially as the IPL's status as domestic tournament meant other countries' international schedules were not in sync with its season, creating one conflict after another for players worldwide and leading to that age-old debate of professional sport: country or club? The IPL seemed to have started to play the role that Europe's rich professional soccer leagues had played vis-à-vis South American soccer clubs in the past: luring the best, the young, and the promising away from national duty.

The IPL's potential to establish or at least serve as a template for a global franchise or club system was perhaps the most revolutionary threat to established structures, for it could subvert the usual motivational schemes for players, and not just by offering fat pay cheques to rookies over veteran internationals, to brawny hitters over Test cricket's classiest batsmen, to trundlers who could swing the bat over Test cricket's ace predators, its strike bowlers. Fame within the new league could be delinked from the international game; a successful sports league, as evident in its many successful American and European incarnations, creates its own mythologies, its own stars, its own legends. If the Twenty20 franchise world expanded, contingent on a sustained friendship with television viewers, by team and season expansion—as in the case of the IPL—or by copycat leagues such as Australia's Big Bash League (BBL), each demanding their own season windows, then the oft-wished-for extinction of the ICC could rapidly become a rather mundane reality.[6]

Indeed, the IPL's promises made the entire geography based structure of global cricket administration seem archaic. Perhaps cricket fans all over the world could enjoy the spectacle of a truly international league, made up of clubs employing the world's best players, not shackled to country or state, paid fair wages, free to contract with the highest bidder. Fans could enjoy a standard of cricket that might be higher than the one

sometimes visible in international cricket, which all too often, even at
the supposedly highest level of the Full Members of the ICC, regularly
featured poorly-attended mismatches. Here, Bangladesh and Zimbabwe
scrambled for respectability, and former cricketing powers like the West
Indies—handicapped by dysfunctional administration—struggled to
regain past glory. (India's embarrassing away run in Test cricket in
2011–12 in England and Australia had, for some, almost relegated
them to this level.) Cricket would be following the seemingly exemplary
example of soccer, whose international clubs, Champions League, and
World Cup have long been the envy of the sporting world. Perhaps
unbridled commercialization, hopefully professionally managed, and
without duty-to-nation-and-the-game posturing, could revitalize the
game. Corporate management seemed like a judicious move—away
from the sight of national boards run as fiefdoms by politicians.

These possibilities understandably provoked genuine fears about
a subversion of the game's ethos. The traditionalists' worries about
the IPL's clear obsession with the monetary bottom line—evidenced
in its too-tight embrace of the commercial sponsor, or its casual take
on transparency and honest governance—seemed vindicated after the
horrendous, scandal-ridden close of its third season, as it offered an
unflattering contrast with the games it supposedly sought to emulate.[7]
The suspected overreach had turned out to be true; other professionalized
sports had managed to successfully triangulate the balance sheet,
the need to provide entertainment and the monetary ambitions of
players. But the BCCI and the IPL had set themselves apart in rather
unflattering distinctiveness; their relationship with the sport seemed to
have been infected, deeply and offensively, by the proverbial filthy lucre.
That most irritating of situations for a cricket fan had been allowed to
transpire: there was not much cricket to be talked about, just tales of
financial perfidy and political skullduggery.

The IPL's 'fall' in the third season was to have an adverse effect on
those who saw its success as a vindication of their nationalist spirit,
as cause for Indian pride. For the IPL seemed to have turned into
the usual Indian showcase for corruption, politics and cronyism, the
problems every Indian was sick and tired of hearing about. The IPL
was supposed to be a symbol of an ever-more influential, dynamic and
prosperous India, a highlighter of its organizational skills and wealth.

To be told there was yet other scam at its heart, involving familiar litanies of resignations, suspensions and scandal, was to traffic in severe disillusionment. The BCCI and the IPL in the third season had shown too, how cricket seemed unable to find a golden mean between the shamateurism of the past, with all its associated inefficiencies and disingenuousness, and the rambunctious, seemingly morality-free entrepreneurship of the present.

Concerns about the IPL, thus, were expressed in several dimensions, by Indian and external commentators alike; expressions of virtuous commitment to Test cricket and the international calendar were greeted by a chorus of approval from the English and Australian media; every announcement of a retirement from Test cricket to concentrate on the IPL stretched the worry lines just a little tighter on all visible brows; Indian superstars like Rahul Dravid refused to rate it higher in its cricketing dimensions than a domestic tournament; and even a non-established Test cricketer like Yuvraj Singh was quick to point out the effect the IPL could have on international cricket and player commitment.[8]

The most dramatic proof—for Indian worriers, and others like them, of the pernicious influence of the IPL, over and above the long list of players choosing the IPL over Test duty, or emerging injured from an IPL season unavailable for international duty—were the Indian Test team's catastrophic defeats at the hands of England and Australia in 2011–12. Blame for this, for some, could be laid squarely at the IPL's doors: it had ruined Test techniques for batsmen, bowlers and captains alike, and sapped the desire to play long-form cricket. And as sponsors spoke of abandoning the Indian cricket team in the wake of these disasters, others wondered if, ironically, the IPL, rather than being the harbinger of greater wealth for Indian cricket, might induce penury instead.

What the IPL had done was propel competing visions of the game to the fore and force the oldest questions about its nature to be asked, whether in the making of the critical responses just noted, or in the defences of the league offered by its proponents. It also meant that these questions had to be answered before the IPL's revolutionary potential could be evaluated, for the promised revolution would mean naught if it left little trace of the game in its wake.

Cricket: Sport, Entertainment or Business?

The primary worry about the IPL is money, that irritant which ensures the constant presence of sports in our lives but manages to infuriate, annoy and offend nevertheless. The role of money in sport cannot be diminished but the acknowledgement of its importance has brought with it the uneasy feeling that the previously incorruptible has been rendered unclean.[9] This incorruptibility is a myth, but like all good myths, its origins are shrouded in obscurity and it is surprisingly resilient.

Cricket and commercial interests have always gone hand in hand. Even a cursory reading of the history of the game reveals talk of guarantee money, gate incomes, player fees, ticket prices, and contracts; talk, in short, of all the financial and managerial trappings of a game. These histories reveal too, clashes uncannily similar to contemporary ones: exhortations to play the game for the game's sake; worries about distortions of nation-and-game-first priorities and accusations of greed and overreach. A fan hoping to find exclusive focus on Olympian aspirations in the history of his beloved game might be crestfallen to find them accompanied by rather mundane tales of monies and balance sheets; it is part of the inevitable disillusionment of growing up as a sports fan to find out that one's heroes have a touch of the mercenary to them, that the grand amphitheatres of sports, the stadiums, are symbols of economic, not just sporting, power. The relationship of the fan to money in sport is thus a little schizophrenic: appreciative of the facilitation it provides and yet resentful that the attention paid to it constantly threatens to upend his most beloved of passions. This schizophrenia is all-pervasive, best evident in fans' sincere desire to reward players as professionals while simultaneously expecting them to successfully comprehend and internalize fans' needs, many of which are far removed from player priorities.

The disillusionment of the sports fan, his recurring worry about corruption, speak to a deep-rooted belief that what is being corrupted is no mere enterprise, but something that can command allegiance, respect and fervour. In this reckoning, sports require, almost conceptually, the subordination of individual interests to a larger, more abstract whole;

it is an understanding of sports that is in fundamental clash with the raison d'etre of profit-seeking enterprises.

Modern cricket faces the possibility of being framed in a manner sharply at odds with the ways its idolaters would have it. These take two particular forms: the first, that it is merely business; the other, probably more insidious and harder to dismiss, that it is merely entertainment.[10] But these framings of cricket are not likely to work in the way their most ardent advocates would like; such descriptions fail to do justice to the passion, commitment and dedication of players and fans. Their dismissive words work as a rhetorical ploy to cut off argument at the pass because once it is granted that sports is entertainment, all else follows: all entertainments are run like businesses, therefore, so should cricket. Quod erat demonstrandum.

The description of cricket as a business, and a business alone, does severe injustice to an activity termed a game, but which triggers responses decidedly less secular.[11] The 'it's only a business' argument, while likely to gain some traction just because all contemporary arguments employing market logic will, is unlikely to appeal to a significant constituency, one aware of cricket's history and its embedding in particular cultural practices.

In such a setting, the identification of cricket with the standard corporate tropes of 'products' or 'properties' induces a severely myopic distortion. A 'product' conjures up images of quality control and ISO-9000 certifications; it fails to tickle the sensibility of a fan worrying about the loss of a peculiarly personal relationship. A 'property' speaks of ownership, of proprietary relations; a curious set of descriptions to attach to an entity that appears to require conscientious collective stewarding instead. It is no coincidence that some putatively commercial entities—like a wildlife refuge for public use, for instance—are run by the state or understood as a public trust; the application of the financial bottom line to them can lead to management decisions that distort the activity on hand.

Nowhere is the self-defeating nature of the claim that cricket is just a business more visible than when the role of the national cricket board is viewed as that of a business corporation and the two are supposed identical. The board of directors of a languishing enterprise is always eminently justified in focusing its attentions on the most immediate, profit-generating move. But it is implausible that the world's cricket fans would rest content if boards of cricket control were to be diverted by the pursuit of more lucrative ventures. General Electric's decision, several years ago, to pursue corporate leasing and finance, and reduce its manufacturing footprint was not a noteworthy news item; such transfers of allegiance are common when the corporate bottom line is at stake, its shareholders are content, the disgruntled employees are small in number and in any case, increasingly irrelevant in a corporate calculus. But the failure of the Brooklyn Dodgers to account for the feelings of their fans in deserting Brooklyn explains the intense dislike Walter O'Malley, the then owner of the Dodgers, still inspires in Brooklyn. This animosity is part of the cultural history of the borough. No mere business can inspire this reaction. Perhaps even devotees of the market, loudly proclaiming its right to be the final arbiter of every cricketing decision, would not be reconciled to the decision of national cricket boards to simply seek greener pastures. The application of cold market-based rationalizations to sport reaches its limit when we consider hypothetical situations like these.

Thus the rush to commercialize a game in the name of entertainment runs up against some irresistible barriers. We are edified and possibly entertained when we visit a national park with soaring mountain peaks, verdant forests and clear rivers; we are grateful the park's financial viability is sustained by engaged corporate sponsors; does this licence the steady, ugly, defacement of its roads by billboards, or the beaming of laser shows on its visible cliffs? Must this village too be destroyed in order to save it? The cricket fan's suspicions are evoked because cricket's recent rush to untrammeled commercialization, its hurry to pay homage to the market, whether in the reckless pursuit of an ever-bigger role for Twenty20 cricket, or in the subservience to the television rights deal, pays little attention to empirical realities, i.e., the actual relationship fans have to the game. Such sensitivity might judiciously attenuate the commercializing urge and induce a temperance that could enrich the game for the fan while preserving the commercial imperative for its underwriters.

The irony inherent in cricket in being excessively beholden to the commercial corporate ideal is reinforced by a simple journey to the cricketing nurseries of the backyard, the street, the school, and the park with its weekend competitions. It is singularly impossible to describe the activity witnessed there as 'just a business' or 'just an entertainment'. The indispensability of money is not to be confused with cricket's raison d'etre; that is to confuse dependency with purpose.

As such, the eager rush by some Twenty20 devotees to dismiss the built-up traditions and understanding of cricket, to straitjacket cricket into the generic template of all mass-produced entertainments, beggars belief, for no game that was treated as a business alone could ever have tolerated the anachronism of the Test match, cricket's most singular and glorious contribution to the world of sport.

The sense of the corruption of cricket by the commercial nexus of the greedy administrator and the media corporation is not comprehensible then, in the reductive frameworks of 'just business' or 'just entertainment'. The protectiveness the game provokes speaks of a far deeper emotional investment by the fan. From the sporting point of view, it is precisely when a sport is not treated purely as entertainment that sporting excellence flourishes; the emotional commitment of the fan follows in the wake of such treatment. The exploitation of a sport as a business too, only works when the sporting aspects are given prime importance. When the business becomes the end in itself, the game is up, and the deception is revealed for all to see.

So cricket remains first and foremost a game, with the substantive dispute at hand one about the best way of running it so as to preserve its character, evident from its history, its actual playing and following. Such an understanding permits a selective borrowing from the worlds of entertainment and business. This jerrymandering could be wholly positive: draw on the energy, the drive, the bustle of the business world; draw on the entertainment world's concern for the spectator; but be wary of their excesses. Draw on the discipline of the corporation, the verve of the entertainer, but reject the crudity of the low-brow, and most importantly, do not disdain the game itself as something requiring such elaborate disguise in its 'marketed' and 'packaged' form that it is obscured and rendered well-nigh invisible.

Thus the IPL—and any Twenty20 league like it—rightly provides entertainment, but it must provide cricket too. At some point, the cricket should take centre stage, and if it does not, the Twenty20 league idea will have failed. Not because it did not provide enough entertainment, but because it did not provide enough cricket. Concentration on cricket and its competitive ideals will be how the Twenty20 league will establish itself as more than a weightless diversion; otherwise little will be retained in fans' minds beyond the odd six-hitting escapade, and none of the devotion of the fan, so necessary to the success of a sporting enterprise, will be expended on its offerings.

The IPL, at its best moments, had promised a great deal. The most alluring prospect was the provision of a template for world cricket that could provide cricket of high quality (via its multinational teams), pay its players fairly (its pay scales promised a genuine spreading of the wealth), exploit the new media appropriately (as in the innovative use of YouTube for live streaming of games), and preserve the game's most essential contest, that between bat and ball (well, that one needed some tweaking). That new entrant on the scene, the franchise, has much to do with the possible fulfilment of these promises, but it faces challenges aplenty in reconciling cricket's many competing imperatives.

CHAPTER 2

Patriots or Professionals?

The disruption and possible displacement of international cricket by the Twenty20 league from calendars and priorities alike has many ramifications. The most salutary effect of the IPL's persistent posing of the question of club and country, of the possibility it suggests for a professional league not confined by the strictures of national boards, is the spotlight shone on questions about how different the ICC-run cricket world is from standard templates for professional sports leagues, how players could or would be treated in a genuine global professional sports league, and how they were treated by their boards and the ICC instead.

Cricket's modern dispute about sports as entertainment or business, about nation versus franchise, does not mask the fact that the cricket player needs to be paid for his services and treated as a professional, something the cricket world is yet to fully realize, especially when that tired old term of abuse, 'mercenary', gets trotted out, and whenever allegiance to the nation is questioned. What the IPL had done, as had various competitors for the ICC and 'official cricket' over the years, was raise questions about fans' understanding of players as professionals or patriots. Treating the player as patriot lent itself to the fervour of the fan; it enabled the creation of 'national teams'; it gave cricket a sometimes-problematic edginess; any displacement of this centrality of the nation would need very good reasons.

The Brave New World of No Nations

The most positive outcome of cricket's move away from a nation-based organizational structure to a city-based professional league might be an emotional detachment from the nation-based game. If nothing else, the franchise system promised to deliver a clearly needed chill pill to the perfervid nationalism that sometimes appeared to be cricket's most depressing companion. After the incessantly nasty, immature, and boorish India–Australia spats of 2007–2008, or the Darrell Hair–Sri Lanka–Pakistan feud, which are merely two examples of disputes infected by nationalist edginess that had acquired an ugly tinge, the IPL was a relief. Conversations about deals, parties, cheerleaders and Bollywood felt like a soothing balm to those who had had their fill of cricket whose passion was nation-driven. The sound of clubs clashing sounded rather more melodious than that of nations locking horns. The singular positive effect of the fiasco of John Howard's failed bid for the ICC presidency—with its reminder that racial barriers remained ever-present in the world of cricket, that the same old depressing divides riven into the history of the game had not gone anywhere, and had indeed taken on sharper focus while being amplified by modern media—was that it might have made fans, administrators, journalists and writers thoroughly sick of the nation-based divide in cricket.

Many in the world of cricket thus found the constant nationalistically-inflected bickering whether offline or on—shot through and through with charges of racial insensitivity and thin-skinned excessive sensitivity—wearying and offensive to their sensibilities. No other professional sport seemingly featured so much virulent wrangling between its post-colonially divided fans who expressed their unvarnished emotions so eloquently, profanely and vigorously, using every single affordance of modern media available to them. If this outpouring was any indicator, the world of cricket was painfully racked by a conflict only likely to be exacerbated by the continued baleful presence of the nation. The introduction of the franchise system seemed like a tempting cleansing solution, one that would make the nation irrelevant as a basis for cricketing arguments.

AT LOGGERHEADS, ON AND OFF THE PITCH

Nationalist feuding is inevitable in a game unique in treating bilateral international encounters as the highest form of the game with no worldwide, international league to allow the mingling of players into multinational outfits. The growing pains of World Series Cricket (WSC) in the 1970s were almost entirely due to the rigid association of 'top-class cricket' with 'official national teams' opposing each other. The cricket fan aches, more than any other, for the stamp of 'Certified International Contest' upon the game that he is watching.

The entrenchment of nationalist sentiment in cricket is particularly visible when national character, or a particular nation-wide psyche or characteristic, is praised (or blamed) for success (or failure) in cricket, or used as explanatory device in tales of perfidy in cricketing conversations, whether journalistic or amongst fans. Indian fans are quick to indulge in long bouts of theoretically dubious psychoanalytic speculation about the lack of national 'killer instinct' when it comes to finishing close games, with their diagnoses ranging from weather conditions to colonial histories to religious inclinations. Pakistani fans have a long tradition of regarding their country's endless production of fast bowlers as a vindication of national aggressiveness and a rejection of Indian 'Hindu' vegetarianism. Australians would have us believe that a particularly Antipodean brand of 'mateship' contributes to 5–0 Ashes victories, nowhere better exemplified than in the Australian team's visits to Gallipolli and John Buchanan's boot camps. The self-flagellation of the English fan is well-known. The list goes on. Thus, much speculation, conjecture and theorizing about nations and their alleged characteristics infects discussions about failure and success in cricket; many an afternoon can be whiled away finding examples of such deployments in cricketing rhetoric.

Some of this quasi-social-science theorizing is entertaining. It is mirth-inducing, after all, to be informed of the linkages between vegetarianism and failure to produce fast bowlers or between military victories and defeats and performance on a cricket field. Sometimes it is in the most allegedly serious of claims that one can find the most humour, precisely because of the tiny germ of truth blown up to grotesque proportions. Caricature works because it seizes upon a tiny feature and exaggerates it. These wonderfully entertaining theses, masquerading as deep analysis, often provide moments of hilarity. But the joke runs out eventually; too many of these claims are infuriatingly reductive, too many of them polarizing.

Nationalism's blessings have been decidedly mixed for cricket. Cricket has often not been a healing agent in patching up nationalist divisions. For every pair of cricketing fans who hail from distinct countries and have found friendship via the game, there is another that despises each other's team for all the wrong reasons, and is not shy of saying so, often anonymously, on the world of blog comments, Facebook Wall scribbles and Twitter tweets. Far from being a facilitator of friendships, cricket seems to provide a wonderful forum—if current online conversations are any indicator—for xenophobic displays of ignorance.

The healing power of the game of cricket thus, often, appears a rather sentimental, over-optimistic assessment. Despite cricket diplomacy, despite multinational games played all over the world between ragtag bunches of expatriates (the South Asian-dominated leagues, whether on university campuses or in suburban parks, in the US are now legend), despite the presence of large immigrant communities playing cricket in England and the US, despite oft-told tales of transnational bonhomie in stadium bleachers, there is little evidence that cricket has increased the level of co-operation or mutual trust between the members of the cricket fraternity. India and Pakistan might resume cricketing ties and play as many games as they used to in the bad old days of the over-scheduled 1980s, but it is unlikely that cricket will engender any diplomatic success not contingent on the success of other thaws in the countries' relationship. Despite the gushing encomiums written by the legions of Indian cricket fans that crossed the Wagah border for the 2003–2004 Test series, or the paeans sung to India–Pakistan friendship during the 2011 World Cup, the India–Pakistan relationship remains in precisely the same state it has always been: a febrile mix of distrust and suspicion, nicely spiced with a generous helping of mutual paranoia. After the India–Pakistan clash in the 2011 World Cup semi-final, and after many, many schoolboy tales of cross-border mingling, it took precisely one, admittedly crude, televised remark by Shahid Afridi to get things back on drearily familiar tracks.[1]

Similarly, despite the burgeoning business relationship between India and Australia, the entanglement of cricketing priorities, the growing Indian expatriate population in Australian metropolitan centres, the much-touted Australian admiration for Sachin Tendulkar, the establishment of Indian food on Australian palates, or the presence of Australian cricket stars in Bollywood, the cricketing rivalry between the two nations often seems to have done far more to worsen mutual misunderstanding and rancour than any other force. It is unclear even now, whether the violent, murderous attacks on Indian students in Melbourne in 2009–2010 were racially motivated. What was abundantly clear was that they would instantly serve as rhetorical ammunition in debates between the fans of the two cricket teams. 'Australia' is often on an Indian's lips; how much of it has acquired a bitter taste is, more likely than not, related to the cricketing rivalry between the two countries, whipped up by the hyperactive Indian media and the Murdoch Empire Down Under. The game is not to blame; but the playing of it in a format that pits nation against nation might easily be the culprit.

PUT THE FLAGS AWAY

The professional Twenty20 franchise's most salutary contribution to this state of affairs would be to provide a template for how cricket might be played, away from the anachronistic notion of a nation, with its depressing reminder of the toll it exacts every time a frenzied display of patriotism, that most passé of emotions, threatens to swamp rational discussion of the game's administration or future.

Thus the IPL, for all those who enjoyed the spectacle of former opponents playing on the same team, promised something genuinely liberatory: a chance to appreciate cricketing talent packaged in a form more amenable to universal appreciation. Those fans tired of suspecting cricketing arguments to be tainted by nationalist prejudice could rightly dream about a cricketing conversation where such prejudice was banished to the margins. Cricket fans have often cast envious glances at the multinational congregation of talent routinely available in the EPL or the NBA, and resigned themselves to making up World XIs for parlour games, online disputation, or tracking fantasy cricket leagues. So why not let the IPL grow as a model for a one-day international league or even more ambitiously, a Test cricket league? Away with England, away with India; in with the Delhi Dynamos versus the Pretoria Predators playing a Super Test at the Wanderers, with Mohammed Asif opening for Pretoria, bowling to Eoin Morgan playing for Delhi? Was dreaming of that all so bad?

At the least, cricket could aspire to manage the balance professional football has found between a club system that commands a passionate following spanning national divides while retaining space for nation-based tournaments, including the one-and-only quadrennial World Cup, the adulation and worship of which is unparalleled. Such an appropriate balance might be found and struck between franchise-based one-day and Twenty20 cricket in an international league, supplemented with a nation-based World Cup every other year for each format. Test cricket could perhaps survive in dedicated windows of time, in rivalries between countries that showed the talent and interest necessary to support it. Even if this would not banish nationalist bickering entirely, it would give it a reduced stage on which to peddle its not-benign wares.

A post-nation world for competitive cricket seems especially alluring when one considers that the lack of a nation to represent has never seemed to affect the willingness of a sportsman to display commitment or skill on the field. The possessor of sporting proficiency plays the game hard because of pride and competitive instinct; the game is often the arena for an overcoming of his own weaknesses, for a coming to terms with his mastery of its challenges. Michael Jordan's drive for an NBA title ring does not suffer in comparison to Sachin Tendulkar's quest for a World Cup; the notion that the absence of a nation in Jordan's motivational apparatus made it inferior to Tendulkar's would seem ludicrous to any serious sporting fan. The IPL's games have not lacked competitiveness either as its participants rapidly discovered new incentive schemes: a bigger pay cheque, a more secure future, less labour, and most importantly, competition against, and possible domination over, their sporting peers.

For some, the post-nation future promised by the IPL was predicated on evidence that in India it was helping fans develop allegiances indicative of a refreshing transcendence of national and state boundaries. Perhaps the IPL could serve as the matchmaker between cricket and a culture visible on the sports channels that youngsters in India's large urban centres devotedly track, that of the EPL's and the NBA's international jamborees. Perhaps support for the IPL franchise could be likened to support for Real Madrid, because it eschewed the parochial passions of nationalism for a more inclusive pluralism.

These claims about plurality, which invoke soccer teams and leagues, are curious, of course, given the ample evidence of the tribalism built deep into their structure of support; a post-nation future built on soccer-style tribalism seems especially ironic. Thus, in sharp contrast to optimism about the IPL's influence, many Indian commentators worried about its effect on 'regionalism'. How would a nation, used to the sometimes depressingly common news of religious or ethnic violence being broadcast in the coded template of conflicts between 'members of a particular community and another', respond to the aggressively jocular and possibly insensitive advertising of the IPL franchise?

These worries highlighted one problem with the promise of a post-nation future for cricket. The demise of the nation has often been foretold, but the nation has always been persistent and is unlikely to go away any time soon, especially in cricket, and especially when the entity driving most of the modern change in cricket was most definitely a nation, and a very particular one at that.

The Resilience of the Nation

For cricket fans bred on a diet of international cricketing rivalry, whether as old as the Ashes, or as new as the recent India–Australia encounters, a non-nation-based version of the game is not fervent enough to evoke those emotions they would most like cathartic release from when watching cricket. Part of the IPL's struggle for acceptance in the sensibilities of many fans, and not just those of Test cricket, has been to provide cricket in a form that tickles the fan's sense of the game's history, of a meaningful cricketing tussle; clashes between clubs do not seem to pit the appropriate opponents against each other. The cricket pitch is bound up in this kind of fan's mind, almost conceptually, for better or worse, with the battle of nations.

I FOR INDIA, FOR INDIAN

Moreover, even the success, current or eventual, of the IPL appeared to be dependent on an underwriting by a particular nationalist pride, possibly strong enough to float it even when economic realities did not. It appears necessary then, to be prepared for the supposedly market-driven IPL to make demands on nationalist sympathy and support. Sometimes it seemed that for all the revolutionary changes franchise cricket promises, in its initial years it will rely on the same tropes as nation-based cricket. This is not as surprising as it might appear.

The history of cricket is replete with stories of national aspirations finding expression on a cricket pitch, of post-colonial self-discovery, of race relations and class. To read cricket history is almost automatically to read the social histories of the nations that play the game. Transcending this history in favour of a club-based structure is not a trivial task. This is especially the case in India where the story of cricket is simultaneously the tale of a nation; speaking of a post-nation future of cricket in India assumes the nation is a done deal. But to visit the Indian north-east and the south, to read of the formation of new states, to witness the growth of new social classes, alliances and formations in response to India's new economy, is to be informed of a nation still in the making; nationalism has an unfinished agenda in this part of the world. In this context the IPL becomes merely a section in the latest chapter of the intertwined story of the Indian nation and Indian cricket.

Unsurprisingly, the most prominent and powerful positive reaction to the IPL in India was pride and wonderment at its Indian authorship, its visible flexing of national economic nous. Proud Indian responses to the IPL pointed to the irony of its promise to take cricket into a post-national world being reliant on the nationalist passion of the Indian fan, eager to put his weight behind the BCCI and the economic force of the nation, and to seize a place on the international sporting stage denied him thus far. The IPL had sparked an efflorescence of pride in the ability of the country to put on a globally noticed show, where the 'foreigner' came to receive payments and stopped being the dispenser of largesse.

Sometimes, with especial irony, Indian pride was particularly tickled because the IPL sparked praise from those familiar quarters still very important to the supposedly secure Indian self-esteem: the international media. For when cricket, via the IPL, did make it to the mainstream media in the US, it was in those venues like *Forbes,* the *Wall Street Journal,* or the *New York Times,* whose praise was likely to set the corporate patriot's heart racing. Praise in these quarters was not to be taken lightly; it still excites the Indian imagination.

So the IPL's promises and threats were implicitly or explicitly connected to national agendas. For some, it was an agent of cultural change, promising not only the professionalization of Indian sport but even the possibility that its cheerleaders would make Indians more comfortable with the female body; for others, it was the perfect showcase for the new cricketing India, for the stage it provided for the display of Indian cricketing talent, not just that of the world.

Thus, for more reasons than one, had a Twenty20 franchise-based league been the brainchild of anyone other than Lalit Modi, the new corporate symbol of India, or the BCCI, or not featured Indian players front and centre, it would not have enjoyed such passionate defences from its Indian fans. One breed of IPL enthusiasts had no problems with the IPL's blemishes on the playing field, the danger it posed to Test cricket—now increasingly viewed as an archaic form of the game—and the upending of the world's cricketing order, precisely because of the national identity of the agent of change. The perversity of this argument reached remarkable extremes with some Indian fans happy to talk down Test cricket, largely on the grounds that it appeared to be most enthusiastically supported by those two cricketing powers, Australia and England, which they saw as opposed to the rightful hegemonic role that India should occupy in the world of cricket.

This protectiveness towards the IPL was also visible in the fear and distrust directed at the foreign 'mercenary', whether manifest in the form of the disinterested international player punching his time card and collecting his pay cheque, or in cricket's equivalent of the mumbo-jumbo spouting management consultant, the team coach. This view saw the IPL ripe for the plucking by those wanting a piece of the action, a snout in the IPL trough. When Sunil Gavaskar sounded a particularly trenchant note in accusing John Buchanan of being a 'failed former cricketer... [who was] made out to be a super coach by the Indian media [and was] milking the owners of his franchise through nepotism',[2] he was not just noticing the age-old unseemly spectacle of the unworthy jostling for position in a gold rush, much like the profusion of semi-literate youngsters claiming to be networking experts during the dot-com boom. More astutely, Gavaskar had tapped into an old Indian worry, the fear of exploitation by the foreigner. For someone like Gavaskar, brought up on a diet of the rejection of India's advances by the fair damsels of the West, the rush for prostration at the IPL altar with one eye fixed firmly on the Indian pay-packet must have been galling.

Thus, one aspect of Indian defensiveness about the IPL, of the prickliness of the Indian fan, was grounded in a very real pique when it came to understanding his place in world cricket; he viewed the modern mercenaries, the national boards, players and media personnel alike, as paying dutiful obeisance at the Indian temples of money while simultaneously, resentfully, unable to shake loose an ossified attitude grounded in disdain for the Old India.

This Indian fan was also quick to notice a strain in the critiques of the IPL that seemed unnecessarily patronizing and dismissive. Some of it was revealed in the oft-expressed disdain for the presence of Bollywood stars at IPL games, the paradigmatic symbols of the supposed gaucherie of Indian cricket, especially in the derision directed at Shilpa Shetty and Preity Zinta, who by virtue of being attractive women, could simply not be interested in cricket, or at Shahrukh Khan as an owner of an IPL franchise (those familiar with his days of sporting glory in Delhi school tournaments would have been entirely unsurprised that this fan would have bought a sports team once he had the means to do so). Indian fans were not unaware that sports fans buying sports teams, even if they happened to be connected with the film industry, would be an entirely unremarkable phenomenon in the now-so-critical 'West'. Neither would celebrity presence at a game be taken as proof of the lack of sporting seriousness of the encounter at hand; Jack Nicholson's constant presence at LA Lakers' games or Spike Lee's presence at the New York Knicks' games did not seem to diminish the NBA one iota (and neither did Australian Rugby League fans think that Russell Crowe's involvement with the South Sydney Rabbitohs made them a less serious team).

So while the 'I' in the IPL was, for the patriot, a guarantee that he would support it, that same 'I', conversely, often seemed a handicap in the IPL's acceptance in the Anglo-Australian media; many who wrote or commented on the IPL could not apparently separate it from preconceived notions about India, home of greedy, wily, plebeian, gauche subcontinentals. It was hard to imagine English or Australian journalists being quite as contemptuous of the sporting and economic prospects of a team called the 'Sydney Surfers' as they were of one called the 'Rajasthan Royals'.[3] This sort of scepticism about the IPL centred almost exclusively on expressing doubt about whether anyone in their right minds would care about teams whose name consisted of a pairing of an Indian city and some other noun; our cricketing pundit would wonder aloud in a tone of pitch-perfect incredulity about the singular implausibility of cricket fans developing an attachment to teams called the Rajasthan Royals, or the Chennai Super Kings. The basis of this particular rhetorical pitch seemed the evocation of two moods: one, a post-colonial hangover that associated the names of Indian towns with distance, remoteness, a peripheral existence; the second, a genteel distaste for the in-bad-taste excess of marketing mavens.

But teams in the EPL or the NBA are named after English and American towns, often scarcely locatable on a map, paired with just as unlikely monikers. It was not inconceivable that some perfectly normal human beings, even today, imagining Arsenal was the name of a quarter in Paris or a place where anarchists went to load up for the revolution, might be surprised to find out it was a club based in North London. Vietnamese teenagers in Saigon that sport Arsenal shirts care about the players that bring it glory and have already succumbed to the marketed creation of a sustained fantasy; very few of them too, might be able to locate the headquarters of the club. Such scepticism about the IPL, based on an archaic notion of an India permanently located in the margins of the sporting world, was interestingly revelatory about an entrenched mindset in the cricket world's reaction to things Indian.

So the IPL seemed only to have provoked dreams of post-nation futures when the cricket action began on the field. The off-field action remained resolutely cast in templates provided by the nation. The IPL did not, for instance, dispel nationalist worries during La Affaire Pakistani Players in 2010; if anything, the IPL exacerbated the crisis. The fiasco of the 2010 IPL player auction, when no Pakistani players were picked up, showed that perhaps the Indian fan was still inimical to them post the 2008 attack, therefore no franchise was willing to risk displeasing financiers and commercial partners. In doing so, they handed over an 'instrument of coercive diplomacy' to the Indian Ministry of External Affairs.[4] None of this spoke of a post-nation future.

But the crisis in India–Pakistan relations—which continued after the 2011 World Cup when Shahid Afridi, clearly suffering from foot-in-mouth disease, suggested that gestures of generosity offered by Indians to Pakistanis visiting Mohali for the World Cup semi-final were not of Pakistani Muslim standards—was also sought to be handled by the IPL. For the very next day, Afridi, now cast as fireman after doing duty as arsonist, was making the rounds suggesting that IPL teams hire more Pakistani players as a way of resolving the rapidly growing crisis in mutual relations. The IPL had thus been deemed both balm and inflammatory for the nations concerned.

A constant illusion of those indulging in post-nation fantasies has been a failure to realize the resilience of the trope of the nation. Nationality still persists as the most important and visible indicator of identity after religion; the query 'What nationality are you?' has not lost any of its importance. It seems almost as likely to establish identity as the question 'What religion are you?' Nationality stands pegged as an almost hereditary acquisition, so successful has its associated ideology been in our modern consciousness; to not have a nation seems almost to deny oneself full personality. The status of the Palestinian in the modern imagination is bizarre precisely because in a world of nations and passports, he has none; the Palestinian is not lacking in bodily shape or form or any other human attribute, but he will never be complete, possibly, in his own eyes, and definitely not in those of others, till a passport is at hand.

So too in club-based sports. The planeloads of Japanese tourists arriving at Seattle during the years Ichiro Suzuki played for the Seattle Mariners were not there just because they loved baseball; otherwise they would have made the trip sooner. Major League Soccer games in the US between a 'Canadian' franchise like Toronto FC and an 'American' one like New York Red Bulls are still preceded by the playing of the national anthems of the respective countries. (Whose? Not all the players on the roster.) And even when there is no sign of club or nation in a sport, as in tennis' Grand Slam tournaments, fans will often cheer along national lines: Novak Djokovic and Rafael Nadal's legions of loud Serbian and Spanish fans are legendary. Given such visible entrenchment of nationalist sympathies, it is implausible that nation-based affections will wither away in sporting domains, especially in cricket.

PROPPING UP THE NATION

Even in the IPL, international cricket plays a significant role. Besides the creation of player auras, it bolsters player remuneration, and indeed, has to, if the BCCI is to maintain control over Indian cricket.

The BCCI and the IPL currently incentivize international cricket via tiered auctioneering. Fees for Indian players at IPL auctions are differentiated on the basis of previous Ranji Trophy or international experience. A three-tier system of salaries places non-Ranji players at the bottom layer, the Ranji player at the second, and the international player at its apex; a tyro with one international cap could make more money than a seasoned Ranji pro unlucky enough to not have made an international debut; a rookie earning the lowest salary in his first year could treble his fee by the second year by the simple expedient of winning a Team India cap between his first and second IPL seasons.

A crucial move towards the post-nation future would be to remove this tiered system of payments at IPL player auctions (or indeed, to do away with the player auction altogether and to let franchises scout for and recruit their own players via a league draft).[5] Once that happens, franchises' bids on players would reflect their perceived or actual Twenty20 skills as opposed to their international experience. Franchises could start to develop their own Twenty20 stars, independent of an international presence, via their own farm systems and minor-leagues, aware that such investment is justified because they do not have to pay excessive amounts for players with international experience.

Such a move is unlikely because once the incentive of the higher salary via international cricket is removed, the BCCI ceases to be the conduit to riches for the Indian player; the IPL franchise would beckon instead. Under the current system, the BCCI, by setting up a tiered auction, and operating under the façade of paying homage to the primacy of the international game, is able to guard against the devaluation of its most prized offering to Indian players. Here, the nation does double-duty in propping up the BCCI's power. Moving towards a post-nation future in cricket would appear then, to require nothing less than toppling the BCCI and the ICC, the entities that stand to benefit the most, financially, from nation-based cricket. In the Indian context, it would require the linkage between the nation and the BCCI to be broken. That would require showing that 'the Indian team' and 'the team selected by the BCCI' were not necessarily identical, that in fact, the former was a construction, an idealization, one that could be delivered by entities other than the BCCI.

In the history of cricket, such severance of linkages between organizations 'in charge of national cricket', the national boards, and the so-called 'national team' has been carried out by private promoters like Kerry Packer and Subhash Chandra. If the post-nation future is to come about, it will not be because of the ICC and BCCI allowing it. Rather, it will have come about because a promoter has managed to put together a breakaway scheme that flourishes, that does not make a deal with a national board like Kerry Packer did, nor get hounded out of town like Chandra's ICL. Both Packer and Chandra were able to show how tenuous the link between the 'national team' and the national board was. They were also able to force an engagement with the question of how players were to be treated, not just by boards, but by fans as well.

The Strange Case of the ICL

Whatever the IPL's influence, it cannot be fully understood without considering its predecessor, the ICL, a fledgling organization that was forced to shut shop, but one that forced the BCCI to execute a smart running jump onto the Twenty20 bandwagon as it rolled by. Nothing quite made clear the hold the BCCI has over Indian and international cricket like the ICL did. As an Indian, if you did not understand the difference between 'official' and 'unofficial' cricket, the ICL induced comprehension. For those historically inclined, it reminded them of the BCCI's monopoly over cricket in India, asserted as long ago as 1946 when it had shut down the wildly successful nursery of the Pentangular tournament.[6]

Most notably, the ICL showed that player power was close to non-existent, whether in India or overseas, that the Federation of International Cricketers' Associations (FICA), for all its pronouncements, had little agency in determining national boards' actions.[7] The ICL also demonstrated, vividly, how cricketers could make money outside the current international system where only a hundred or so centrally contracted players make a good living off cricket, an arrangement that abides by the Matthew Principle of 'those that have get more'.[8] Thus the very best players are well rewarded, while the rest are left to fight for the scraps. The ICL's success lay in offering players a chance to make money playing outside the ICC's constraints; its failure, at least as far as players were concerned, had everything to do with the BCCI's threats and bullying, and very little to do with the merits of the way it was organized.

The BCCI–ICL imbroglio thus laid bare the structure of the player-BCCI-ICC relationship and showed just how passionately and quickly the BCCI and ICC could respond to something—'unofficial cricket'—they considered a threat to their positions of power. In its resolution, it reminded players and their associations that the Kerry Packer revolution was as yet unfinished. Now, there is another, perhaps more disquieting, lesson for those inclined to imbibe it: if the ICL was capable of disrupting the BCCI's monopoly on Indian cricket, the emancipated genie of the IPL—the moneyed corporate franchises it brought in its wake—is capable of rendering the BCCI and the ICC irrelevant.

The cricketing monopoly of the ICC has been challenged most fundamentally twice, first by Kerry Packer and the WSC, and then by Subhash Chandra's Zee network and the ICL. The WSC created a parallel world of cricket, including tests between representative sides; the cricket was real, the statistics were not. Those who signed up for Packer were banned with varying degrees of severity, attenuated by local labour regimes, from official cricket, but on settlement of their dispute, went back to playing Test and first-class cricket.[9] By then they had ensured discourse about players and their standing as professionals had changed. For many fans used only to international cricket played by semi-professional players, the idea that there could be allegiance to any but a national or domestic side, or national board, was a new one. Justice Slade's ruling against the Test and County Cricket Board

(TCCB) in their 1977 court dispute with the WSC (*Grieg vs Insole*)—triggered by the TCCB's dropping and banning of WSC players from the English team—told cricket fans the world over that players draped in the national flag could also be understood as tradesmen seeking greener pastures to ply their trade. The name-calling of that era might have receded from some fans' minds, but for those old enough to remember, the fury provoked by players' decisions to pursue the attractions of club-based Twenty20 and not focus exclusively on international cricket is nothing new. It reminds them that the player's place at the cricketing table is still not set.

The initial portion of the ICL story is uncannily similar to that of Kerry Packer and the WSC: a series of failed bids for television rights and the mounting frustration of a businessman, eyes firmly set on lucrative advertising and subscription revenue, facing a monopoly that actively blocks one's entry. Through the first decade of the new millennium, Subhash Chandra's Zee Telefilms submitted bids to the BCCI for cricket telecast rights and was turned down repeatedly despite often making the best offers. When the smoke had cleared, Zee Telefilms had lost out on the rights to broadcast all BCCI-sanctioned cricket matches in India until 2011.

Chandra's response was the same as Kerry Packer's. Denied content, he made his own: the ICL, featuring six teams playing Twenty20 with prize money of one million US dollars for the winning team. The ICL commenced with a roster made up of retirees or fringe players; its two seasons included tournaments between four international teams—The World, India, Pakistan and Bangladesh—nine domestic teams, and the Lahore Badshahs. The ICL dreamed of expansion to fifty-over matches; the realization of its various schemes would have made it the most moneyed professional league in India. Eighty-five Indian and sixty international players, enamoured of its monetary potential and given a chance to extend paid careers or share in the pie that was the exclusive preserve of international cricketers, were to sign with the ICL, swelling their wallets, but rendering themselves pariahs in the process.

From start to finish, the ICL was doomed because it had dared to step on official cricket's turf. It collapsed in 2009. The response to the league was immediate, swift, and draconian, for the odour of 'unofficial' cricket was strong and demanded resolute cleansing. The BCCI quickly banned ICL players from all forms of official cricket and from using its facilities. Sixty-four Indian ICL cricketers found millions of rupees owed to them by the BCCI as match fees and prize money on the official domestic circuit not forthcoming. Non-ICL players received their dues for the same period from their state associations.[10]

The BCCI also ensured that other national boards cracked the whip on ICL recruits as well: the Pakistan Cricket Board (PCB) banned ICL players from playing domestic cricket; several English counties refused overseas ICL players contracted to play for them the documents necessary to play in England. Why a player who had fallen out of favour with his board was not allowed to ply his trade elsewhere seemed mysterious. (The same question was raised in 2011 when, after yet another dispute between player and board, the PCB refused to issue Shahid Afridi a no-objection certificate (NOC) that would have enabled him to fulfil his contractual obligations to Hampshire.) Cricket Australia (CA) then joined the BCCI and Cricket South Africa in banning ICL players from the Champions League.[11] Later, the BCCI decided to not invite English counties to the Champions League as the England and Wales Cricket Board (ECB) had dared to allow ICL players into county ranks after the ECB faced legal action from the players. The outcome of that dispute might have been to the players' advantage given England's muscular trade laws (and the precedent set by *Grieg vs Insole*). Having memorized the dictator's playbook, Lalit Modi stated that counties with ICL players in their ranks would not be allowed for the tournament 'under any circumstance', even if those players were dropped for the tournament. Redemption was not on the menu.[12] Still, legal or sporting realities intervened: some ICL players in Pakistan and New Zealand were admitted back to domestic cricket.

Appeals to national pride and loyalty sometimes ran alongside these sanctions: when the ICL added a team from Bangladesh, the Bangladesh Cricket Board (BCB) banned its players for ten years, but recognizing the potential gutting of its international team, asked Bangladeshi players to reject the ICL and stay 'loyal' to the board and the national team.

The ICL, displaying an almost charming naivety, asked the ICC to have the ban revoked; the ICC, only too happy to maintain the fiction that it could actually influence the BCCI, set up a meeting between the league and the BCCI. Its outcome, failure, was a foregone conclusion. The ICC then formally rejected an application by the ICL for 'authorized unofficial' status; this rejection was backed up by some deft buck-passing, as the ICC stated it would not recognize the ICL unless the BCCI did. Cue talk of porcine aviators.

Back in India, the BCCI, as if striving to attain formerly unattainable heights of autocracy, stepped up its crackdown. Kapil Dev, as chairman of the Executive Board of the ICL and the chairman of the National Cricket Academy, was viewed as a particularly egregious Judas-incarnate; Dev was sacked from the Academy, and the BCCI tried not to commemorate the silver jubilee of India's 1983 World Cup victory for fear of involving him. Thanks to interventions by members of the 1983 squad, who made it clear that the celebrations were not dependent on the participation of the BCCI, the body was forced to participate on pain of appearing to be petulant marionettes. Then, relying on that old trick so beloved of despotic states, the BCCI went in for memory effacement, effecting a removal of a portrait of Kapil Dev from the Punjab Cricket Association Stadium in Mohali.[13]

Next up, the ICL players were treated as lepers, as if playing in close proximity to them would ensure contagion. During India's tour of New Zealand in 2009, the Indian team management withdrew Sachin Tendulkar and Dinesh Karthik from a benefit Twenty20 match in Wellington because they would have had to play alongside and against the ICL's Hamish Marshall. A similarly flavoured restriction was placed on V.V.S. Laxman's appearance for Nottinghamshire in 2008 because the county had ICL players in its ranks.[14] To many, the BCCI's actions seemed considerably less benign than Heath Mills's description of them as 'a bit silly'.[15] The word 'zamindar' was thrown around freely; images of bat- and ball-wielding serfs flickered across fans' minds.

The first edition of the ICL had commenced on 30 November 2007; in 2008, the ICL expanded; the first edition had six teams; the second, eight, with another team added in the second half of the year. A third edition added two teams and two venues. The second season acquired an international tinge as the Lahore Badshahs competed and won. In Pakistan, the ICL was a raging success. Denied international cricket, the Pakistani fan found his cricket fix taken care of not by the charity of official cricket but by the chutzpah of a buccaneer.

The first ICL final was a success as the IPL–Twenty20 entertainment template was quickly established: the plethora of sixes, the DJ'd music, the presence of Bollywood stars, beauty queens, cheerleaders or 'dancing girls', pop star performances, and an age-and-gender-diverse audience. Populism had its bright points: tickets were reasonably priced; heavy-handed security was absent; there were no restrictions on bringing beverages into the stands.[16]

Though the ICL was denied access to many cricket facilities, thus severely constraining its revenue-generating capacity, those supposed communists, the West Bengalis, still agreed to rent out the Eden Gardens to it. The thought of an ICL final taking place there must have filled the BCCI with horror. The inimitable Lalu Prasad granted the league access to the stadiums governed by the Indian Railways, described the ICL as 'a good initiative' and suggested mischievously that teams selected by the BCCI and the ICL play against each other for top-dog status.[17] In making this remark, Prasad had hit upon the truth: the BCCI and the ICL were merely two competing entities trying to organize cricket and provide cricket players a living.

In August 2007, the ICL accused the BCCI of anti-competitive intimidation, and requested a legal injunction against the BCCI's interference with the ICL's attempts to hire players and use cricket stadiums owned by state governments. Displaying acute common sense, the Delhi High Court ruled in favour of the ICL, noting the adverse effects on players' livelihood in this tussle between 'promoters of the game', and issued injunctions to corporate sponsors, state cricket associations and the BCCI against terminating valid contracts of players joining the ICL.[18] The Monopolies and Restrictive Trade Practices Commission (MRTPC) of India in turn, asked its Director-General of Investigation to investigate the BCCI's actions against ICL players.[19] It is not clear if a report was ever submitted, and sadly, the MRTPC was to be wound up in August 2011.[20]

Despite its financial worries and the concerted harassment by the BCCI, the real endgame for the ICL began with the BCCI announcing an 'amnesty' for all Indian ICL players, who, it said, could return to official cricket provided they cut all ties with the ICL. They were deemed eligible for international and domestic cricket after 'cooling periods' of varying lengths. The BCCI was clearly determined to humiliate the

ICL players just a little more before relenting, forgiving, and permitting career resurrection. Other national boards, like those of Pakistan and New Zealand, for whom it meant a restoration of their national sides, followed suit. The ICL put on a brave face and said the right things. Its business head, Himanshu Modi, stated, 'As cricket professionals, they are free to decide and explore their options.'[21] Players might have fervently hoped that such wisdom had informed the actions of all concerned throughout the sorry display of unrestrained managerial and organizational power.

The dislike that the BCCI's behaviour created was palpable in many cricket fans, Indians included.[22] Unsurprisingly, the BCCI's actions were defended using the same logic that underwrote the ICL: sure, the players were professionals and should have been free to ply their trade anywhere; but the BCCI was their employer; it ran a business; it bore no duty to tolerate a competitor. Forgotten in this defence was the role that the BCCI was supposed to have been playing: as promoter of the game, not controller of those who played cricket. And the BCCI did not treat its players as professionals. The real structure of the BCCI's labour relations with its players displayed depressing traces of the feudal, hierarchic top-down, non-egalitarian arrangements of the past.

In debates about the judgment to be passed on the BCCI and Lalit Modi, comparisons were inevitably made with the behaviour of corporate giants like Microsoft, who single-mindedly pursue economic glory and zealously guard their turf against any potential invaders. Such comparisons should have given everyone pause. Microsoft's marketing and technical talents are indisputable, but thanks to its monopolistic behaviour—as evident in its long troubled history with anti-trust laws in both the US and Europe—and the damage caused to the public practice of computer science by the aggressive promulgation of a proprietary model of ownership in software and software patents, virulent dislike for Microsoft is not rare in many quarters of the computer science community, be it at the corporate, academic, or users' level. Most importantly, it did not seem as if there was an improvement in the lot of cricket if one set of imperialists—the old ICC—was replaced by another, in the form of the BCCI.

The BCCI was lucky that no substantive legal challenge arose in response to its monopolistic behaviour. Indeed, the ICC and its national boards' cartel-like behaviour seemed to require legal assault. It would have been interesting if Australian, New Zealand, Indian and Pakistani players contracted to the ICL had challenged their disbarment from domestic cricket. Courts would then have had to decide whether this 'ICC-sanctioned ostracism' had the force of law or whether it constituted 'an infringement of a person's right to livelihood, or a restraint on trade'.[23] Alas, many courts were never called on to define the powers of the national cricket boards. A prolongation of the BCCI–ICL dispute might have resulted in some seminal court rulings, established legal precedents, and clarified the nature of the board–player relationship. (Interestingly, the raising of the possibility of the alternative economics of the ICL had one immediate salutary effect: the BCCI sharply increased the prize money for winners, runners-up and losing semi-finalists in its domestic tournaments. It also replaced honorary selectors with paid professionals in September 2008, a change long desired in the eventual professionalization of Indian cricket.)[24]

A properly resolved legal dispute between the BCCI and the ICL would have sparked a discussion on the terms of the contracts players all over the world sign with their national boards, and enabled a closer look at the murky foundations of organizations that function like monopolies and are not above recourse to the rhetoric of nation and national duty. (Unsurprisingly, BCCI–player contracts are not available for public inspection.) It could have shown how demands that are not placed on professionals in other sports are placed on cricketers just because they play for 'national boards' and 'nations', and would have enabled a closer look at the ICC and its members, who convey the impression of wanting to run cricket as a business, but only in ways that most suit them.

SUBVERTING THE NATION PARADIGM

What the ICL had shown was that nationalism in cricketing manifestations such as the 'national team' rested on slightly shaky ground, especially when confronted by the question of whether Indian players were 'unpatriotic' for joining the ICL and owed 'duties' to their country, or whether the cricket played in the ICL was 'unofficial'.

For the ICL raised the awkward question of what it was that made the national teams 'official', and why a player owed a 'duty' to his 'nation' when playing cricket for a national board, rather than the more mundane responsibility an employee bore to his employer. Invocation of the nation is the oldest trick in the book; that did not seem to have made it any less effective.

For many, the ICL, like the WSC before it, introduced a fundamental subversion of their allegiance to the nation. The key moment was the creation of the ICL India XI complete with the regalia of the navy-blue India caps handed out by Kapil Dev. It showed something formerly understood as a conceptual given, the 'national team', was a conventional arrangement. As long as the Indian fan has known cricket in India, it was assumed there was only one 'Indian team', its relationship to the BCCI glibly assumed but rarely understood. But nominally, the ICL India XI was an 'Indian team' as much as Team India; the definite article 'the' does not apply to 'Indian team' unless the fans recognize it as such and place their allegiance squarely behind it. Team India, the 'Indian team', the 'BCCI India XI', the 'ICL India XI', all form part of a continuum with the 'English team', the 'MCC XI', and the notion of possibly terming the present English team the 'ECB XI'. The Marylebone Cricket Club XI reminds us how a club XI acquires the aura of a national team; the stories of the WSC and the ICL remind us that a franchise, which included 'India' in the title given to its team, would have taken the first steps to commanding nationalistically inflected allegiance from its fans.

The self-identification of a fan with a group of players taking the field is with a team put together by the organization 'in-charge', be it a club or a national board. The former demands allegiance to the club alone; the latter links itself to the nation. In the case of national boards, their being 'in-charge' has also meant 'doing it for long enough to become official'. Over that period of time, the board and its team can become identified with the game as 'national representatives'. But this is a matter of convention established by time, constant reference, and community norming, not otherworldly linkage. These connections remain 'official' only in the absence of competition.

The hold of these conventions can be hard to shake off. Many cinema fans remain convinced that the annual Oscars pick out the year's best movie. But it does no such thing. It merely names the movie that the Motion Picture Academy selects as deserving of the title. The title 'Academy Award' acknowledges this. To note this is only to point out the obvious, and yet, it is a revelation for some. 'National' cricket teams, similarly, are picked by an organization—whose history itself may be poorly understood—the members of which, by a variety of contingencies, have become the 'national' organizers of the game. The 'national team' is one selected by them to do duty. When players realize that they need to be paid for their services, whether by club or national board, that there are mercenary aspects to both arrangements, and when national boards run the game like a business anyway, then the affiliation with the 'national team' can be considerably weakened. Players, to their credit, are increasingly never confused by the notion of competing allegiances in the modern era. In this clarity of mind, cricket players are no different from those lining up for overseas employment visas at consulates and embassies worldwide. The demands of the nation do not seem to have quenched their thirst for a better life for themselves and their families.

Had Kerry Packer's WSC stuck around long enough to fully permeate the consciousness of a generation of Australian spectators, the confusion over which Australian team was the 'real' Australian team would have been acute, especially as the WSC featured 'Tests' between teams named 'Australia' and the 'West Indies'. The WSC had fought to convince fans that its cricket was real and serious; some fans were convinced by David Hookes's broken jaw, others by the palpable efforts of the players on the field. The cricketers too had not failed to notice that the competition was intense and the money real, the same kind as paid by the national boards.

By the time the WSC Australian XI went to the West Indies in 1979 for a series of Super Tests, the confusion had become palpable. What was described on the sporting pages of newspapers sounded like Test cricket. The tour even included the seemingly obligatory Caribbean riot in Guyana. The players' competitive spirit did not seem lacking in the five Super Tests and twelve one-day matches that both teams declared were the best they had ever played. The 'West Indies' and 'Australia' ended the series 1–1; the series had representative sides; it had the world's best players putting on outstanding performances, especially

Greg Chappell, whose batting in the series is still reckoned as one of the finest performances against the 'West Indies'.

Australian fans confessed genuine dissonance at this state of affairs. At home during the 'official' summer, the English team had thrashed the Australian Cricket Board's 'official Australians' 5–1 in the Ashes; later, the 'unofficial' WSC Australians drew with the mighty, albeit unofficial, 'West Indies'. Unofficial cricket was more exciting and competitive; it showed Australian cricketing talent in better light. Perhaps the nation could be identified with success, wherever, and in whatever form it was found; yet another wrinkle in the landscape. Nothing, in matters of allegiance, was ever straightforward.

The WSC experience suggests a simple thought experiment. Imagine the Packer-ACB dispute had not been settled in time for the 1979–80 pseudo-Ashes; imagine the ACB and WSC had remained at loggerheads, and more cricketers had signed up with the WSC for better pay cheques, leading to more tournaments, more tours, and a longer season. Imagine too, that the older world of national board-sponsored cricket continued apace. Before too long, fans would have started wondering which side—the Packer XI or the ACB XI, the Packer West Indies or the WICB XI—made claims on their allegiance and support. Which one was the 'real' Australian team, which one the 'real' West Indian? Whose statistics should be considered 'official'? Would a score of 366 in a Super Test between the Packer Australian XI and the Packer West Indies have been a 'world record'? Perhaps Australian and West Indian fans would have supported both sets of teams as they took the field in their respective domains of competition, but the intensity of their nationalist ardour might have been dimmed and diffused somewhat.

The raising of the question of which Australian team was the 'real' one would have brought the awkwardness of the answer to the fore. There is no 'real', 'official' Australian XI; to expect one is to expect that anything could be more 'official' than what is already at hand: a bunch of players selected by the—hopefully only—organization in charge of the game.

When there is more than one organization in charge of a sport, the confusion begins. Consider boxing. Surely there must have been an official world championship in the glory days of Mohammad Ali and Joe Frazier? But all we ever had was the championship of the dominant boxing council emerging from the primordial alphabet soup of the NABF, IBF, WBC, and the WBA. Hence the urge to find unification champions to resolve the confusion. When the dominant boxing council was no longer so, and when unification efforts failed, boxing fans were treated to the spectacle of multiple world champions. The chess world championship underwent similar confusion in moving from the FIDE to the unification championship, all in the name of finding the 'official' world champion. The NFL, comprising the American Football Conference and the National Football Conference, and the MLB, comprising the National League and the American League, bear witness to histories of competitive leagues, of moves towards unification and consolidation in an effort to avoid similar dissonance and ensure the greatest prosperity for the leagues. This account is considerably oversimplified, but the rough similarity of the crisis of multiple leagues – Packer in the world of ICC and Chandra's league for the BCCI – should be clear.

The ICL India XI had thus served as a reminder of the origin of 'the Indian team' and its entirely contingent linkage with the BCCI. The BCCI is not the same as 'Indian cricket'; the 'Indian team' currently happens to be 'its' team. Indian fans support it because it is the one that makes claims on them, but it is worth acknowledging the convention at hand, one propped up by the enduring, enforced presence of the BCCI in Indian cricket, and by appeals to 'nation' and 'national duty' and calls to 'represent the nation'. Conventional arrangements, of course, are nothing to sneeze at. Think of how languages got to be the way they are. But that same example, laden with stories of languages coming to be and passing away, should serve to demonstrate how some other entity—perhaps the ICL India XI—could come to be associated with the 'Indian national team'.

The ICL failed to survive, but it brought to light the existence of a monopoly in Indian and world cricket. In its worst moments during its relationship with the ICL, the BCCI rapidly regressed to the mean of monopolies in displaying ruthlessness, complacency and greed. The manoeuvrings of the ICC, the BCCI and other national boards, and the reminders of the WSC also rendered transparent a simple fact about world cricket: the ICC and its national boards currently run cricket worldwide like a self-interested cartel would, but they are not the only possible administrators of the game, and certainly not the only ones capable of putting teams on the field which could command the allegiance and devotion of fans.

A truly nightmarish possibility for the ICC and its constituent national boards is that the current IPL franchises or those of some other Twenty20 league might morph into genuine competitors for the BCCI and ICC, perhaps by finding international partners which sponsor Test matches, fifty-over games and Twenty20. But to the surprise of all concerned, they do not dispense with the nation, and indeed call on it in the formation of a league featuring national XIs in competition. Then the national boards and the ICC would be displaced by franchise-based leagues, a change in management that would be reliant on the same old tropes while committed to the profit motive and all its attendant risks. There would be some initial discomfort for the puzzled cricket fan but he would switch allegiance soon enough, for in the end there would still be cricket on the field, albeit propped up by a different set of abbreviations than the BCCI, the ICC, CA, ECB or WICB.

Or perhaps the breakaway league would not bother with the notion of a national team at all, and simply structure the game around the club system. Such a league could, just like the rebels before it, pay enough to deplete the official structures of cricket of their best players and set up their competitions using the same three formats as in the current world of 'official cricket'. Fans would find a new set of allegiances here too, given enough time to develop a relationship with players and to find a space within the competition that would take care of their appetite for cricket.

To prevent the possible evolution of such a system, the ICC and the national boards could strengthen the hold they have on world cricket. They can do this by imposing a variety of legal and extra-legal measures on cases like the WSC or ICL. Or they could make nation-based cricket as it exists today, the most attractive financial option for a modern-day cricket player. If that were to ever become less lucrative—as it often seems it will—the BCCI and the ICC could face a genuine threat to their existence.

The ICL and the WSC have ensured the creation of a template to be followed by anyone with the time and the inclination to take on that 'cartel of monopolies',[25] the ICC and its constituent national boards.

A modern-day Packer or Chandra, perhaps an ambitious Mukesh Ambani or Vijay Mallya, fed up with the restraints of the current IPL by the BCCI, the ICC and international cricket, and armed with deep money bags and the resilience to hold out and not compromise is all that is required to upset this particular applecart.

No More Bonded Labour

The ICL saga threw into sharp focus the need to regularize the labour market in cricket, to spread the wealth generated by the game a little more broadly than its current concentration at the top of the international pyramid. It emphasized players' status as contracted professionals, subject to the legal protection of employment and labour law, which many national boards often seem blissfully unaware of. Here, the regularization of player labour relations does not mean a simple increase in player salaries, but rather a deployment of those structures that place professional sportsmen in appropriate power relations with their employers. These concerns are pertinent when disputes about over-scheduling and commitment to Test tours are a regular feature of the modern cricketing headline.

The need for appropriate labour relations in world cricket is especially acute if player involvement in cricket administration is to be enhanced. One might view the tendency towards corruption via match-fixing to be based on players' perception of the game as a foreign enterprise, run by distant administrators, relationships with whom breed resentment rather than partnership. Quite straightforwardly, players need to be involved in, and given ownership of, the game's problems. The fidelity to the game that could be bred by such a partnership would be of a qualitatively different nature. A player used to thinking of the game as a temporary revenue-maximizing enterprise could then approach it with a sense of ownership, involved as he would be in the game's administration. Given the highly politicized nature of most national boards, this might seem a distant dream, but bold player initiatives, whether substantive, like Anil Kumble and Javagal Srinath's election to a state association in India, or rhetorical, like Kumar Sangakkara's epic Cowdrey lecture in 2011, are a hopeful start.

UNIONS AND FREE AGENCY

The BCCI's dispute with the ICL emphasized that players need, first and foremost, adequate legal representation. A cricketer used to concentrating on willow and leather might be staggered to find that sports professionals require representation with expertise in contract, labour, employment, worker's compensation, antitrust, tort, and tax law; they also need access to strong contract negotiation and drafting skills, and knowledge of the arbitration process when disputes with employers require arbitration.[26] In particular, the language used by the BCCI when referring to players either during the ICL crisis or on other occasions is instructive[27] and suggests that Indian players need a union or player association, one that would 'promote and protect the interests of the members...with a view to the abolition of all restrictions which affect the social and financial position of members',[28] display the will to fight for their rights, and perhaps diminish the posturing characteristic of the BCCI, which struggles to understand players as freely contracting agents with rights in an employment marketplace. The problem of labour relations in cricket, of course, is to reconcile the commercialization of labour with the maintenance of the status of a game run not just as a business. But to acknowledge the difficulty of this balancing act is not to concede its impossibility.

The right to form a players' union, unsurprisingly, was established long ago in the homes of professional franchises. For instance, in 1967, the US National Labor Relations Board (NLRB) ruled that players have the right to form unions or players' associations to negotiate collective bargaining agreements with the owners of franchises. Players and owners must, in particular, negotiate hours, wages and working conditions.[29] A comprehensive agreement specifying playing schedules and commitments over the various cricket seasons—in essence, agreement over working hours—would have rendered unnecessary not only Alastair Cook's dramatic threat of a strike in April 2011 in response to the onerous schedules placed on the English cricket team by the ECB,[30] but also the persistent squabbling over IPL-contracted players' availability for international games. It would put an end to the spectacle of national boards constantly making pronouncements to restrict players during the course of the year, be it participation in

English county cricket, or the abortive Sri Lankan Premier League (2011)[31] and coming up with new restrictions on players according to their whims and fancies, or scheduling one pointless, context-free one-day international tournament after another.

With a union to back them up, players could bargain collectively and demand the legal vetting of the contracts they sign with the BCCI (or any other national board). Are its terms of employment and 'workplace conditions' permissible under the various relevant legal regimes? Are player responsibilities and commitments not excessive, and clearly specified? Is the player free to exercise his trade during those periods when he is not otherwise contractually obligated to the national board? Is he protected against retaliation by the national board in case he does choose to work elsewhere? In the absence of such a body, the answers to these questions remain ambiguous today.

The apparent imbalance in the power structure between Indian players and the BCCI—and indeed, that of many international players with their national boards—prompts questions about the extent to which players are free to choose their employers. More formally, do cricket players enjoy free agency? Free agency ordains that teams do not own rights to players beyond the actual terms of contracts entered into with the players: a player is to be understood as the proverbial contractor of standard free market theory, at liberty to contract for his services, with any constraints requiring careful justification. In plain language, in the context of the modern sporting world, a free agent is a player whose contract with one team has expired and who is eligible to sign with another.[32] When there is no contract to begin with or when there is ambiguity in the terms of the contract, the question of players' rights become more interesting. In mundane, familiar employment situations, consider the nine-to-five worker who moonlights on weekends or engages in consulting work after hours or on vacations. Any restrictions on these activities need to be part of the original contract, and to be strongly motivated. Not all such restrictions will pass a legal test for fairness.

In North America, free agency came about after sports leagues surrendered reserve clauses, which allowed clubs to renew player contracts at terms favourable to themselves but did not allow the players to terminate. These reserve clauses, ostensibly to reward owner investment in player recruitment and training and to permit competitive balance, an essential item for the sporting credibility of a league,[33] had meant that players could rarely leave their original teams by their own choice. This put them at the mercy of their owners when seeking employment elsewhere. In cricket, national boards enjoy something like a reserve clause in their prerogative to deny a contracted player an NOC for, say, county cricket or a Twenty20 league. This ensures that movement between the various employers in the cricketing world is restricted.

In cricketing contexts, the claims made by national boards on player loyalties—via their restrictions on player activities during the year—are rendered partially justifiable because of their cultivation of player development in their domestic systems. In major-league baseball, owners assume the risk of training a player in the minor-league farm system in the hope that their investments reap dividends in major-league championships. In cricket, the national boards have taken on the role of grooming players and thus have a vested interest in protecting their investment by, for instance, preventing a player from playing in a Twenty20 league. Arguably, the IPL's drawing freely upon international players with only 10 per cent of their fees paid to the national boards as compensation is poor reward for the years put in by the national boards into player development. Conversely, the player in question might already have generated sufficient income for the boards through gate revenue and television rights.

An open labour market, bolstered by free agency, pays scant attention to national or state boundaries: an Italian basketball player is free to play in the NBA or in the European leagues; an American baseball player can move to Japan to play in Nippon Professional Baseball. In these situations, there is no national board to cast aspersions on a player's patriotism, nor an international system which enjoys a primacy such that he owes a higher allegiance to it.

With players free to move to the highest bidder for their services, labour markets become skewed in favour of the sellers. The resultant rise in player salaries has often bred suspicions amongst fans that players are overpaid. But more often than not, in holding this view, fans are reacting to a highly visible generous contract for a top player, and paying little attention to the ranks of the journeymen who constitute the vast majority of sports professionals. And free agency does little more than leave the choice of the best employer to the player; the market does the rest.

SALARY CAPS AND THE PRESERVATION OF INTERNATIONAL CRICKET

However, leagues may constrain individual player or team roster total incomes. These limits reflect an awareness of the pernicious effects of free agency: bidding wars for players decrease owner profits and, more problematically, richer teams can consistently outbid other teams for players. If players were free to sign with the wealthiest bidder, the wealthiest owners would buy up the best players, skewing competitive parity grossly. This can also occur if salary caps are set high enough for teams in large media markets to leverage their greater incomes.[34] Hence the popular dislike of the New York Yankees, which is often able to outbid less well-endowed teams in the MLB and persistently stack its rosters with the best, most expensive players.

While salary caps are a standard feature of negotiations between league management and players' unions as they restrict player salary growth, there are no salary caps in the world of the ICC; it does not, and cannot, take on the task of restricting the salaries that national boards pay their players. The ICC does not view itself as a professional league, which needs to maintain competitive balance, and in any case, players play for country not club, so there is little or no movement across its members' rosters. English players cannot easily move to India to play Tests for the BCCI; strict national residency rules have to be satisfied, not just the mundane regulations for a worker's visa. In such an arrangement, the BCCI's gigantic coffers do not allow it to simply purchase the world's best players for its Test team; it has to develop its own from available local talent. In the world of cricket, national boundaries, not salary caps, do the work of maintaining competitive parity.

The current salary cap in the IPL does not just attempt to preserve competitive parity in the league. It ensures that a player looking for the best cricket employer in India will always pick the BCCI (for journeyman cricketers the IPL's salaries will be good enough), that franchises cannot be better paymasters than the BCCI. The BCCI thus retains its ability to provide the best pay cheques for the best players via a path through the official system to international cricket. Were the franchises allowed to become better paymasters, Indian players, even the best ones, could skip much of the official system, including international cricket, and simply play for their franchises. In contrast to the BCCI, many national boards do not pay their players enough or offer them adequate security via long-term contracts;[35] these players will always find the IPL, or a Twenty20 league like it, a better employer.

So while the BCCI retains its international strength through the salary cap and the prioritization of international cricket for Indian players in the IPL auction, other national boards could, and often do, find their teams weakened by the allure of the IPL, unless they are able to raise salaries for their players to a level similar to that of the BCCI. This could be viewed as a positive development if national boards are incentivized to increase player remuneration for not just national service but also for domestic tournaments, thus preventing longing glances constantly being sent the IPL's way.

IPL LABOUR RELATIONS

IPL labour arrangements, which include restrictions on salaries, roster composition, timings of player transfers, and which are dependent for player supply on a cartel of national boards, are a curious hybrid of open and closed labour markets.

The current structure of IPL franchise–player relations is most similar to that of a loaned employee working with a temporary employer: the BCCI and other national boards allow their players a second master for a limited period. Each player is required to furnish an NOC from his national board in order to be eligible to play. The IPL compensates the board with 10 per cent of their players' fees as a quid pro quo. IPL players sign contracts whose template is supplied by the IPL council. Once the auction is complete, the player's name and his pay are filled out in the blank contract; there is little or no negotiation with franchises over contractual terms.[36] IPL players are thus employees of the BCCI or some other national board temporarily working with a different paymaster, under terms set by the IPL council.

As franchises do not sign individual customized contracts with players, there is little room for an agent or a union in franchise–player relationships. The IPL council devises every term of the player contract; a franchise requiring extra services from a player has to negotiate it in Indian fashion, informally. An Indian player, used to taking orders from board officials over his playing career, is probably not even aware that he could turn his franchise down if asked for duties not specified in his contract. Thus, in the IPL, franchise owners may demand from players services over and above those contracted for. (The imagining, by employers, of terms of service not actually specified in a contract is, of course, a perennial feature of the modern workplace.)

The BCCI's invitation of franchises into Indian cricket allows partners, carefully circumscribed ones, into a monopolistic domain, and permits them a six-week window to exploit player 'property'. But franchises and their numerous commercial partners—eager to leverage one of the biggest forces on the Indian economic scene into ever more lucrative spin-offs—are keen to exploit this 'property' for longer periods. These commercial ambitions, indeed, the very long-term prospects of the IPL, will remain on tap till national boards release their hold over players for more than just the IPL season. One way this could happen is via a clarification of players' terms of employment—which, for instance, constrain their movement in cricket's labour market via NOCs—with the national boards. The lifting of some of the contractual restrictions which national boards place on players could make them available to franchises at other times during the year for promotional activities, fan cultivation, and so-called 'brand-building' exercises, all necessary to entrench the franchise more firmly in its local region.

The BCCI's hold on Indian players in particular could loosen if international cricket, which is available thus far through the BCCI, became less important for players and if its allure were diminished. International cricket is the BCCI's trump card and it will remain important as long as the salary cap of the IPL is in place, as long as the player auction is rigged to reward international and 'official' cricket, and as long as the sensation of playing for the country remains a desirable one. Given the pre-eminence of the Indian team in the Indian fan's imagination, this hold is likely to be retained for the foreseeable future. But current protestations of commitment to international cricket, and especially Test cricket, aside, there is little to indicate that players reared in a cricketing world whose legend-making is increasingly driven by limited-overs cricket and where the biggest pay packets are available from franchises, will not be content with a career devoted exclusively to that form, playing under the banner of the club. Such a player, making a living from a Twenty20 club career, will not be beholden to the official structures of cricket any more.

For Indian players who will never play international cricket, the IPL could continue to showcase their talents and provide an income better than that available through current domestic cricket. For overseas players too, the IPL and leagues like it could serve as an alternative path to riches, one that might lead to them disregarding official international cricket if their national boards do not pay them enough. Lasith Malinga's decision, in 2011, to give his knees a break from the demands of the long form of the game and concentrate on the shorter forms, including, obviously, the IPL, was underwritten by the realization that club, not country, was the best guarantor of a more secure personal future.

The BCCI, by promoting one-day internationals and Twenty20s internationally, and insisting on IPL salary caps and the current system of auctioning players, could theoretically have its cake and eat it too. It could retain exclusive access to international cricket in the format seemingly most palatable to players and fans, and maintain international cricket's allure for domestic players, while continuing to reap profits from the IPL. The BCCI's best revenue maximization model is one that prioritizes international cricket just enough so that a loyal following of the IPL, with the presence of international Indian stars, is guaranteed. This imperative would rescue Test cricket if the BCCI sees glory in the longer format as enhancing the value of the Indian team for its television rights deals and if Indian fans indicate their desire to support not just any international Indian stars but just the successful ones. This could well be Test cricket's saviour in India. As the furious backlash against the BCCI and the IPL after India's heavy defeats in England and Australia in 2011 and 2012 showed, Indian fans do not want the IPL's success at the cost of humiliating defeats in Test cricket. The BCCI, ironically, might have to pay more attention to Test and, concomitantly, domestic cricket, for the sake of the IPL's continued prosperity.

A WORLD LABOUR MARKET

In general, Twenty20 leagues, delinked from any larger mission to produce a 'national team', demonstrate the potential for a world labour market to emerge in professional cricket players; they promise a livelihood to players who might never have entertained dreams of a professional career, especially if that career was premised on international cricket arranged by a national board through the ICC.

A straightforward and not implausible effect of this could be a promotion of the game worldwide that the ICC has been unable to bring about, and sometimes, as its dealings with Associate Members shows, seems uninterested in. Ryan Ten Doeschate has already demonstrated that Associate Members can supply players to the IPL; the Irish 'O Brien brothers, Kevin and Niall, raised hopes—ultimately dashed—of IPL contracts based on their 2011 World Cup performances; the Canadian Hiral Patel, who smashed a six off Shaun Tait in the 2011 World Cup, should have jolted a check loose from an IPL auction buyer as well; his presence in the 2012 IPL would have been a bigger boost for Canadian— and possibly Gujarati—cricket than any ICC-sponsored initiative so far. Most intriguingly, it is entirely plausible that one Afghani player in the IPL could lift cricket in his benighted country from the level of curiosity to that of street-level passion. While IPL franchises remain fixated on Indian players and more established international players, the presence of several players from the ICC's Associate Members—such as Alex Kervezee (the Netherlands), Kyle Coetzer (Scotland), Rizwan Cheema (Canada), Niall O'Brien (Ireland), Hamid Hassan (Afghanistan) and Freddie Klocker (Denmark)—in the 2012 Bangladesh Premier League (BPL) showed that such a movement of players and possible global development of the game could get underway in Twenty20 leagues. (The BPL requires each of its six franchises to buy at least one player from an Associate country.)[37] For the time being, these players will hope for promotion to the IPL, but if other Twenty20 leagues take hold worldwide, they might find employment elsewhere as well.

The closest cricket has come to a world labour market has been English county cricket. But not quite, for county cricket still incorporated restrictions on the number of overseas players in county sides. And the modern-day reaction to the presence of the so-called 'Kolpak' players in English county cricket shows that a genuine world labour market does not easily get established when a nationalist or geographical structure is in place in a local sport system because cries of 'foreigner' greet the presence of the 'mercenary' in the ranks of its teams.[38] Football avoids this problem because the delinking of clubs from the role of nurseries for national teams is almost complete. Counties are still seen as contributing to the national mission of enhancing English cricket and its national team, and the presence of the sports professional plying his trade by playing in another country engenders nativist talk. England as such cannot shake loose the accusation that it is a mere importer of players as opposed to a canny recruiter of professional services. The older restrictions on overseas players in the ranks of the English county were important precisely because of their explicit connection with nationalist interests; to restrict the overseas player was to promote the home player. But there has never been a cricketing reason to restrict overseas players in a domestic cricket scene, only nationalist ones.

In cricket, national origin still makes a difference, and the tolerance for the globe-trotting professional is a little low. In contrast, cries of 'foreigner' do not arise quite as often when a non-native represents a country in other domains; an Indian-American doctor who carries a US passport after naturalization and represents the US at the annual conference of the Red Cross is quite straightforwardly an American. For a true world labour market in cricket to emerge, cricket leagues would have to be freed from any imperative to produce a strong national team. The global structure of cricket would have to evolve away from the current primacy of international cricket created by the arrangements of the ICC and its constituent national boards.

The IPL, the Champions League, the BBL and the BPL show how this may occur in the not-too-distant future. Currently, thanks to the IPL and Champions League, which make it possible for a player to play for different sides during different competitions, the outlines of a world labour market made up of players not beholden to any nation are visible and highly suggestive. Worries about the motivations of potentially conflicted players—torn between their state sides and their IPL franchises when they play in the Champions League—arise precisely because of the conflict between 'home' and elsewhere. These would not be raised if the nativist link between them and their 'home state' was severed. As professionals, the players should perform as well as they can; they would not owe their domestic sides any more than what any employee might owe his former employer.

Problematically, for nations other than India, for national boards other than the BCCI, the IPL has made it possible to skip the traditional nurseries of state, county, city, province and country. Dirk Nannes showed how easily traditional player growth models could be disrupted: players can find a road to the national side via a Twenty20 league, or they can settle for its duties in preference to service in national and first-class sides. The IPL, BBL and the Champions League ensure players can refuse central contracts with national boards and play instead for clubs and franchises in international competitions. The two Andrews, Symonds and Flintoff, were good examples of this new-found freedom; a situation preferable for them, and their agents, because of their disciplinary and fitness problems respectively. Being a freelancer also means not having to supply an NOC furnished by the 'home' board; the player sets his price and looks for willing buyers, unencumbered by the board.

Cricketers in this situation seem like free agents, working for self, offering their services on the international market, and considering and rejecting contract terms on the basis of their self-interest with no national board making claims on their loyalties. The glimpse of the Promised Land afforded by the Twenty20 league has been startling. It will veer into ever sharper focus if more leagues like Australia's BBL take hold in their respective domestic cricket scenes. But again, this was a glimpse first afforded by the WSC and the ICL, which showed how a cricketer could earn an income outside of the strictures of official international cricket.

The role of domestic cricket structures is already considerably attenuated, for the crowded international schedule leaves little time and passion for cricket at a lower level of competition. The peculiarity of this situation is apparent: currently, domestic competitions and international cricket produce players who gain fame and reputation through their structures and economies and then abandon them to go play in franchise-based Twenty20. Such an unstable scheme raises the question of whether franchises, those of the IPL or others, will be able to build a road to their future on the back of geography-based cricket, and how long it will take before they will want or need to produce their own players from their own domestic systems. But IPL franchises have no interest in developing farm systems if they have to pay premium prices for international players in an auction; they would be more interested in grooming players for their teams if those players were not being drawn from a pool of labour controlled by entities with their own economic interests.

The current relationship between the IPL and domestic competitions worldwide thus highlights a crucial difference between the IPL and other professional sports leagues. The world's greatest sporting franchises—the New York Yankees, Manchester United, the Los Angeles Lakers—were, and are, part of the very structure of the sport. They have served as both showcases for the best players and nurseries to raise them to the level of international sport. The IPL perfectly inverts this process; it exploits an existing professional sports league—that of the ICC and the BCCI—skims its leading players, and throws them into a super-series. Here, the IPL appears as an imposition with an external cost. (The Indian team and its fans felt this acutely given the injuries to Virender Sehwag that kept him out of action for the first half of the team's disastrous 2011 Test tour of England.) English county cricket functioned much like the IPL, with the tacit understanding that imported players' exposure to English conditions and experience in competing against many of the world's best players was suitable recompense. The IPL's compensation to the national boards, in contrast, is largely monetary, for it is not where future international players are groomed, at least not for anything other than Twenty20 cricket.

Besides the IPL, copycat leagues like Australia's BBL, born of the compulsion to claim a share of the apparently limitless Twenty20 pie, place further strain on international cricket scheduling and exacerbate the club–country divide, while pushing the world of cricket towards a global, boundary-less, labour market. A 'hot' Twenty20 player—as Chris Gayle appears to be demonstrating—could conceivably make a living by securing contracts from just these leagues. A franchise with a stake in several of these leagues would be on its way to being a true global entity and could start a farm system for Twenty20 cricketers, independent of the national domestic systems. The investment in such a system would be justified because of its pay-off in the worldwide system of Twenty20 leagues. The players produced would play in multiple leagues, earning their home franchises sporting glory and increased revenue from better television deals.

On the flip side, the proliferation of these leagues will devastate domestic cricket in countries unable to match their pay packets. As a particularly stark example, consider the perennial scrapper and poor cousin, New Zealand, whose domestic cricket scene risks evisceration unless the national board improves remuneration and contracts to retain players who may play only casually for New Zealand so that they can play in more lucrative venues. Precedents abound: Shane Bond and Daryl Tuffey opted to join the ICL; Iain O'Brien retired to move to England and pursue local cricketing options. Lacking the financial means to offer attractive contracts, smaller cricketing countries will continue to haemorrhage their best players to Twenty20 leagues.[39]

The ICL's most significant achievement was to make it possible for cricketers all over the world to take the first steps towards functioning like independent entrepreneurs, earning a living wage not tied to the national board. It exposed the general disaffection amongst players condemned to spend time in unglamorous domestic circuits, hoping to eventually enjoy the riches of the international player. The ICL had made it possible for many players to make a living playing cricket; it did not seem to matter that it was 'unofficial'. The restrictive, nation-based, international-cricket-centric world of cricket was a severe disadvantage for these players.

As Shahid Afridi's case demonstrated in 2011, the need for players to be delinked from their national boards—whose co-operation with each other in restricting player movements for employment opportunities makes them a cartel—was never more apparent. Afridi was denied an NOC to play for Hampshire—with whom he had a signed contract—after his dispute with the PCB.[40] He could have taken the ECB to court as he had already signed for Hampshire and claimed collusion on their part to deny him a living. Later, the PCB relented and granted him an NOC. The Afridi case suggests that a crucial legal clash between players, boards and the new Twenty20 leagues will occur when a franchise seeks a player's services and the player agrees, but his parent board does not grant him the NOC. At that point, the player could breach his contract with the board, and the board would take legal action against the player.[41] If the court in question then rules that the contractual demands are untenable, not only would the player be free to play for the franchise, but the court's ruling would have established an important precedent in weakening the hold that boards currently enjoy over players. (A dispute along related lines is brewing between the WICB and the WIPA; its resolution will bear watching.)[42]

With the ICL, the franchise model had served to highlight the weakness of the nation-based structure of cricket in providing adequate employment to cricketers. And talk of the nation—and of loyalty to it—had, most importantly, also prompted talk about how franchises in a truly international league could put an end to nation-based cricket's trading in the most problematic of twentieth-century obsessions, nationalism. The longer the IPL persists, the more successful it will be in raising the club–country question, and in raising the kind of questions raised by the ICL when it formed 'national' teams, and the more attention it will bring to national boards and the ICC and their claim to be the best guarantors of cricket's future.

Thus, the most important move towards a post-nation world in cricket is the persistence of the IPL and the success of other leagues like it. And there it faces many challenges, not all of them immediately visible when confronted with tales of IPL player riches, premature retirements of Test cricketers, extravagant valuations of the league and bonanza television rights.

CHAPTER 3

The BCCI–IPL: Prognosis and Prescription

Thus far, an assumption of the rise of the IPL's fortunes has been axiomatic in most discussions on cricket's future. But there are internal and external problems, sporting, financial and administrative, that the league needs to surmount. Indeed, as the fifth season of the IPL approached, it seemed in disarray thanks to the Indian Test team losses, the cancellation of the Sahara deal and Lalit Modi's whistle-blowing about, among other things, rigged IPL auctions: 'One IPL team has pulled out, two more are in arbitration, a fourth in litigation, the BCCI has dissociated from its broadcast partner Nimbus, lost its team sponsor Sahara, the team itself is losing and rights are hard to sell.'[1] And worries were expressed too, whether it could generate the same television rankings as before[2] and whether its management had learned from the fiascos of the third season to become more professional and transparent, especially when it came to constantly making rule changes to accommodate one interested party or another.[3]

In the worst case, the IPL's economics could be disruptive enough to pull Test players into retirement, to distract youngsters, but not robust enough to survive beyond a few years, in which time severe,

if not irreparable, damage might have been done to domestic and
international cricket worldwide. Such a fear has already been expressed
with regards to the Australian BBL and its effect on Australian domestic
cricket.[4] A milder version of this scenario would have the IPL and its
emulators vanish, having provoked conversation and possible thoughts
for reconfiguring cricket. But if the IPL succeeds, expands, is copied,
disrupts international cricket in structure, then some of the most
ambitious—and possibly disturbing for some—changes alluded to in
these pages might well be on their way to being realized.

The Indian fan will play a crucial role in deciding the IPL's eventual
fate; the global audience will play a significantly smaller part. More
than anything, the IPL will test the appetite of the Indian fan for a
cricket league that is not fully international, does not necessarily feature
the best players in the world, and whose cricket might not be of the
highest quality. The IPL, in these formative years, will also depend on
the Indian team doing well in international cricket. Without success
in that domain, the IPL, in the eyes of the Indian fan, will showcase
failure. In this regard, the shake-out from India's 0–8 thumping in
2011–12 remains to be properly assessed; the BCCI will have to act,
and soon, to assure the Indian fan that it has not ignored Team India in
its obsession with the IPL.

Equally crucial is the IPL's dependence on the Indian economy,
since the IPL's allure for its commercial partners is primarily financial.
Its business model is not complicated: it earns revenue through the
sale of media rights, the title sponsorship of the tournament and
merchandise licensing, and then distributes it amongst the franchises.
Franchises earn revenue from gate collections, sale of advertising space,
ticket advertising, and sponsorship on team uniforms. IPL franchises,
some of whom are now in the black, are clearly banking on a boom
economy to make their extravagant investments worthwhile. As the
now-defunct Kochi Kerala Tuskers found out, the IPL was not simply a
case of 'money for nothing'; and as the case of the Sahara sponsorship
dispute showed, the BCCI has to work harder to keep its commercial
partners happy.

Thus, given its reliance on the backing of one national, gold-rush
economy featuring plenty of giddy investors and a sense of never-
ending revenue streams, because valuations often race well ahead

of reality, bringing busts in their wake, and because even in the fifth season, management problems continue to plague the IPL, a moderate scepticism is a healthy response to the IPL's proponents' most vigorous claims. This is especially true because the vagaries of the world's finances may still deal a wicked uppercut to the IPL's backers who are, invariably, large multinational consortiums enmeshed, inevitably, in the world financial system's affairs. But to hitch one's wagon to the business world is to suffer the derailments of stock markets underwritten by collusion, insider trading, systematic fraud, deceit, and the invocation of voodoo charms. The devastation of US middle-class retirement funds in 2008 by a grossly mismanaged, deregulated and dishonest financial community bears adequate testimony to the plausibility of this worry.

Cricket's longevity, despite it being a largely marginal sport at best, might well trace some of its provenance to its unfashionable delinking from the external business world. Such total abstinence is perhaps neither possible nor desirable now, but it is worth keeping in mind when the future of the IPL is pondered. What the investor and the market give, they might very well take away.

If You Build a Franchise, They Will Come

The earliest criticism of the IPL pointed out that the league suffered a crucial, possibly crippling weakness, especially in comparison to professional leagues whose audiences had been built, maintained and sustained for extended periods of time, starting with the particular and highly specific relationships their member clubs bore to their fan bases and local neighbourhoods. These local followings are what sustain the club, enable its prosperity and make fan loyalty a reflexive gesture. In this picture, a global franchise like Manchester United or the Los Angeles Lakers represents a locally successful club transformed into a global 'brand' with a non-local following. Some professional leagues, of course, never aspire to global standing and are perfectly happy, arguably, with their local footprint. Such a claim might be made, for instance, for the Australian Football League (AFL) and the Australian National Rugby League (NRL).

The IPL, when it began, was confined to the urban centres of India, and consequently disregarded those regions that have been the most productive in terms of recent cricketing talent and provide large television audiences in India—the mid-sized city and the small town. Furthermore, because of their short season and their unfamiliar and rapidly changing rosters, IPL franchises had little scope to develop extended relationships conducive to the growth of partisanship within their local terrain. A new franchise like the Pune Warriors faced especial difficulty in playing catch-up as an expansion team in a league that could not promise it instant popularity. (Later, the Warriors faced even worse problems as the Sahara–BCCI dispute preceding the fifth season showed.) The Kochi Kerala Tuskers, of course, never managed to solve this problem.

Thus, one straightforward difficulty faced by the IPL is of generating a loyal, committed and passionate fan base. This is not an insurmountable barrier for a well-marketed, lavishly promoted league. But neither are its challenges to be discounted, and the high failure rate of sports leagues worldwide—and the canning of the Kochi Kerala Tuskers by the BCCI—sounds an appropriate note of caution.

Anecdotal evidence suggests that fan identification with IPL teams proceeds in a fashion found in other sports: the presence of a favourite player, a controversy that required the taking of sides, star personalities, and so on. Initial fan reactions to the IPL, though, were reflective of genuine confusion. Cheering for an overseas player playing for 'your' franchise, when he was engaged in a personal tussle with an Indian star, was a strange experience for many. Would a Delhi fan cheer for David Warner's assault on Mumbai's Harbhajan Singh?

Ironically, given the post-nation dreams engendered by Twenty20 leagues, it was India's 2007 Twenty20 World Cup win that initially drove the IPL to average an attendance of 58,000 in its first season.[5] Some of this success had little to do with the cricket but everything to do with the glamour associated with a team: it would have been hard to imagine a team with Sachin Tendulkar not attracting a large following. The Mumbai Indians and the Kolkata Knight Riders, the latter perhaps riding on Saurav Ganguly and Shahrukh Khan's fame, in particular, quickly acquired a local and loyal base.

In such a fledgling league, now five years old, rivalry between clubs and their fans is often tenuous, artificially propped up by the excessively contrived franchise advertisements that start doing the rounds well in advance of the season. But the IPL needs to attract the kind of loyal committed fan whose constant passion has enabled cricket to weather times of economic penury. It cannot hope to survive on the drive-by fan. A fan reared on international cricket, who thinks cheering for large professional franchises is a bit like cheering for Ford vs Chrysler, might find the IPL's inter-city rivalry contrived and fail to engage emotionally. IPL franchises will have to convince such a fan that his attention is fruitfully diverted to their offerings. It will be cricket that will do the trick, and not just the IPL's stadium entertainment package.

For an average Indian cricket fan, domestic cricket comes with villains and heroes clearly defined. For this author, it was bold, bustling Delhi against those stodgy, tiffin-packing Bombay-wallahs. Delhi players went to local colleges and played in local clubs with names familiar from the local newspapers. Throwing one's lot in with this fraternity seemed natural and reflexive, even if, as years went by, thanks to domestic transfers in Ranji Trophy cricket, loyalties had to be modified to accommodate the out-of-state 'mercenary' or the 'local' transferring out. During the IPL's first few seasons, the Delhi team seemed a curious, unfamiliar hybrid, one that did not allow instant adoption even by loyal Delhi fans. The overseas hires ensured that the nationalistic fervour that marked international cricket was absent and the Delhi team did not seem 'Delhiite' enough.

But a loyal fan is born when he senses players' fidelity to the game, their skills, and his club. By the fourth season, the players seemed to have convinced some IPL fans that the cricket they played was serious, that they cared about the outcome, that winning and losing was of crucial importance to them; some franchises started to acquire reasonably loyal fan followings. This process seems destined to continue as long as cricket is pushed to the centre, and not to the margins in the rush to commercialize and exploit the action in the middle.

Here again, IPL franchise owners might seek limitations on players' free agency precisely so that fan identification with a club can be built over a period of time. Current IPL transfer rules have been disruptive of such hopes. In the fourth season, player movement between franchises disturbed many player–fan associations. Delhi boy Gautam Gambhir's move to the Kolkata Knight Riders from the Delhi Daredevils and Punjabi puttar Yuvraj Singh's move to the Pune Warriors from Kings XI Punjab were the most glaring examples of moves that tested fans' identification with their teams.

But the generation of a team's fan base in the Indian context is not entirely unproblematic because it would thrive on the construction of inter-city rivalries in a country where 'regionalism', that delightful Indian word like 'communalism', which has a special meaning in the Indian context, is not an idle worry. Jocular remarks made by north Indians about 'Madrasis' or by Punjabis about 'Bongs' are not innocent in the Indian context for this lot. Would the harnessing of advertising with sport along 'regional' lines be benign, for club marketing thrives on contriving differences between cities, teams and fans? Would the Mumbai Indians be happy to receive public, vocal support from the Shiv Sena, which might suddenly decide to project it as a visible symbol—in whatever imagined dimension—of Mumbai's superiority?

The BCCI–IPL's decision to facilitate player transfer amongst IPL franchises, to permit the inclusion of overseas players, have thus far acted to limit a 'local' presence in IPL teams and prevent the overly strong identification of local fans' ethnicity-based identities with that of franchise players. Such has not been the BCCI's explicitly avowed motive, but it could be its effect. A franchise like the Delhi Daredevils would be a very different package for residents of the Indian capital if its XI included more locals able to stay on the team's roster for extended periods.

The IPL could breed, most promisingly, rivalries similar to that of the Yankees–Red Sox where, despite the apparent rabidity, or the occasional story of beer poured on Yankees fans at Fenway Park, the odd brawl between Red Sox and Yankees fans at Yankees Stadium, and the expectedly edgy clashes between fans online, there has always seemed to be an implicit, unspoken understanding that it was all a bit of a lark (well, at least among the more sober fans). Or, more worryingly, intemperate IPL marketing could generate the vicious tribalism of the Rangers–Celtics football rivalry.

Thus far, fan rivalry in the IPL remains benign, for the atmosphere at IPL games is still more carnivalesque than gladiatorial. Older rivalries with their greater emotional hold will take over; the Delhi Daredevils fan returns to hoping David Warner will fail when he plays India. Perhaps this is unsurprising because such a fan is easily diverted by the cricket world's other offerings once the short IPL season ends. This tenuous hold of the IPL franchise could prevent rabid fanhood, a blessing for the concerned Indian patriot and a curse for the IPL marketer. It could change if the role of franchises in Indian cricket is expanded, as would be the case if they were to become involved in domestic cricket, for then they would have a longer-term relationship with both players and local fans.

However, IPL marketing has generated visible fan loyalty, perhaps better than Ranji Trophy teams have if attendance at IPL games is compared to that at Ranji, Duleep or Irani Trophy games. Some of this is due to change in format, but the rest may be traced back to aggressive marketing, merchandizing and the provision of a party at the local stadium. This situation has the salutary side-effect of forcing attention to the fact that the BCCI's efforts to promote domestic cricket are not comparable to the IPL franchises' promotional activities. The BCCI and its state associations have failed to market the Ranji Trophy and other components of domestic cricket adequately, even failing to do justice to the riveting 2009 Ranji Trophy final between Mumbai and Karnataka played to a capacity stadium in Mysore. State-level cricket might do well too, if a fraction of the energy, passion and commitment that administrators show for format proliferation and television rights could be devoted to thinking about how the long-format domestic game might be promoted by the same combination of tactics employed by IPL marketers. Nothing works quite as well as a T-shirt in this regard; Ranji teams do not sell them, IPL franchises do. The fate of domestic cricket might rest on the willingness of its managers to dispense, for a price, colourful sloganed apparel.

The IPL's best friends are the Indian economy and the absence of Indian success stories in sports other than cricket: if the Indian economy flourishes, if the urban Indian continues to have leisure time for the IPL, if other sports fail to generate success stories that compete for the Indian fan's attention, if the Indian team can climb back from its recent Test defeats, the IPL will slowly but surely build identification with its local fan base. The presence of a local, just-international-enough franchise showcasing successful Indian cricketers is all this group needs as diversion. In particular, a large urban population, which, given its time commitments and disposable income, is best suited for watching an IPL game, will ensure a large IPL following in the cities. But whether the IPL will ever command a loyal following outside major metropolitan centres is questionable, for it could alienate those Indian fans who, not living in the regions covered by the IPL franchises, and experiencing a lack of representation in their teams, simply tune out the IPL. This problem, as we will see below, is also crucial when thinking about whether IPL-style franchises could supplement, or even supplant, extant domestic cricket structures in India.

Expansion and Saturation

For those familiar with tamasha, the IPL's success has not been surprising. But even tamashas can go stale, and worries about the injudicious expansion of the IPL and the possible saturation of the Indian cricket market are not unfounded. Worries about an unsustainable boom in the IPL, for instance, were quite reasonably triggered by the addition, in 2010, of two new franchises—the Pune Warriors, bought by the Sahara Group for US$370 million and the Kochi Kerala Tuskers, bought by Rendezvous Sports World Consortium for US$333 million[6]—both of whom needed to attract commercial partners and sponsors to generate IPL-related spin-offs and were reliant on the continued growth of the Indian economy. A year or so later, the Kochi franchise was history, the BCCI having terminated it for failure to meet its financial guarantees. Its failure is the most serious indicator of a limit to the IPL's fortunes. The Pune Warriors, in turn, were floundering as the Sahara Group withdrew its ownership, its once-happy relationship with the BCCI on the rocks.

Extravagant investment in franchises is not necessarily evidence of serious brain dysfunction. A sports franchise is a visible demonstration of wealth first and foremost. The value of the franchise for its owner— as Mark Cuban will readily testify—is not so much its balance sheet as its ego-propping capabilities. The good doctor, Herr Freud, would have had a field day analysing the propensity of businessmen to buy large, expensive properties in urban settings and to make well-endowed athletes perform publicly for them. Young men, poorer versions of those that buy sports teams, have long known that economically mysterious activities such as dropping out of school to pick up a guitar yield dividends not translatable into straightforward financial terms.

In the case of a sports franchise, the ownership of one can enhance the business prospects of other properties. Sport still carries a cachet unlike any other trade; a business expansion into a related industry makes a few headlines in the business section, but the purchase of a sports team features in two sections of a newspaper. Cricket will continue to retain its glamour quotient for Indian investors in the foreseeable future, especially if the Bollywood connection is maintained or enhanced, and crucially—this point cannot be emphasized enough—if the Indian cricket team remains a visible symbol of sporting success. The urge to spend millions of rupees to enable cavorting on television with cricket and Bollywood stars, and the opportunity to associate a corporate 'brand' with a successful sporting one will remain irresistible for many in the Indian business community.

While the Indian economy is large enough to sustain more than one professionalized sport, it still features disproportionate investment in cricket by sponsors and advertisers. While the chances of other sports serving as a diversion for their budgets remain slight, some Olympic sports such as shooting, weightlifting, boxing, and wrestling, as well as hockey or soccer, might still serve to take away a part of such funds. These sports, along with basketball, cannot be discounted—especially if the seven-foot four-inch Indian-Canadian youngster, Sim Bhullar, gearing up for an NCAA career in the US, earns an NBA contract. If they, along with golf (where Arjun Atwal, the first Indian to win a PGA tour event, or Jeev Milkha Singh, the first Indian to qualify for the European Tour, could inspire a new generation of Indian golfers) and tennis (if Indians perform as well in singles as they do in doubles) start to snip away at sponsor dollars, the IPL's financial health could take a beating.

The IPL council's biggest worry might be the commission of Golden Goose Homicide, a crime of which cricket administrators worldwide might justly be accused: the number of IPL franchises will need capping, as will the length of the season. Problems with saturation were most visible in the flatlining television ratings of the IPL's fourth season, as struggling Indian fans, caught in the inevitable trough that followed the euphoric high of the 2011 World Cup, found their attention faltering as the season wore on;[7] later that same year, even attendance at one-day internationals plummeted to new lows. Many Indian fans have already complained of the length of an IPL season and spoken warily of the prospect of a second one in the same year. But season length does not seem wholly determinative of a league's success. The MLB (with 162 games from April to October) and the NBA (with eighty-two games stretching from October to June) feature seasons that are often accused of being too long. Here, the quality of the sporting contests often makes up for concerns about season length or an excessive number of games. The IPL—and other Twenty20 leagues—would do well to emulate these benchmark leagues in this regard. They could too, consider diversifying their offerings via a fifty-over tournament or even a five-day one.

If other Twenty20 leagues worldwide come to resemble the IPL in structure, content, format, and perhaps salaries, the IPL could lose its uniqueness for its commercial partners and television audience. Australia's BBL is likely to be the IPL's most serious competitor (especially if Indian cricketers are invited to play). Its expansion in 2012 will bear close watching. While its success will inevitably depend on Indian investors and Indian television audiences, it could contribute to a surfeit of Twenty20 and perhaps overexpose Indian cricketers. The BCCI might prevent Indian cricketers from playing in the BBL and other Twenty20 leagues to prevent pernicious overconsumption and subsequent devaluation of their most valuable property.

What About the Cricket?

In sporting terms, there is the question of whether the IPL is indeed the showcase for the world's best talent and, consequently, the stage for the highest-quality Twenty20 cricket in the world. Franchises might need to assert this for advertising purposes but claims that the IPL was an adequate training ground for the rigours of international cricket would have appeared ludicrous when India, supposedly the favourite for the 2009 Twenty20 World Cup in England, and the 2010 Twenty20 World Cup in the West Indies, did not feature in the finals of either; the top

IPL teams, in the inaugural Champions League, playing on home soil, won only three matches out of ten.

There is a precedent for this, of course. The EPL has not resulted in England winning another World Cup to add to its 1966 triumph, and neither did the presence of international stars in English county cricket turn England into the world's strongest team. If anything, it merely strengthened other teams—the 1970s West Indians and Pakistanis being classic examples—by exposing them to English conditions. But the EPL's standing does not diminish with England's failure to win a World Cup as it has long lost any pretensions to being a nursery for English football; rather, it is merely a stage for the exhibition of the football skills of some of the world's best players. However the IPL, in the presence of overseas player quotas, is not yet as international as the EPL. For the time being, its evaluation will be done like the evaluation of any domestic cricket league: does it groom its participants adequately for the rigours of international cricket? Soon, it will be judged rather more simply: is the quality of cricket on display good enough?

This worry about the IPL's cricketing quality is neither new nor uncommon, especially as the quality of its bowling attack has often seemed below international standards. The IPL might continue to regress if its rosters—padded and filled out with Indian players to keep up with quota requirements—serve as showcases for mediocrity rather than excellence. (These quotas allow three BCCI party lines to be maintained: first, the IPL is a domestic tournament, and as such, the highest standards of the game should not be expected from it; second, its primary function is to reward Indian players and to bring new Indian talent to the fore, even if thus far Indian team selections have not drawn too heavily on IPL-generated talent; lastly, the BCCI bears no responsibility for any problems of prioritization for players committed to international cricket by their national boards.)

But this numerical dominance by Indian players in the IPL rosters has generated greater competition among overseas Twenty20 stars for the four available slots With the commencement of Australia's BBL, more Twenty20 specialists will be looking for work. This competition, from both Indian players and upstart Twenty20 tyros, has sharpened the edge of established overseas stars who initially conveyed the impression of time-card punching cheque collectors deigning to put in an appearance when international commitments allowed. Greater commitment has been on display as more overseas players now perceive the IPL as a serious career option. Twenty20 specialists like Aiden Blizzard of the Mumbai Indians will push established internationals hard; the IPL's new breed of the Twenty20 free agent, dependent upon the shorter format for a living, is likely to be an eager beaver keen for contract renewal and a higher price in the player auction, and will contribute mightily to the format's cricket retaining a competitive edge. The ICL had already demonstrated how many cricketers would like to make money outside of international cricket; the hunger of players like them, both Indian and overseas, is the IPL's best bet for the future.

After the IPL's third season disasters, its most pressing concerns remain matters of administration and governance. But as the franchise expulsion fiasco[8] of 2010 and the Sahara dispute of 2012 demonstrated, to talk about the reform of the IPL is to talk about the reform of the BCCI. Indeed, the entity in question is more accurately referred to as the BCCI–IPL: the IPL is now a subcommittee of the BCCI, its governing council has been shrunk and its powers limited, while franchise representation remains minimal, a strange state of affairs for a professional league. So incestuous is the relationship of the IPL to the BCCI that it features gigantic conflicts of interest in violation of the BCCI's charter:[9] BCCI secretary and president-elect N. Srinivasan is a member of the IPL governing council and the owner of the Chennai Super Kings,[10] while during the first three IPL seasons, national selector K. Srikkanth served as brand ambassador for the same franchise. These blatant conflicts of interest, many more of which were discovered during the third season scandals, are staggering violations of any respectable standards of transparency.

Reform of the BCCI is necessary, but not just for better administration of the IPL. An overhaul is required because of the BCCI's importance in world cricket. Any meaningful prescription for world cricket will necessarily include the BCCI in its to-do list. But this change is seemingly intractable for a variety of reasons: the history of the BCCI, its identification with Indian cricket, its politically powerful leadership, and the nature of player power in India.

Reforming the BCCI

The BCCI takes some explaining. Its status is that of a club, a charity, one dedicated to the promotion of a healthy outdoor activity that would uplift the country's youth. These paeans to the gymnasium are sharply at odds with the reality of the BCCI, which, thanks to the Indian passion for cricket and its gigantic television rights deals, has come to resemble a media corporation, with all its attendant ruthlessness and short-sightedness. Wealth and power; what else can one think of when powerful politicians head an organization that traffics in multimillion dollar media deals? Such a combination of sporting, financial and political power is perhaps only comparably present in the Silvio Berlusconi–AC Milan combine, an unflattering comparison Indian cricket would do well to stay away from.

The most important events in Indian cricket history in recent times—in their economic implications, at least—have been the winning of the Prudential World Cup in 1983, the hosting of the Reliance World Cup in 1987, the winning of the Twenty20 World Cup in 2007, and the freeing of the BCCI, by the Supreme Court of India, from the onerous income-restricting provisions of the colonial-era Telegraph Act.[11] That last momentous intervention set the BCCI loose to trade in the market for television rights deals for cricket. From then on, riding on a magic carpet of lucrative partnerships with media companies, the BCCI has enjoyed all the power, if not the competence, of the rich. And in true plutocratic fashion, it often deems itself above the mere mortals' world of accountability, transparency and reform.

The presence of politicians and powerful businessmen in the BCCI's councils of power has meant Indian inegalitarianism has been reinforced in cricketing administration; its players are not managed as much as they are ruled by figures that in India are inextricably connected with power and influence. The ability of a small-town Indian player to transcend this particular power relation, to speak up, to assert himself, is limited at best.

The BCCI's riches—coupled with its often heavy-handed, sometimes arbitrary actions—thus breed a peculiar relationship with players. While the BCCI now gives Indian players, international and domestic,

26 per cent of its gross annual revenues, it has done little to promote player autonomy or ownership of the game. The Indian player, cognizant of the fickleness of the BCCI, is predisposed to make the most of his possibly truncated relationship with riches and fame. He is well aware that the BCCI, whether in dealing with temperamental talent or with professional ambition, has not been afraid to be ruthlessly autocratic. There is ample historical precedent in the tales of Lala Amarnath's return from England after the 1936 tour, Vinoo Mankad's troubles in playing for Haslingden in the Lancashire Leagues in 1952, the various difficulties Indian players have faced in representing English county sides, the banning of half-a-dozen Test cricketers for playing unauthorized cricket in the US in 1989, the denial of permission to players to participate in the Sri Lankan Premier League in 2011, and of course, the ICL.

The BCCI has never fought a battle with players it has not won. The players, aware of this history of compromise, co-optation and defeat, have seemingly resolved to make the most of their temporary fame and fortune and to then move on. Indian cricket remains for the player a temporary employer, one to perhaps be commented upon after retirement, but not one to be engaged with from the grassroots; reform and struggle with the upper echelons of power are secondary concerns. The BCCI has at least managed to successfully alienate most players from harbouring any pretensions to greater autonomy or administrative power.

While a players' association or union, which could take up collective cudgels on the players' behalf, looms as a partial solution to this state of affairs, it faces seemingly insuperable barriers. Player associations have started up before and have run aground; the Association of Indian Cricketers (AIC) did not last long after its founding in 1989, and neither did the Indian Cricket Players' Association (ICPA), which attempted to get off the ground in 2002.[12] Indian players often appear too divided—by class, sporting seniority, language—to come together under a collective banner. As the histories of the AIC and the ICPA will reveal, the BCCI's 'divide-and-rule' policy with players has paid it rich dividends in controlling any of their aspirations to power.[13]

Neither has a strong leadership role ever been played by an Indian player, no matter what his seeming influence. Sachin Tendulkar, while obviously aware of his tremendous rhetorical power and the guaranteed media impact his reformatory pronouncements would have, has stayed resolutely clear of controversy and avoided substantive confrontations with the BCCI. A reform-demanding speech like Kumar Sangakkara's Cowdrey Lecture will not be made by an Indian star, even one as well-ensconced as Tendulkar, in the foreseeable future. To be fair to the Indian player, his awareness of the fickleness of the Indian fan is also likely to be a discouraging factor. What guarantee is there that a 'rebel' player will not be perceived as a 'traitor' by them? (The recent BCCI versus the Rest of the World debate has also produced a new variety of Indian fan, keen to defend the BCCI against the perceived slights of all and sundry, thus further complicating any assessment of the possible incitement of Indian fans to 'rebellion' against the BCCI.)

The BCCI thus enjoys an immediate advantage in its relationships with Indian players. This power relation would be interestingly attenuated were most of its administrators ex-cricketers. The awe and respect for an apparatchik would then have a genuine cricketing tinge to it, and there might be more empathy for the player's lot from administrators too. Thus, one of the most promising potential changes in Indian cricket is the attainment, by former players, of positions of power: Anil Kumble and Javagal Srinath, for instance, are now office-bearers of the Karnataka State Cricket Association (and thus eligible for BCCI offices). If there is hope for reform of the BCCI, it lies in moves like this one, where players feel sufficiently invested in the game to return to its caretaking. Dilip Vengsarkar did run for office in the Mumbai Cricket Association elections in 2011 but lost, unfortunately, to a politician candidate, Vilasrao Deshmukh, the Union Minister of Science and Technology.[14] But retired players bold enough to bell the BCCI cat need to know they are entering a professional sphere where their very particular set of skills and talents are desirable and valuable; for that, a critical mass of professionals and players will be required to accompany the ex-player's efforts.

While player power has been neutered by a mix of financial inducements and displays of administrative might, the BCCI's member state associations are rendered benign and perhaps even dysfunctional by generous revenue-sharing that demands no accountability. The BCCI's fortunes supposedly flow back into local development schemes for cricket because regional cricket boards depend on the BCCI for hand-outs of funds for infrastructure and grassroots development. But these state associations do not return to annual meetings of the BCCI with detailed reports of expenditure and outcomes. Unsurprisingly, the list of state associations whose cricket remains mired in mediocrity is a long one.

The BCCI's revenues, earned by cricketers' performances on the field, go into state association coffers and pockets. Except for a few of the justifiably famous and productive age-group tournaments which showcase young cricketers, or the new academies that supposedly promote and train fast bowlers and encourage development of coaching techniques and sports medicine, there is little evidence that the BCCI and its member state associations are breeding future stars. Not do they seem to be nurturing existing ones.

The repeated inconsistency of the Indian team can be attributed to several factors, both at administrative and performance levels. Persistent over-scheduling, selectorial flakiness, failure to establish IPL versus international duty priorities and planning Test tours without time for adequate preparation are to be blamed on the administrative level. At the performance level, preparing death-bed pitches affects bowlers' desire to bowl fast and batsmens' ability to perform on fast overseas tracks. Every single one of these familiar problems contributed to India's 0–4 thumpings at the hands of the English and Australian teams in 2011 and 2012. If the BCCI can be forced to reform its cricketing management in response to these twin disasters, perhaps some good will have come out of one of the most depressing events in recent Indian cricket history.

BCCI office-bearers appear thus to be engaged in a rather comfortable line of business: they dispense largesse, no questions asked, in exchange for votes during its elections, which permit them to continue to occupy their positions as controllers of the huge Indian market in television rights. But this hands-off attitude with regard to the state associations ensures that besides creating a mediocre environment for cricketing excellence, cricket is administered in curiously disjointed fashion. The abandonment of the one-day international between India and Sri Lanka in Delhi in 2009, or the riots in Guwahati during England's 2006 tour should have been greater embarrassments for the BCCI than they seemingly were. The responsibility for the grounds in question rested with the Delhi and District Cricket Association, and the Assam Cricket Association, but all of Indian cricket was besmirched. The pretensions of state association decentralization and autonomy are self-serving in this regard. When the BCCI wants to exert nation-wide power, it is able to do so, swiftly and efficiently. But to exert too much managerial control over non-performing state associations might be to lose a guaranteed vote during election time, a risk perhaps too great to take.

The BCCI's internal structure and functioning, lacking standardization and consistency, remains opaque. Some member associations of the BCCI are registered under the Societies Registration Act, others under the Companies Act. The former forbids voting by proxy; the latter does not, and in the resulting system, proxy forms can be misused. During its elections, there is no independent supervision. A more transparent state of affairs would require an 'independent returns officer' such as a retired jurist to conduct the elections.[15] Reform is unlikely, of course; it would immediately deny entrenched feeders-at-the-trough their positions of comfort and power. Change only appears likely if externally imposed.

Though politicians are often office-bearers in the BCCI, it is officially a 'private body', a status that seemingly renders it immune to external reform. However, the Indian constitutional provision of a Public Interest Litigation (PIL), while sometimes misused to frivolous ends, has resulted in at least one cricket fan forcing reform upon the BCCI. In 2000, Delhi lawyer Rahul Mehra filed a PIL against the BCCI in an attempt to ensure public accountability from the board, accusing it of being the 'private empire of a business and some traders'.[16]

The resultant legal encounter ended in victory for Mehra as an Indian High Court rejected the BCCI's argument that it was a wholly private body not subject to governmental regulation, and pushed it towards instituting some reforms—such as pension schemes for retired players and revenue sharing with current players—suggested by Mehra's PIL. Mehra's comprehensive wish-list of reforms—which makes, in particular, a passionate plea for full-time professional administrators—remains fascinating reading;[17] some reforms have been implemented while many others remain in the queue, awaiting new leadership at the BCCI.

Mehra et al. vs BCCI et al. also ensured that the BCCI is subject to other PILs lodged by those invested financially or emotionally in Indian cricket. A comprehensive, well-documented account of the cost of the operational opacity and poor governance at the BCCI could still form the basis of a PIL—like Mehra's—in the future. The 2011 National Sports Development Bill[18] could have imposed further mandatory governance requirements on the BCCI—along with other sports associations in the country—which could, in turn, have led to not just a players' association, but also a greater professionalization and regularization of the BCCI's workings; the bill, unfortunately and unsurprisingly, was shot down by the Union Cabinet, which includes four BCCI members, when it first went up for consideration.[19] The Indian sports fan will continue to keep several fingers crossed, hoping for a renewal of efforts to pass such legislation.

NURTURING THE NURSERY

The BCCI, while claiming tax exemptions as 'a charitable activity', devotes just 8 per cent of its revenues to the actual promotion of cricket.[20] This scandal is a well-known one, but Indian fans have grown strangely numb to it, perhaps because of the giddiness and the national pride generated by the size of the television deals the BCCI keeps signing. These matters of revenue and expenditure obscure another unpleasant fact: for far too long, India's status as the world's richest cricketing nation has only been possible thanks to television money. Its translation into comparative strength on the cricketing field is a relatively recent occurrence, and its domestic system's ability to produce sustained excellence remains questionable. Talk of the dollar value of television deals, or the salaries paid to Indian players or IPL pay-packets, does not prevent gossip—made louder by India's horrendous Test cricket thrashings in 2011–12—about the unflattering state of affairs: after several years of the financial domination of the BCCI, important balance sheets pertaining to Indian cricketing wealth do not stack up well. The BCCI distributes a disproportionate percentage to those at the top, including salaries for Team India's esteemed overseas coaches, with little regard for those that underwrite their current wealth and guarantee their future: the run-of-the-mill recreational or amateur cricketer.

While showing commendable interest in sponsoring the India A tours, or in organizing age-group tournaments, which have brought to maturation many Indian stars, the BCCI is yet to upgrade cricket facilities—whether at the level of school, village cricket ground, district maidan, or city club—across India so that the next generation of its cricketers grow up with ready access to the game. The notion of a community cricket net, available in every major urban neighbourhood, is a very distant dream, as is the possibility that the BCCI could upgrade cricket facilities for public schools or famous nurseries of cricketing talent (the clubs of Mumbai or the universities of Delhi, for example).

Here, graphically, is visible the skewing of the BCCI's priorities by the IPL; rejuvenation of domestic cricket in India appears to have skipped several rungs lower on the totem pole ever since the IPL kicked off. Of course, domestic cricket languished even before the IPL showed up. The Duleep Trophy, the Irani Trophy and the various Challenger tournaments had long been obscured in the rush to schedule one-day internationals. The golden goose metaphor is relentlessly flogged in this context, but its usage is unavoidable, so vividly does it demonstrate the dangers of the BCCI's current obsession with the loud organization of money-spinners as opposed to the quiet, unglamorous cultivation of the game. Clichés about mighty oaks and their undernourished roots thus unavoidably spring to mind when thinking of the BCCI and its handling of the Indian domestic scene.

The BCCI's unique position in the world of cricket places an interesting wrinkle in its responsibilities towards the domestic cricket scene in India: the growth and nurturing of Indian domestic cricket, which is necessary for the success of the Indian team, the quality of the Indian domestic cricketer and the wealth of the IPL, and thus, concomitantly, the overseas cricketer, is a vital component of the ecology of world cricket. Without a steady stream of high-quality Indian cricketers to lavish his devotion on, the Indian fan stands to have his attention diverted by the ever-changing offerings of the entertainment world. Denied this adulation, the IPL will suffer, and so will cricketers worldwide, prevented from earning more than their national boards or domestic systems can pay them.

Given this ecological framework, the BCCI bears an equal responsibility to nurture strong opponents: without adequate competition, the lustre of international contests and the Indian team will diminish. Thus, it would appear in the BCCI's interest to support cricket in Pakistan, New Zealand, West Indies, Sri Lanka, Bangladesh and Zimbabwe. The cricket boards of these countries are unavoidably already dependent on the BCCI's generosity; too often, this assistance has been regarded by overenthusiastic Indian fans as the mere dispensation of largesse. But the spreading of the wealth of the BCCI is an investment that can only benefit Indian and world cricket in the future. One, possibly reductive though not unjustified, way to think of the world's cricket fans is as a television audience for the BCCI's team; it redounds to the BCCI's benefit to assure this audience competitive cricket by taking care of its own team and that of its partners.

For long, the BCCI's riches, associated as they were with a team that performed brilliantly but erratically, placed it in an uncomfortable position. That team's increased consistency in recent times did more to bolster the BCCI's reputation than any of the organization's displays of wealth; when it falters, as the Test team did during its tours of England and Australia, the BCCI's reputation suffers too. The BCCI would do well to remember that it was cricketing success in 1983 that set it down its current path to financial glory. The Indian fan is just as likely to ask 'What have you done for us lately?' as any other fan. The BCCI can only count on continued wealth and power if the Indian team continues to bring it glory on the cricket pitch. Despite the inconsistent performances of the Indian team since 1983, the cricket market in India has grown. This situation is not likely to persist forever when the Indian fan develops a greater sense of expectation, especially in the wake of the 2011 World Cup win and the rise to the number one position in Test cricket. The sharp howls of protest that greet every lacklustre effort by the Indian Test team to drive home an advantage in a Test and settle for a draw is ample proof of such sentiment. A lack of continued success of the Indian team will result in sharper disillusionment and rejection of the BCCI and 'its team'; the BCCI ignores the aspirations of the Indian fan at its own peril. The anger directed against the IPL and the BCCI as the Indian team slumped to heavy defeats against England and Australia during the 2011–12 season and lost its top Test ranking was proof of this backlash. If the BCCI wants to protect the value of the IPL, and its pre-eminence in Indian cricket, it will have to make sure that a successful Indian team is prominent in the Indian fan's mind.

For that, domestic cricket, the nursery of Indian cricket, cannot be ignored and here perhaps, rather than being a problem, the IPL can come to the BCCI's aid.

Franchises Begin At Home

A perennial sore and sticking point for the Indian fan is the perplexity raised by the question of why, given its large player base, India has had such difficulty in producing champion teams over the years. Indian fans have not failed to notice that the tiny nation of Sri Lanka, outmatched in its demographic and economic dimensions by India, is able to produce some of the world's most distinctive batsmen and bowlers, who over the years have made possible a strong Test team and a one-day outfit that has won a World Cup (and reached its final on two other occasions).

Perhaps the much desired reform of the state-based structure of cricket could be best achieved if state associations were replaced by franchises (reorganization along similar lines has been carried out in South Africa and Zimbabwe). This could conceivably lead to a concentration of the talent pool in an environment managed according to 'professional' and 'corporate' standards.[21]

There are two prima facie problems with the argument for franchises to rejuvenate domestic cricket in India: they appear neither necessary nor sufficient.

First, the franchise system is not necessary to produce a high-quality champion cricket team. Australia is a major cricketing power without a franchise system, and it does not lack in player quality. The Australian state cricket championship is a tried and tested ground, and a strong coaching culture and a well-managed, well-equipped, scientifically oriented cricket academy has produced champion teams whose stranglehold over Test and one-day international cricket has only recently weakened. Despite the gloomy assessment of the Argus report, or the alarm bells rung about the possible weakening of Australian cricket by the BBL, only an utter fool would take an Australian team lightly when it steps on to the ground, a fact that says a great deal about a cricketing culture that has cultivated champions despite the lack of a corporate franchise system.

Secondly, a franchise system is not sufficient to rejuvenate Indian domestic cricket. Too many arguments for franchises to replace the current Ranji system assume that a 'professional' attitude can only be cultivated in the context of a 'corporate' atmosphere; that it is somehow part and parcel of the 'corporate ideology' to produce results.[22] This straightforward privatization mantra is unlikely to convince anyone familiar with the state of the railway system in England, but in India it still carries considerable weight. In the Indian context, 'corporate' functions as a synonym for 'professional', as if all the attributes associated with that tag were the exclusive province of the corporation. When an Indian corporation shows itself capable of running anything as complex as the Indian Railways or the general elections, this claim might have more weight. Neither does corporatization inevitably bring cleanliness in its wake, a quixotic hope, given the entrenchment of 'Enron' or 'Satyam' as shorthand for corruption. The IPL in its worst moments, as in its third-season scandals of terrible administration and poor governance, can seem stunningly non-corporate.

So an argument for why franchises would succeed when state sides have not consistently done so needs to rest on grounds other than privatization of Indian cricket. Otherwise this argument is remarkably similar to the generic ones offered for economic liberalization in the Indian context. The merits of such a proposal need to be made independent of corporate boosterism; claims that corporate management would rejuvenate and refurbish Indian cricket often ignore cultural aspects of the Indian cricket scene that will not respond in straightforward fashion to the imposition of a new management structure.

Consider, for instance, the idolization of the senior player in the dressing room and on the cricket field, and the concomitant lack of upward-directed feedback from junior players. The corporate culture in India is no more egalitarian than that of the society it is embedded in. No Indian manager is likely to be addressed by his first name by a junior associate in any workplace in the country. The IPL players currently addressing franchise owners by first names are not Indian. The problem of the lack of an egalitarian dressing room would not be solved if board-room inegalitarianism is imported into the cricket franchise.

But franchises in Indian domestic cricket could certainly create a smaller pool of cricketers at a higher level of competition by replacing the twenty-seven state associations that currently participate in domestic cricket, perhaps by combining several state teams into one.[23] (Entrenched state associations are likely to resist strenuously unless franchises incorporate their existing infrastructure and provide employment to their current staff—not an impossible task.) The IPL's franchises could participate in four-day and one-day tournaments with two hundred players—a considerable shrinkage of the current pool—competing for spots on rosters. Franchises could retain as much of the current domestic tournament infrastructure as required, and prune redundant tournaments.[24] They could, and should, retain the age-group competitions, which have produced many of India's greatest players.

But franchises will need to do justice to the geographical representation of Indian cricket fans, since the current IPL franchises are almost exclusively city based. Fans of the West Bengal Ranji Trophy team might be assuaged by the presence of the Kolkata Knight Riders, but it is not clear whether other states' fans will be so easily mollified. Some change of branding or nomenclature might be necessary as it is implausible that Haryana, Himachal Pradesh and Uttar Pradesh fans would be content to be represented by the Delhi Daredevils. The franchises will also need to develop a farm system which, with youth programmes and scouting systems, could further develop the talent currently available to state associations through small towns and rural centres.

Franchises entrusted with domestic cricket in India will need to bring fans back to the four-day game, provided Test cricket remains a continued priority for Indian cricket. While the Ranji Trophy, as in its 2009 final, can still pack the rafters occasionally, by and large, the four-day game languishes. Here, franchises could do precisely that which Ranji teams and their state associations have failed to do over the years: build a fan following by merchandizing, fan contact and loyalty programmes, and market the game more aggressively.[25] They might experiment with day–night matches especially at warmer times of the year as well. Franchises could consider placing overseas players, from neighbours like Pakistan, Bangladesh and Sri Lanka, and possibly even ICC Associate Members, on its rosters. A day–night four-day and one-day domestic system of tournaments, with a lucrative prize money component, could provide not just entertainment for the crowds but good training for Indian first-class cricketers. If IPL franchises' promotional energies, so clearly visible during the IPL season, could be made available to the longer versions of the game, then it is not inconceivable that Indian first-class and Test cricket could prosper.

Most promisingly, if franchises can enter into agreements with the BCCI to reserve windows for domestic cricket, especially for the four-day game, they might be able to solve a problem plaguing Indian cricket for long: the absence of the local international player called away to represent the national team in a crowded international schedule. Indeed, to enhance the value of their four-day 'product' franchises could demand that international players be available for a domestic window.

This need for agreements with the BCCI highlights the most important change that might be induced: franchise representation in domestic cricket should make the administrative structure of the BCCI more like an owners' council of the MLB than like the current BCCI–IPL relationship which features limited franchise representation. It would also make for a welcome change from the BCCI's current pick-up-payment-but-submit-no-reports relationship with state associations. Franchises could infuse some honesty into dealings with cricket players as professionals, especially if they modelled their labour relations on extant professional leagues worldwide. Most promisingly for IPL franchises, an expansion into a domestic system geared towards producing international players would radically expand the current tiny window of the IPL season afforded by the BCCI, making their commercial partners' investments more economically sensible.

The promise of the franchise model rests largely on the possibility that it could affect a wholesale change of the domestic scene, perhaps more expeditiously than might be possible via piecemeal reform of the BCCI and its state associations. A happy co-operative, hybrid model—of franchises and the BCCI working together to produce international cricketers for the BCCI while safeguarding the commercial interests of the franchises via the domestic tournaments and the IPL—would represent a golden mean in this context.

The BCCI's problems are not restricted to the way it handles Indian cricket, for it also handles world cricket via its problematic and fractious relationship with the ICC. Here, the BCCI cannot be blamed for all the ills of world cricket. In the relentless, myopic obsession with the bottom line, both are equally guilty; speculation about the game's current governance and evolution needs to include and indict the BCCI and the ICC equally.

CHAPTER 4

Cricket's Future Form

The concerns of cricket historians, worried about its modern lurch towards avaricious commercialization, and those of law professors, writing on Internet regulation for the brave new era of cyberspace, are quite distinct. One area where these unlikely twain converge is on the concept of 'governance'.[1]

Current debates on Internet regulation tend to revolve around the dualism of the Hamiltonian versus Jeffersonian models of governance,[2] on whether regulation should flow from a strong, centralized authority (the Hamiltonian model) or from decentralized, autonomous groups evolving modes and methods of co-operation and power-sharing (the Jeffersonian model). The success of the Internet seems to be explainable in terms of the latter, while worries about the loss of its 'unique' nature stem from the fear that the former model will come to predominate.

The ICC–national board structure possesses the features of the Jeffersonian model: there is no strong centralized authority, and executive power resides with its constituents, the national boards, each a local monopoly in its own domain, and each, unfortunately, representing a country, a national interest, and not the game. This sounds delightfully laissez-faire, till one notices that in practice, it results in lassitude and ineffectiveness, for the ICC can do little to affect the efficiency and transparency of the governance of its national boards. And in terms of disclosure, corporate governance standards, financial controls and freedom from political interference, most ICC members come off poorly. The BCCI, PCB, the Zimbabwe Cricket Union (ZCU) and the Sri Lankan Cricket Board have all been in the news for one scandal or the other in recent times; each is heavily politicized and ripe for reform and professional management.

The ICC could seek to improve the governance of its member national boards, perhaps by insisting on professional administrators —as it insisted Pakistan do in 2011—rather than the motley crew of politicians and businessmen who appear to be in charge worldwide.[3] But these directives or requests, issued from a distance, oblivious to local ground realities, are destined to fall on deaf ears—there is no carrot to be dangled, no stick to be shook. The persistent embarrassing dysfunction of the ZCU and the PCB—and some might say, the BCCI— and the resigned acceptance by the ICC is a particularly graphic case in point. The ICC also echoes some of the dysfunction of its members, for while it distributes revenue from major world tournaments to various national boards, it demands very little by way of accounting.

In general, since the ICC can only function as well as its national boards do, and take no decision that is not favourable to them, or to a particularly important member of the board that can build an alliance to resist such a decision, calls for the ICC to act decisively on the latest crisis riling the minds of players and fans alike, whether match-fixing, the state of pitches worldwide, or lately, the Decision Review System (DRS), are inevitably met either by inactivity or by an unwieldy compromise.

This situation has come to pass in cricket because—despite the lack of a centralized authority and the devolution of power to the national boards—cricket's political economy does not forbid the subsequent concentration of power in the constituent units. The political structure of votes and committees and rotating presidents does a poor job of masking the cricket world's worst-kept secret: the BCCI, thanks to its pre-eminent economic position, for all intents and purposes, runs the show. Thus the cricket world has been treated in recent times to the sight of a largely decentralized unit seemingly pushed hither and thither by one of its members, which, ostensibly, in voting terms, is no more powerful than any other.

But blocs can form in the ICC; the colour divide in the ICC is now a well-known fact, visible in: the ICC's tolerance of South Africa over the objections of its Asian members in the bad old apartheid days; the voting for the 1987 World Cup; or in the bickering over security for the 1996 World Cup. Power-brokering and alliance-formation are thus unavoidable, especially if one is to curry—no pun intended—favour with the BCCI. Another perspective on the ICC's blocs is that they are not colour blocs as much as they are economic ones, with a Big Four clearly identifiable: England, Australia, India and South Africa. The structure of the Future Tours Programme announced by the ICC in 2011, which prioritizes cricketing contacts between the Big Four at the cost of the development of cricket worldwide, and the ICC's machinations for the 2015 World Cup, which prioritizes the continued, unquestioned participation of Full Members at the cost of possibly more deserving Associate Members and the need to globalize cricket, are indicative of the influence of this economic bloc and its pernicious impact on the ICC's handling of cricket.

In a truly decentralized arrangement like, for instance, the Internet Engineering Task Force, the structures of governance do not permit any concentration of power. But political economy can interfere even in this case: the astronomical growth in the value of domain names led to the enrichment and disproportionate empowerment of Network Solutions Inc. and the Internet Corporation for Assigned Names and Numbers (ICANN). In the world of cricket, the twin blessings of demographics and economy have made the BCCI the cricketing power it is at present; and in the past, historical priority and colonial sensibilities allowed the Anglo-Australian combine to rule with a benevolent iron hand.

Cricket and the Internet demonstrate the challenge, then, of devising a model of governance that is in accordance with the Goldilocks principle of regulation: enough control to prevent undue concentration of power but not so much that individual constituents cannot self-regulate. Any loss of local autonomy must be strongly motivated. Constituents might desire rule by a local despot for the achievement of shared ends; it is their decision, and theirs alone, to devise the most appropriate means for achieving them. If the benevolent dictatorship of the BCCI is felt by the cricket world to be its preferred mode of leadership, so be it.

But any power is subject to the moral requirement that shared ends are determined by consensus building. For if the agreement on ends is not democratic, the importance of the ends becomes moot. There is often little evidence of a democratically achieved consensus or consensus building, as opposed to consensus assumption or imposition, in the governance of cricket today. For instance, there was little attempt at consensus building in the creation of the IPL which, despite protestations to the contrary by Lalit Modi, did not look, feel, walk or talk like a domestic tournament and whose scheduling immediately set several large felines amongst the pigeons. Such a public disregard of the ICC contributes to unflattering perceptions of it and leads to lack of respect.

The ICC has always only had a peripheral relevance to cricketing administration; its power has always been that wielded by its most powerful members.[4] Previously, this was the Anglo-Australian bloc; now, Indian power is loud and visible. The older alliance spent as much time propagating a particular self-image and its cultural ideals as it did promoting the game worldwide.[5] The former mission seems to have been successfully achieved, if the world view of an older generation of Indian fans—who imagine England to be a land of village greens and county ovals, and who have internalized the locations of English cricket grounds in their mental geography—is any indication; the newer breed of Indian—or indeed subcontinental—fan does not look to the Anglo-Australian axis any more for moral or cultural guidance in cricket. As for promoting the game worldwide the ICC, and concomitantly England and Australia, appear to have failed spectacularly. Cricket remains a fringe game worldwide, with many Associate and Affiliate Member teams dominated by expatriates from Full ICC Members and still struggling to achieve competence in the game. Global expansion of the game appears not only a rather forlorn hope, it has even been made to seem undesirable, as if the exclusivity of the 'highest form of the game' would be tainted by the admission of too many neophytes. The BCCI–IPL might do better with regard to the financially solvent growth of cricket in newer markets and demographics. (Mention of solvency also serves to remind us that the ICC was close to bankruptcy when its Indian managers took over. The pendulum has swung, and the calibration between the extremes of the inefficiencies of the past and the rapacity of the present remains a stern challenge for its office-bearers.)

The rise of the BCCI and the resultant uneasy—sometimes resentful, sometimes grasping and greedy—relationships other members of the ICC have formed with it signals a change from a situation where love of the game and unwritten 'primary rules of obligation' were an adequate cohesive and managerial force in the world of cricket. But cricket's new commercial imperatives—or rather, its new, seemingly singular imperative of maximizing the dollar value of the television rights deal—sits rather uneasily upon such holdovers. The mythology of the game clashes ever more loudly with this visible pursuit. A rough analogy might be drawn with the university, which is considered a home of learning and of free, untrammelled inquiry, a mission that jars uncomfortably with its modern role as supplier of labour for corporate workforces and incubator of technology for industrial research and development. This entity's grab for intellectual property rights, its relentless hustle for patents, is sharply incongruous with that original romantic, pedagogic and intellectual notion. Under these circumstances, worries about the undermining of the educational or intellectual mission by economic or corporate imperatives are to be expected.

This transition to its new commercially inclined form has not been easy for cricket whose administration is often spectacularly unprofessional. But a facile corporatization of the ICC and its operations will not work either. Indeed, if the current over-scheduling of international cricket is any indication, we have ample proof of what can go wrong when cricket is corporatized. This sort of destructive corporatization is not restricted to cricket: England's national university system lies devastated thanks to such initiatives and a similar imposition is underway at American universities. Ironically, in these settings, corporate influence is a bureaucratic intervention that stifles academic innovation and sidelines pedagogical imperatives: it imposes management structures impervious to the fact that an educational institution cannot be managed like a factory unit. In short, it subverts the educational mission. A similar fate might await the world of cricket if it fails to address the issue of how much change is possible in its administration and its mission so that the essential nature of the game and its relationship with its fans is preserved. Cricket does need to be commercialized, and managed by full-time professionals, but this most definitely does not mean a wholesale import of corporate management techniques. Rather, it means management sensitive to the nature and differing priorities of the 'product' managed. (As the ECB's Giles Clarke showed in his ill-directed rant against Internet sites providing 'pirated' live streaming of cricket matches,[6] some corporate Kool-Aid seems to have been rather overenthusiastically consumed.)

If franchise power were asserted more vigorously thanks to the expansion of IPL-like tournaments worldwide, it could reconfigure the ICC, perhaps via franchise representation in the ICC's governing council, or even possibly supplant it. Talk of reform might be moot then; there might not be anything left to reform if franchise power grows unhindered. The BCCI and the ICC might be replaced by entities still committed to organizing, sponsoring and making money from cricket worldwide; the commercial objective would at least be straightforwardly visible.

The Escape of the Franchise Genie

If the power of the franchise in the world of the Twenty20 league grows, with expansion of seasons, either through length or frequency, so will its influence on world cricket. The constant worries about the setting aside of a window for the IPL shows that the IPL has already skewed the ICC's agenda. No domestic tournament has ever required the creation of such a specific window for its commitments. And a second IPL season, of equal duration and economic incentive as the first, might effectively torpedo the entire international calendar.

Once such a window is created in the international cricketing calendar, the pretence that the IPL is a domestic tournament will have to be dropped by all concerned. Given the absence of conflict with the international calendar, franchises could request an increase in the number of international players in a playing eleven. If that is agreed to, the effects already noticed in player commitment to international Test and ODI cricket will be exacerbated as movement towards a global labour market will accelerate due to the availability of these new roster slots. A second IPL season would make exclusive commitment to the

IPL more likely; many more players might find two seasons of the IPL all the time they want or need to devote to cricket.

Thus, without exaggeration, the most important steps in the growth of the IPL and the possible development of the cricket world towards an international franchise system are: dropping the tiered system of auctioneering—perhaps in favour of a draft—that prioritizes international appearances for Indian players (for reasons alluded to earlier), the creation of a window for the IPL in the cricket calendar, resulting in an increase in the number of overseas players in IPL rosters, the starting up of a second IPL season, and lastly, the possibility of international franchise partnerships across the world's various Twenty20 leagues.

With an international franchise-based league officially entrenched in the game's calendar, the path will be cleared for its further expansion, as international—as opposed to exclusively Indian—ownership of a franchise will become more likely (more international corporations, for instance, will find players to serve as faces for their brands). There would be a worldwide stake in the fortunes of the new international league as opposed to thinking of the IPL as an Indian affair;[7] more importantly, the franchise could become as much of an administrative entity in cricket as the national board since its argument for formal representation in the ICC will be strengthened.

The earmarking of a window for the IPL could also lead to suggestions that the league expand with more franchises. Thus, the internationalized IPL could spark the growth of franchises in Test-playing countries and facilitate the growth of franchises in smaller, non-Test–playing ones. Ireland, the Netherlands and the UAE could conceivably field franchises in a larger, international league. The development of this group of franchises into an entity that is solely committed to its financial growth and tolerates the international calendar for only as long as it needs its star players and till it can generate its own stars is inevitable, given its overriding financial imperatives. The growth of franchise power worldwide is therefore unlikely to be altogether benign for the ICC and BCCI. It is likely to entail demands for greater involvement with cricket administration; and a worldwide council of franchise owners and ICC administrators—with a changed set of priorities that might not include sticking to older structures of the game—could replace the current ICC.

The transformation of the IPL into an international league could appear as a tempting way for the ICC to control cricket's calendar, ensure less congestion—there would be no need for copycat leagues competing with the IPL—and more evenly distribute revenues worldwide, especially if the BCCI cedes control of the IPL to the ICC.[8] But given the Indian ownership of the IPL, and its place in the Indian imagination, there is little chance that the BCCI and the Indian cricket fan will tolerate what will look like the usurpation of an Indian entity. Indeed, one response to this proposal would head in a converse direction.

Could India Go Its Own Way?

In August 2009, the Indian blogger Shrikant Subramanian made what, to many, seemed like an absurd suggestion: that India withdraw from international cricket to create its own internal cricket league:

> Does India need international cricket?...[C]hanneling our attention and energies towards domestic cricket will do India a world of good. Ideally... the Indian domestic scene [would] be structured like the NFL...the game will be played on our terms, devoid of any outside interference, including the ICC. As the...IPL showed, the BCCI has the capacity to organize and to market the game...No more having to kow-tow to all and sundry within the ICC...No more trying to shore up the ICC by contributing up to 70% of its monies while having to incur all the opprobrium for its inadequacies...Our game, our terms, our way.[9]

Many Indian cricket fans had not failed to notice that, given the size of the Indian cricket market, the BCCI's revenues from overseas markets suffered in comparison to those of other boards from their interactions with the BCCI.[10] The Indian economy, in their view, sent millions of dollars to the coffers of various cricket boards around the world; those BCCI–IPL-generated revenues could flow back into the Indian economy instead. Thus the IPL promised a swadeshi product—cricket matches produced by an Indian enterprise with a tax debt to the Indian government—that could even, as in the proposal above, enable the avoidance of the baggage-and-debt-ridden presence of international cricket.[11] The importance of the BCCI's monies to the ecology of world cricket is of no concern in this perspective, neither is the fact that if the 'brand value' of the Indian national team is riding high—as it was after the 2011 World Cup win—the BCCI could make more money from international cricket even after it had finished subsidizing cricket played elsewhere.[12] The cost of international cricket was perceived as a new colonial plunder of India's cricketing wealth, an inversion of the international cricket world's position that India looted the wealth of the world's cricketing talent via the IPL.

The proposal above does suggest, over and above its 'India versus the World' pitch and the possibility of India withdrawing from international cricket, a possible evolution of the cricketing world by making explicit the notion of an entity termed the International Premier League, a 'new IPL', based in India, much like the NBA is based in the US while being a truly international league. This proposal has the salutary effect too, of exposing problems with international cricket today. Thinking about such a domestic-yet-international league, larger than the current IPL and more geographically representative of India's regions, exposes vital truths about the nature of Indian cricket consumption and the dependence of the world of cricket on it.

While Indian cricket would be poorer without international cricket, and Indian domestic encounters prima facie do not seem to set the pulse racing the way a top international encounter might, some Indian domestic encounters are still likely to be more compelling for the Indian fan than some of the mismatches typical of international cricket in recent years. Some domestic encounters would generate more passion amongst Indian fans than so-called 'neutral' encounters[13] and even more pertinently, more passion than those matches evoke in their home countries. The 2011 West Indies–Pakistan encounters in the Caribbean, for instance, were notable for poor attendance even at limited-overs games. The 2009 Ranji final shows how a top-class Indian domestic encounter can easily produce a larger crowd than such an international encounter. The IPL's popularity with Indian crowds is not solely reliant on the Twenty20 format; it is also propped up by what often seems like extremely unappetizing fare served up from overseas, consisting of empty stands, slow pitches, mediocre cricket skills, indecisive Test matches, and one-sided one-day internationals.

Furthermore, while it might not be possible for India to produce the same level of cricket players without the competition present in international cricket,[14] this situation is not likely to persist if their skills are only being honed for Twenty20 games. As the NFL and MLB show, international competition is not necessary to produce high-quality competition or players. The set of cricketing skills in question are smaller; future players in such a league will not need to learn to build long innings, and neither will bowlers need to exert control for twenty-five overs in the course of a day. The proposed 'new IPL' would generate a new breed of Indian player, competent and skilled at Twenty20, playing on a stage meant for the showcasing of those skills.

While current IPL stars are stars because of international cricket, the 'new IPL' could create its own star system. This is especially true when it comes to thinking about the next generation of Indian cricket fans, raised on a steady diet of IPL games. The fervour of Melbournians for Australian rules football—run by the Australian Football League (AFL)—is not tempered by the lack of international stars in the system; rather, quite simply, the AFL is woven into the fabric of Melbourne life and has engendered rivalries so intense that the average youngster in Melbourne must choose a team to support—perhaps by the time he comes of age—on pain of social ostracism. An AFL fan takes his children to games, buys them paraphernalia and exposes them to the mythology of the AFL franchise; the lack of international competition does not seem to bother its fans. The transition period, correspondingly, for the 'new IPL' to create its own stars, its own mythology, is the matter of true interest. The creation of the league's legend and its further sustenance is not conceptually impossible.

While India's isolation from international cricket might lead to an overseas cricketer not playing in the IPL unless the remuneration is extravagant, it only means that pay cheques of the appropriate size will be required to entice him to offer his services. If the franchises are successful enough, this will not matter. In the 'new IPL', the national boards could be bypassed and international players could work as free agents contracting directly with Indian employers.[15] Indeed, given some Indian sensitivity about international players treating the IPL as a highly paid vacation, some franchises might prefer to have keen Indians instead, a sentiment likely to be enhanced if local populations begin to identify with the franchises and expect to see local players perform. Americans do not seem to care that they are cheering for 'locals' in the MLB or the NFL; the perceived quality of the games and the skills of the players, even if not from the franchise's 'hometown', is uppermost in their reckoning of the worth of the league and the claims it can make on their attention.

The dependence of Indian cricket on international cricket is complex.[16] As far as Test cricket is concerned, between 1993 and 2001, England did not visit India, and neither did Australia, between 1986 and 1996. This absence did not seem to affect the Indian following of the game, which by then had taken on a life of its own, thanks to the 1983 World Cup win, the hosting of the 1987 World Cup and the growth of satellite television. In those years, the Indian fan continued to show interest in the game, in any form, against any opponent. Matters are not so simple anymore, of course. Indian sports fans have many more distractions now, and cricket fans denied international cricket will have plenty of other diversions to entertain them.

The BCCI–IPL could achieve much of the proposal alluded to above simply by creating a second season (the ICC could help by creating a window for both seasons). The BCCI could, as noted before, participate in just enough international cricket to stoke the nationalist frenzy required to stimulate adequate interest in the IPL but concentrate most of its energies on the IPL's development. Whether these actions will be taken and what the BCCI–IPL's future course of action will be should rapidly become clear to all concerned.

A MORE INDIAN IPL

Some outlines of a trend towards a more Indian IPL are visible. By its fourth and fifth seasons, the 'Indian' was back in the IPL with a vengeance: most of the money in the 2011 and 2012 auctions was spent on Indian players. This preference for the Indian over the international player was partially rooted in convenience as many international players could not commit fully to the season thanks to prior commitments. But it might also have been that franchises considered Indian players more marketable in India. The recent successes of the Indian cricket team—

before the Test defeats of 2011–12—meant that the international player's role as the symbol of cricketing virility in the Indian cricket fan's mind was now beginning to be played by Indian entities. This displacement is especially significant if the IPL fan expects the local franchise to provide the frisson that international cricket once provided.

There are cultural reasons too, why the international player might not be significant in the IPL's eventual evolution. The relentless Indian tendency to Indianize everything is evinced by Hinglish, Indian–Chinese food, and masaledar pastas; imports in India need to be homogenized and Indianized for consumption and absorption into the larger culture. Thus, despite the legendary Indian proficiency in English, it is no coincidence that Brett Lee learned Hindi in an effort to improve his marketability in India. Where such homogenization does not work, the import remains confined to the margins. An international player might therefore represent too much effort for an IPL franchise to make him truly palatable to an Indian audience, especially one not located in a major metropolitan centre. Perhaps the overseas player, in order to enable a true connection with an Indian audience, would have to perform the cricketing equivalent of a Tom Alter and slip into the figurative garb of the local.

Thus, amongst Indian audiences, an IPL franchise's 'brand identity' is likely to be made up by local players who could enjoy a loyal, personalized fan following. Most importantly, an Indian player instrumental in helping a beloved franchise win will most assuredly win a fan's loyalty. Star power will not matter as much as sporting success. As journeyman baseball player Scott Brosius found out when playing for the New York Yankees, it was his ability to come up with a clutch hit or fielding play in the World Series wins of the late 1990s, and not his glamour quotient, which ensured that New York fans still deify him. Correspondingly, all the glamour of the international player will mean little if he is unable to help his franchise win; indeed, he is more likely to be vulnerable to accusations of carpetbaggery. Thierry Henry's sometimes lackadaisical showing for the New York Red Bulls in US Major League Soccer often earned him jeers from fans who preferred the drive and hustle of the young US star Juan Agudelo, who had barely a few international caps to his credit. Here patriotism and passionate skill comprehensively trump the sheen of the overseas star.

For the new Twenty20 fan, international reputations, built on success in Test cricket, have not mattered very much; Yusuf Pathan, yet to fully establish himself in the Indian limited-overs team, has made more money in the IPL than V.V.S. Laxman. While this payment structure is unstable in that classical notions of the cricketing quality of players visibly do not match their remunerations, this will carry increasingly less weight with fans if Twenty20 and the IPL persist.[17]

If something like the 'new IPL' is to come about, it will in all likelihood be because an existing ambitious franchise owner like Mukesh Ambani (Mumbai Indians) or Vijay Mallya (Royal Challengers Bangalore), chafing at the restrictions of the BCCI, eager to tap into the visible wealth of the Indian cricket market, and confident about his ability to attract enough Twenty20 players to make it worthwhile, finally decides to break free. Whether the BCCI will attempt to quell his ambitions as it did in the case of Subhash Chandra, or co-operate to create a de-facto equivalent by agreeing to a second IPL season, remains to be seen. The course of action the BCCI chooses could determine whether the cricket world will split, or whether it will merely march obediently towards a new leadership.

A MODERN LESSON

The plausibility of the success of the 'new IPL' is bolstered by noticing that nothing works in the world of cricket—except perhaps the Ashes—without India being involved. Even that supposedly magical format, Twenty20, is not a sufficient condition for high attendance: when Pakistan toured the West Indies in 2011, they played their first Twenty20 game at a largely empty ground; the format of the game did not make up for the lack of local interest.

Or consider the contrasting fortunes of the IPL and the Champions League. The latter, aspiring to a status similar to that enjoyed by football's Champions League, featured the top Twenty20 domestic sides in the world. Here, the format seemed crucial; the Mohammed Nissar Trophy features the domestic champions of India and Pakistan squaring off in a four-day game, but this attracts little attention from most Indian and Pakistani fans other than the local supporters of the national champions.

But when the Champions League did debut in 2009, it attracted little attention after the three IPL teams—Delhi Daredevils, Royal Challengers Bangalore and 2009 IPL champions Deccan Chargers—were all knocked out in the group stage. Their departure sent television ratings into a tailspin despite the heroics of the little-fancied Trinidad and Tobago, whose Kieron Pollard made a 54 off 18 balls that made possible an upset against eventual champions New South Wales.[18]

So, the presence of competitive cricket, a torrent of sixes, and an appealing underdog, the supposedly standard tropes of a good modern tournament, were not enough to evoke interest from Indian fans who appeared more enthused by an Indian tournament that guaranteed the presence of Indian teams late into its resolution. The new format for the Champions League thus features organizational tweaks that ensure that IPL teams and Indian fans last longer; its ratings have improved in turn.[19] This response has now been taken to its logical next step: the suggestion, made at the end of the 2011 IPL season, to include another IPL team in the Champions League roster. Such an increase in the number of IPL teams would make the Champions League resemble nothing so much as a second season of the IPL. Like any other cricket tournament in the world, the Champions League needs to cater to the audience that pays the bills. And unsurprisingly, we have been told that Australia's BBL too 'needs Indian players…to boost the value of media rights when they are next sold in 2013 [and for] wealthy Indian investors to sink their cash into a Big Bash team'.[20]

The Champions League experience, the reorganization of the World Cup after the 2007 debacle of India's early exit, the proposal for an India-centric world league for cricket, the dependence of Australia's BBL on Indian players and investors, all remind us the cricket world is controlled by the finances of one national board, whose vast local television audience is largely geared towards watching Indians play. Under these circumstances, any overseas player hoping to make a comfortable living from cricket has his fortunes pegged to the tastes of the Indian cricket fan (and the success of the Indian team).

This state of dependency serves as an uncomfortable reminder of a fact possibly hard for cricket fans to accept: cricket is a minor sport in the world's sporting calculus. The most salutary lesson of studying cricket worldwide is not puzzlement at its lack of success but rather amazement at how it has managed to take hold anywhere. The most visible of the cricket-playing nations—England, Australia and South Africa—treat cricket as a secondary sport. Cricket cannot hope to compete with football in England, with the various football and rugby codes in Australia, or with rugby in South Africa. Even in Australia, while cricket is the one truly national sport, it does not command the kind of allegiance rugby and Australian rules football are able to when their seasons are on. Indeed, if the market research preceding the establishment of the BBL is to be believed, cricket's popularity is on a downward trajectory Down Under. There is a simple test to gauge the populist appeal of a sport: will the bartender turn up the television's volume for a game? Nine times out of ten, for cricket in Australia, the answer is 'no'. Not so for rugby in New South Wales and Australian rules football in Victoria.

The dependence of world cricket's fortunes on Indian fans' likes and dislikes is obviously cause for resentment, though Indian fans might find it quite reasonable to say that matters would be considerably helped if other countries paid more attention to cricket and elevated it in their ordering of sporting priorities. (Perhaps admitting that cricket might have lost its importance in a world packed with manifold attractions might be too hard for some; it can also be guilt-inducing.) For it is not just the number of Indian fans that makes money for world cricket; it is the amount of cricket an average Indian cricket fan is willing to consume and the position that cricket occupies in Indian fans' hierarchy of priorities. This demographic would most like to see a successful Indian team; it does not seem to matter in which format. As the India–Australia Test series of 2010 showed, despite worries about the death of Test cricket in India, large crowds came and stayed, and recreated the atmosphere at Indian cricket stadiums associated with the Test cricket of old. Similarly, the last day of the 2011 Lord's Test, when India was due to bat to try and save the game, and when ticket prices were lowered, witnessed a full house and queues that started at three in the morning. This was testimony both to Test cricket's appeal and to the Indian cricket fan's appetite for the game, for a large percentage of the crowd lining up that morning—some of whom would have failed the Tebbit test[21]—was Indian.

It is a common refrain that the cricket world needs a strong West Indies, or a strong England, or a strong Pakistan. International cricket might need all of those entities to flourish, but most of all, what the cricket world needs is a strong and successful Indian team, no matter what the format. It is the rising tide that will float the boats of the modern cricketing world. In this fact might lie the best hopes for the continued flourishing of Test cricket, often seen as being threatened by recent developments, both sporting and economic, in the game.

Test Cricket: Anachronism or Art Piece?

The death of Test cricket is at hand. Never before in the history of cricket has this oft-repeated claim seemed to have the resonance it does now. If there is some sort of emerging consensus about the possible influences of Twenty20 and its associated leagues, it is that Test cricket is threatened. If there is a serious worry, most conducive to the generation of a profound despair that infects a particular kind of cricket fan, it is the thought that Test cricket might be the victim of the latest developments in world cricket. This should be unsurprising: Twenty20's financial success, its audience-generation, the visible commitment of players to its riches, and correspondingly, the seeming lack of audience response to Test cricket, all do not appear to bode well for Test cricket.

Test cricket has always struggled to assert its relevance in a world struck by the sheer singularity it represented in forms of sporting endeavour or mass entertainment. It made possible a notion of player and spectator that was unique in its privileging of patience and forbearance, in its asking the fan to occasionally find satisfaction and succour in draws. Test cricket is relentlessly not-modern: it exposes fans and players alike to an open-endedness not found elsewhere in sport. The notion of the declaration, the voluntary surrender of an innings to derive tactical advantage, the possibility that a first innings could, in theory, last the five days of a Test, are distinctive within sporting rules. They serve to make a Test occupy a unique tactical and strategic space on the field and in the mind of player and fan alike. The imposition of an overs-per-innings limit in Tests to force results would rob Test cricket of some of its most exciting finishes: the hard-fought fight-back for a draw, which showcases some of Test cricket's greatest batting feats, or the tense one- or two-wicket gap between victory and defeat, of which, amazingly enough, Test cricket has seen several instances in the last few years.

Test cricket has thus not had an easy relationship with entertainment. It has never sought to make the crowd-pleasing routine. Test cricket's disdain for the equation of high scores or fast scoring with good cricket, or the equation of run scoring with something happening at all, is captured well in our chuckling at tales of those who turn up late for a football game, and on being told the score is love-all, exclaim with great relief, 'It's all right then, we haven't missed anything.' The 1998 South Africa–England Test series featured a little spell of cricket pitting Michael Atherton against Allan Donald in which no boundaries transpired, no wickets fell, yet every fan at Trent Bridge who took a bathroom break during that period is still kicking himself; small wonder that the YouTube clip of those emotionally charged dozen or so deliveries has racked up hundreds of thousands of views.

The devotion that Test cricket inspires in its aficionados is perhaps unrivalled in sport; most cricketing mythology is built on a foundation of lore generated by them. For this kind of fan, the moniker 'limited-overs game' supplies the right prefix to forms of the game that seem crucially 'limited': Test cricket alone allows cricket's various possibilities to be fully explored; its nation-based encounters are the pinnacle of the game and all else is poor mimicry. As such, followers of Test cricket have always been prone to anxiety, to fret about its continued viability, and the most visible expressions of these worries in the modern era emerged after the success of one-day internationals in the 1980s. In this regard, Test cricket's oft-heralded decline resembles nothing as much as the oft-bemoaned degradation in civility and other social mores supposedly brought on by every technological change. Modern complaints about text messages and tweets and their pernicious influence on polite conversation find their echo in early twentieth-century worries about the displacement of genteel conversation by the rushed, hurried, frenetic pace of urban life. Yet, somehow, within the hustle and bustle, oases of calm do lurk and may be found by the diligent. Perhaps Test cricket's longevity lies in its ability to tuck itself away in such protected corners, confident in the hold it has over its devotees.

Anxieties about Test cricket are natural, given the awareness in the cricket world that this form of the game is an extraordinary business in a world of sport devoted to the ordinary. The lurking fear of the Test fan is that this abnormality will not be tolerated, will be squashed. Sometimes Test cricket's fans' wailing seems like a pre-emptive display of unprompted self-awareness that Test cricket is an archaic practice.

But there is a danger in such chest beating. Too much self-abnegation can be counterproductive; the Cassandra can, like other soothsayers of doom, help bring about the very phenomenon feared. Anxiety over Test cricket has produced the constant urge on the part of cricket administrators to do something, anything, to make it more appealing. As long as this urge to meddle, to tinker, was confined to the one-day international, the cricket purist might not have felt threatened; but surgical intervention in Test cricket provokes a horror reserved for gratuitous amputation. Coloured clothes, balls, night cricket, perhaps even artificial turf pitches, will change the game in a manner that fans of Test cricket might eventually reconcile themselves to, but what is to be done about the administrators' constant urge to self-flagellate? What if, a decade later, when Test cricket shows another blip in attendance, the urge to tinker rises again? Games display longevity because they start with simple essentials and display fidelity to them. Test cricket's community, that supposed cradle of conservatism, might do well to pay heed to this piece of wisdom.

Perhaps what Test cricket needs is not another fiddling at the margins but some therapy for its fans and administrators who might be urged to stop being such hypochondriacs. For the greatest danger in the refrain 'Test cricket is dying' is that the demise of Test cricket might be hurried on by these rhetorical bleedings, and finally, fatally, by the resigned acceptance of its fate, thus bringing any attempts at persistence with nourishment to a grinding halt.[22]

None of this is to detract from the threat that Twenty20 poses, for the modern political economy of the game is very different from that of a few years ago and Test cricket faces challenges that, if not overcome, could have serious implications. Declining global audiences for Test cricket are an unpleasant reality. Only England, Australia, and on occasion India and South Africa can claim decent crowds at Test matches. IPL pay scales make Twenty20 a far more attractive option. Test cricket's duration, its possible lack of results (made worse by batsman-friendly pitches even if mitigated by the increasing use of floodlights and sophisticated drainage equipment), make it increasingly harder to justify and defend. Nevertheless, the historical resilience of Test cricket demands that the response to the threat of Twenty20 be commensurate, that the medicine offered not kill the patient, that its fans be trusted just a little more, for just a little longer. Perhaps the storm clouds of the Twenty20 leagues will pass. Perhaps they will no longer appear as threatening, bringing nothing more than a passing shower, one that might even conceivably bring relief to a sometimes parched landscape.

Test cricket's problems, old and new, have never just been about the dominance of bat over ball or about one-sided results. The limited-overs versions of cricket routinely produce games where the result is a foregone conclusion after the first half; cricket fans have often wondered what was more stupor-inducing, the draw, or the leisurely stroll to a low target by a team batting second in a one-day international. The supposed decline of Test cricket is linked to a diverse set of factors, and is not simply explainable by the recent success of Twenty20. (It is a fair guess that right after the 2011 World Cup, the one-day international form might have been more popular than either Twenty20 or Tests.)

Indeed, the story of Test cricket in the 1990s and 2000s, which a cricket historian might have described as a phase unremarkable in its variations as compared to others before it, seems to have been utterly forgotten. For in the years leading to the introduction of Twenty20 cricket, the Twenty20 World Cup, and the IPL, there did not appear to be a sense of crisis in the cricketing world about Test cricket. There were worries aplenty about the dominance of the bat, the marginalization of the bowler, slothful pitches worldwide, the decline of a great Test cricketing power, the West Indies, and the failure of Bangladesh and Zimbabwe to assert themselves. But there never was a serious worry about the viability of Test cricket that seemed any more urgent than the fears expressed during the 1950s or 1960s, or the glory days of the one-day international's ascendancy in the 1980s. While many new fans of cricket emerged thanks to the limited-overs game, many were created via some of the greatest Test series of all time, played in the new millennium (the 2005 Ashes, the 2001 India–Australia 'Kolkata' series, the 2008–

2009 South Africa–Australia home-and-away 'world championship'). In the midst of a world churning out speeded-up diversions on a daily basis, Test cricket miraculously continued to turn out a steady parade of golden hits for its all-time charts. There was plenty of dross, but Test cricket moved on. These recent acknowledgements of the continued importance of Test cricket have been rapidly effaced. And since multi-modal explanations are complex, it has become much easier to rely on the laziness of 'Twenty20 attracts larger crowds and richer television deals, therefore, Test cricket is despised and doomed'.[23]

In such a rhetorical space, fallacious arguments abound. A particular clunker is the one that deems Test cricket impractical because 'no one has the time to go for five days of a game'. This view assumes that Test cricket depends for its survival on fans attending every single day of a Test match. But while such patterns of attendance were undoubtedly more prevalent in years gone by, most Test cricket fans select particular days to attend Test matches; some prefer the brand-new match experience of an opening day; others prefer their Test matches well done and elect to go for the third or fourth days. Yet others are willing to go when the match shows promise of resolution, and some, on vacation, still go for multiple days. These sporadic attendances can add up to a healthy number and at times fill up stadiums.

But there is a more fundamental problem with this particular argument. Its proponents persist in the fallacy that a Test should be compared to a sporting event like a tennis match. This is the wrong target. A Test match is more aptly compared to a golf or tennis tournament. These run over several days and do not lack for attention; their fans understand that the action develops over a period of time and their level of awareness of its details can vary. The length of these sporting encounters has never been a reason to deem them unviable in this day and age.

It helps, of course, if the Test match is made the centrepiece of a sporting or cultural season, and the time-deprived cricket fan can plan accordingly. Australia has made the scheduling of the Boxing Day and New Year's Day Tests into an art form; the annual Melbourne and Sydney Tests are social events, and command large attendance from crowds eager to participate in a cultural ritual. India, unsurprisingly, has surrendered its Test cricket calendar to the vagaries of scheduling constraints imposed by one-day internationals, tournaments and overseas tours. India's cricketing calendar, if restored to its traditional winter times around various festivals in different parts of the country—such as Tamil Nadu's Pongal—would allow Test cricket to clamber back, even if only partially, into the pre-eminent position it occupied in years gone by. Scheduling that is sensitive to local environmental constraints would also help: Test matches in the Caribbean and Sri Lanka frequently encroach upon the rainy season, leading to a lack of results. (The recent standardization though—of the use of floodlights in case of poor light conditions, and the increasingly sophisticated drainage equipment—has been a welcome enhancement of the tools available to grounds staff in dealing with Test cricket's oldest and most implacable foes.)

Test cricket did have an easier time in the past, and players and spectators never found difficulty in finding meaning in its encounters. The reasons for this were manifold: cricket games were rare; they were not subject to the demythologizing influence of relentless media coverage; they were played in a world where entertainment options were limited; the nations playing them were often new and still struggling for a sense of national identity reinforced by the game. The primacy of the print media made it possible for an elaborate canopy of imaginative description to be erected over each Test; radio commentary required spectators to work to fill in the visual blanks, an act of participatory construction of fantasy that made the game a more personal experience. In this setting, the meaningfulness of the Test match was the result of the interaction of scarcity, mode of presentation, and the participation of the spectator. The highly technologized modern world with its shrinking vacations, ever-expanding work week, and diverse offerings of entertainment makes demands on our time and attention like few other socio-economic arrangements of the past have. In this setting, it is unsurprising that a segmented, thirty-hour event would have to work hard to draw and retain attention.

In modern cricket, the pressures of cricket scheduling, besides making a Test series just another event in the crammed cricket calendar, have also meant that Test tours, those extended ramblings through a country that bore thrilling similarity for a schoolboy to a military campaign, and that might have allowed time for story-telling and daydreaming, are now rendered archaic. Reading Phil Tresidder's *Captains on a See-Saw*, which recounts the story of the West Indies' 1968–69 tour of Australia, one is struck by the incongruity of Test players playing against the touring side in tour games, sometimes even between Test matches; these all remind us that the Test 'tour' is no longer one, and correspondingly, encourages little story-generation and makes it ever more difficult to construct an elaborate mythology around the modern Test series.

The most salutary corrective for the cricket fan dismayed at the thought of a world ruled by franchise-based Twenty20 cricket is a reminder, first, of scepticism about a post-nation Twenty20 world, which suggests that there might be a continued place in the cricket fan's imagination for that summit of international cricketing encounters, the Test, and second, of the need to pay close attention to the actual history of the game preceding the IPL.

Much ink has been spilled in recent years on clarifying, quite precisely, the nature of the threats to Test cricket. For cricket's multiple formats compete with each other for the same fans, sponsorships and media; player diversion to one format could threaten the others. The outcome of this juggling for market share could well augur the demise of one form of the game. In the wake of the initial success of Twenty20 and the IPL, even the fifty-over game was deemed threatened.

As in any conflict, the usual resolutions are possible: vanquishing the foe, surrender, or peaceful reconciliation. Twenty20 seems invincible, and unlikely to be beaten back. Surrender seems hasty and injudicious; a premature hara-kiri, as it were. What then?

A POSSIBLE RECONCILIATION

The balkanization of cricket into several formats renders the sport different from soccer, which is played in the same format all over the world in all tournaments. Thus, soccer fans do not face the danger of having a particular format of the game being denied them. Lionel Messi's skills in the ninety-minute, two-halves game will always be available for the soccer faithful, whether he plays for Barcelona or Argentina. Cricket's new formats speak to the need for a new ecology of the game, one that would let these three formats flourish, hopefully by mutual reinforcement and enrichment.

Perhaps reconciliation between Test cricket and Twenty20 is possible, in a manner similar to that partially achieved between classical and pop music. Test cricket, as the classical, 'codified, cultivated form... authoritative and definitive'[24] might find a way to coexist, and even prosper, alongside the crowd-pleasing, money-generating forms of pop music. Musicians do not compete for the attention of the plebian and the connoisseur alike, and yet, both groups of fans find their needs satisfied with a rich, diverse, calendar of Big Day Outs, jugalbandis, Mostly Mozart classical music festivals, Lollapaloozas, summer rock and jazz concert series, and of course, the high-society ritual of Philharmonic recitals. Perhaps there is cause for optimism here, for 'if classical music, its virtuosos and its audience have survived...perhaps Test cricket will survive the rumoured demise of the first-class game'.[25] Audiences for pop and classical music have some crossover; the older fan is just as likely to spend his money on both; perhaps cricket fans willing to devote time and money to Twenty20 and Test cricket might conceivably float both. Indeed, the two forms of music are more radically distinct than the two forms of cricket.[26] If there is hope in the world of music for peaceful coexistence, there should be in the world of cricket too.

But a little pinprick of empirical reality might yet burst this hopeful balloon. For popular forms of music can threaten the classical genre; the constant diversion of young, promising musicians to pop music would rightly be viewed as a potential threat to the world of classical music; a budding composer and songwriter might devote himself to writing jingles for commercials; a classically inclined bassist might only find work as a session musician for solo rock artistes. Such worries would especially be enhanced if sponsors of summer concerts decided that their dollars would be better spent on Cee Lo rather than Chopin, on Madonna rather than Mozart, on Jackson rather than Jasraj.

Or consider modes of transportation and competing technologies. When consumers found a superior mode of locomotion, or at least judged it to be superior, they transferred their allegiances all too quickly. And the history of technologies tells us that the technical superiority of a technology has little to do with its adoption. Witness the demise of the Betamax video recording format, or the failure of the UNIX operating system to overcome the Microsoft Windows juggernaut. Rather, many different forces—economic, social, political—combine to enable a technology's adoption; there is little guarantee that the best technology will autonomously bubble up to the top. As the success of Microsoft Windows eloquently demonstrates, inferior technological modes can be aggressively promoted at the cost of the superior.

So too for forms of entertainment; the high priests of culture have little control over the social adoption of a form of entertainment; this is true in politics too, where the vulgar can trump the principled. All the gnashing of teeth, even in conservative circles, did not prevent the dizzying rise to power of that Queen of Poor Taste, Sarah Palin. Similarly, the corporate posturing of Lalit Modi, the 'vulgarity' of the IPL and the BBL, the apparent inferiority of Twenty20 as a form of cricket when compared to Tests, was no barrier to their success.

This means that if Test cricket is to be preserved, it will need active protection and stewardship. It will need active intervention in the conduct and staging of games, and in utilizing the other formats of the game and the new media appropriately. This does not mean fiddling with the rules of Test cricket. It means, rather, finding ways to showcase the game's oldest and richest format, and to be willing to let it incur losses, even if it means reduced profit margins for the BCCI and the ICC as a whole, an imperative that is only likely to be kept in mind by someone inclined to think of cricket as more than a business. Twenty20 owes many of its financial harvests to the fertile ground that was prepared for it by the legend-making of Test cricket; its most popular stars are those whose reputations were built in the five-day game. A sensitive, historically inclined cricket administrator would ensure that it paid its debts adequately by subsidizing Test cricket. The question that administrators need to ask and answer is whether Test cricket is worth preserving for its own sake, not just as a means to the end of the more profitable television deal. If that question is answered in the affirmative, all is well. If not, Test cricket could wither and die from malignant neglect.

A GOLDEN OPPORTUNITY LOST

The irony of the recent 'crisis' in Test cricket is that Twenty20 did not come at a time when fans were tiring of Test cricket; instead, as noted, some of the greatest Test series of all time have been played in the first decade of the twenty-first century. The scoring has often been fast and heavy, the outcricket has been spectacular, and some of the greatest bowlers of all time have mowed down strong batting attacks. More Test matches now end in results than ever before. Batsmen still know how to put up big innings; they just do not 'construct' them any more. The loosening of batting techniques thanks to limited-overs batting has meant that modern batting sides are less able to resist a strong bowling attack; conversely, triple centuries and double-tons have increased, and hard-hitting batting has led to an increase in Test scoring rates worldwide. Thus, even on the standard construal of crowd-pleasing cricket as the fast scoring of lots of runs, Test cricket has done well.

Still, domination by batsmen is not the only theme of the modern era in cricket. The greatest Test side of recent times, Australia, built its success on the backs of not just one of the greatest fast bowlers of all time but the greatest exponent ever of leg-spin, an art form thought consigned to the cricketing dustbin. Indeed, the fact that the most successful bowlers of the modern era have been a leg-spinner and an off-spinner has made considerable claims on a cricket fan's credulity. Bill O'Reilly, who predicted that a leg-spinner would clean up the modern cricket world's batsmen if he ever made an appearance,[27] has been vindicated in the most spectacular fashion possible.

The modern era of Test cricket has featured an increase in bowling strike rates and the greatest wicket-takers in Test history, with both Glenn McGrath and Muttiah Muralidharan enjoying a long, productive career in more than one format of the game. Bowlers have increased their armouries considerably, with talented exponents of reverse swing still able to cause the world's best batting line-ups to undergo considerable trials and travails. It is now common wisdom that no Test batting side in the world can survive a hostile bowling attack in helpful bowling conditions, say Dale Steyn and Morne Morkel on a first-day South African green-top, or an Indian pair of spinners on a fifth-day turning track. Fielding, thanks to modern fielding drills and greater athleticism, has now surpassed all previous standards, and many catches that were put down before are held. Run-outs by direct hits are routine, and close calls never escape the third umpire; technological aids such as video and stored statistics enable batsmen and bowlers to be studied and planned for in greater detail.

While the coexistence of fast scoring with regular fall of wickets is neither impossible nor problematic—indeed, it is the norm in Twenty20 cricket—in Test cricket, it is when the two do not go together that problems start. For in modern Test cricket, the domination of the bat in some cricketing locales is distressing to the discerning and not-so discerning fan. The former seeks balance, the latter seeks result. Both respond with dismay to the prevalence of one cricketing modality at the expense of a vital and necessary other. If Test cricket's administrators do not act speedily to find a balance between bat and ball, mostly by paying attention to the quality of pitches worldwide, it will kill the game, not just because Twenty20 promised more, but because Test cricket began to deliver considerably less. The greed for maximal gate revenue and advertiser fees from the full five days of a Test, ensured by the slow, low, batting road, will bring about Test cricket's demise far quicker than any threat posed by Twenty20.

The limited-overs versions of the game have had much to do with this trend in modern Test cricket. Pitches have changed worldwide to accommodate the supposed batsman-friendliness of the one-day game; they now aim to accommodate high-scoring games. Field settings for pacemen and spinners alike have suffered; the extravagant slip cordons of the past are relics, as are the rings of close-in fielders for spinners. The captain of the erstwhile top-ranked Test team in the world, M.S. Dhoni, frequently bowled his senior spinner, Harbhajan Singh, for long spells in Test cricket with only a slip and a forward short-leg. There was no silly point or silly mid-off for Singh's doosra and at most times, no backward short-leg, a classic field setting for the off-spinner.

Modern batsmen have also started to have the deck stacked for them. They play with heavier bats while wearing helmets on flatter pitches against bowlers allowed only one bouncer an over. The crowded international schedule, meanwhile, flogs the best and the hardest-working bowlers into the ground. Thus, individual batting averages have inflated, a trend commented on ad nauseam in recent times. Here, the undoubted advantage of the limited-overs formats over Test cricket reveals itself; in them, batting domination is as likely to play a role in a result as is good bowling; in Test cricket, the dominance of batting invariably means stalemate. Test cricket needs to be made more bowler friendly, for its open-endedness favours the batsman more than the bowler. More to the point, a batsman-dominated game—as purists of Test cricket never tire of pointing out—is just not as interesting as the alternatives.

The dullness of all batting, all the time, is brought out best by highlight reels of big innings. For these testimonials to batting feasts are infected by a peculiar boredom; it is essential to cricket and to the enjoyment of a stroke that the fan's thoughts never stray too far from the cricketing version of death. Cricket's terrible beauty is that it promises swift and surefire extinction to those that transgress even momentarily. To let this fear infect one's perception of a batsman's endeavours is to sharpen one's appreciation of the skills on display. To simply watch runs piled on introduces a form of deadening ennui instead. While there is a joy in watching mastery, in watching the demonstration of a particular kind of arrogance and confidence by an actor whose march seems unstoppable, it still must happen within a competitive context. Thus, imbalance in batting and bowling in the open-ended version of the game needs corrective measures because to do otherwise is to take the very serious risk of the game losing competitive value and becoming stale, and ready for replacement by a newer, flashier variant.

Still, Twenty20 might do for Test cricket what the one-day international started, as its sensibilities make its way to the Test arena, leading to faster scoring rates. A modern cricketer playing the longer version of the game, while straddling formats, is likely to be more aggressive, more inclined to faster scoring and, as a result, more likely to get out. The inability of the modern Test batsman to produce Trevor Bailey-style stonewalling or Gavaskar-like monument building might also be conducive to the production of results, even if it does offer the spectacle of shots likely to offend the purist. Indeed, Twenty20 cricket could bring about a great equalization simply by infecting Test batting techniques with its own fecklessness. The talented batsman interested in big scores in the longer version of the game might need to solve this problem on the fly if lacking in practice in the longer version of the game, a cricketing challenge likely to be quite enjoyable for the spectator. (David Warner's successful and spectacular induction into Test cricket shows that supposed Twenty20 specialists can solve the puzzle of Test batting in entertaining style.) Similarly, Test bowlers, used to skin-saving variations like yorkers, slower balls, and other tricks of the trade in Twenty20, might find their armoury enhanced for the longer version of the game.

One solution to the conundrum of reconciling the unusually good quality of Test cricket that spectators have been treated to of late and the potential for much more brilliance on the field with the decline in Test attendance is that the modern cricket fan likes Test cricket just fine; he just prefers watching it on television. This, along with batsmen-friendly pitches, might have led to the most depressing spectacle in modern cricket: the empty stand.

A DEPLETED BACKDROP FOR GLORY

For a few years now, in too many Test cricket venues and during too many Test matches, watching a Test has been to watch a rather drab affair, partly because of the looming empty galleries that serve as background for the cricket. In many cricketing locations, limited-overs cricket appears triumphant; its attractions appear to have made Test cricket come off poorly. Often, the aura of an important international game is not to be detected and there is little spectator atmosphere to soak up or revel in. Tests suffer when staged in such forlorn settings. While the game is supposed to provide sporting drama by itself, it is always aided by its environment. That, in modern Test cricket, often seems to be lacking even if the cricket on display is of a putatively high standard.

A classic example may be found in the highlights reel of Virender Sehwag's batting against Pakistan in the 2006 Lahore Test, as he made 96 runs off 89 balls to kick off India's response to Pakistan's mammoth 679-7. While Sehwag's stroke play was a pleasure to watch, the setting and atmosphere were discordant. The light was poor and the stadium took on a gloomy hue of grey, despite the green of the grass and the white of the players' uniforms. Attendance was sparse; only a smattering of applause greeted each shot issuing from Sehwag's blade. The runs came fast; yet one could barely detect drama. There were no cheering crowds, no attacking fields, nothing that would have upped the drama quotient and provided the appropriate backdrop for the crickter's heroics. Actors like their stage to provide some presence; the Gaddafi Stadium had none. The kind of scores put upon the board by Sehwag that day would be considered entertaining cricket in some formats of the game, the kind of effort that should bring spectators back to Test matches. But there was no one to see it.

Now, in India, Test cricket is not yet dead, even if the street-level excitement it generates cannot be compared to the all-pervasive buzz of the 1970s. As attendance during the 2010 Bangalore Test against Australia showed, Indian crowds are still capable of jamming turnstiles and packing the place to the rafters. Television audiences are often gigantic;[28] advertisers and sponsors clearly still think Test cricket fans live on in India. But the spectacle of a keenly contested Test played in front of empty stands rankles; it is of little comfort to know that interest in that form of cricket lives on in the living room or lounge.

The most famous example of a recent big-occasion Test played to an empty backdrop was the 2008 Mohali Test between India and Australia, where the absence of spectators was highlighted by the fact that Tendulkar's run-aggregate record, otherwise gaudily recorded by fireworks in daylight, was witnessed by just about nobody, except some schoolchildren bused in from local schools and impatient Australian fielders. The presence of schoolchildren who were let in for free was read—especially by the visiting Australian press—as further evidence of Test cricket's desperate straits in the subcontinent, reduced now to reliance on pathetically crude populist gestures, akin to politicians busing in supporters for rallies.

But the Mohali schoolchildren experiment provides a very good model for how attendance at Tests could be bolstered in India. It suggests a solution perhaps applicable only in the unique economic context of the BCCI and Indian cricket, though variants of it could be applied elsewhere: admission to the ground should be made free or almost free. Gratis admission would generate the audience needed for the creation of the televised cricketing spectacle, the true financial driver of the game. And the more exciting the televised version, the more likely it is that the television audience might be tempted to go the arena, the scene of the spectacle, and the more likely that the television rights deal will remain a lucrative one—Roman coliseums filled up with crowds eager not just to witness gladiators in action but to be part of an arena of colourful and loud spectators participating in a public ritual. The sports spectator wants to be part of an event; solitary appreciation is a pleasure best reserved for museums and mountain vistas. The most exciting cricket match would be considerably duller if there was no one there to see it. As every television viewer realizes, part of the aura of the televised game is the sound of the crowd reacting to the action on the pitch.

Consider any form of televised entertainment where an audience is needed to complete the spectacle. The David Letterman show derives part of its telegenic appeal from the presence of a crowd that packs the studio and provides an applause track. This audience is not charged for admission to the show, though CBS could, if it wanted, easily charge $5–15 as an entrance fee from the many tourists to New York City that make up the majority of the audience. But the studio realizes that its primary draw is the televised show and lets crowds line up for free entry instead. This results in a no-losers situation for all concerned: the studio becomes a must-see sight on tourists' lists; the show gets its audience; Letterman gets subjects for his pranks and an audience for his jokes.

In cricket, crowds raise a game's importance; they dramatize by their passion the game's excitement; by their absence, they float a giant thumbs-down over the stadium.[29] But in this modern setting, given television's primacy, the spectator in the stands also needs to function as television extra, one that makes the televised spectacle possible. Spending time and money on a game shows commitment; the burden of that commitment can be reduced by sharing the wealth of television rights with the spectator. The spectator will still spend his time; there is no need to lighten his wallet as well.

If Test cricket is worth preserving—presumably the BCCI and the local state association in charge of the cricket ground in question can agree on this—then the mechanics of the 'let-them-in-for-free (or just-about-free)' solution are viable. Tickets generate revenue for the local cricketing association, which earns income too, from advertising hoardings and the television rights deal. In order to make up the loss of gate receipts, the BCCI and the local association could calculate estimated revenues, and add that to the television rights and ground advertising deals. These rates can be adjusted upwards considering the reality of more eyeballs at the ground. The television rights owner gets to show an Indian Test team at home playing in a packed stadium; the state association will see increased revenues from sales of food and drink at the ground. Thus, the rolling back of ticket prices could guarantee other forms of income for sponsors, state associations and the BCCI. These could include, for instance, merchandise sales at the ground and the sale of Test highlights packages on DVDs.

Subsidized attendance at Test cricket is not a radical idea; the 2011 Lord's Test owed its last-day full house in part to the authorities' enlightened decision to let under-sixteens—Test cricket's future audience—in at no charge (the 'last-day-for-free' model is already quite well-established in Australia). Giving away a product to attract a larger customer base, members of which might then go on to become more expansive consumers of ancillary offerings, is an idea starting to take hold in the modern music industry where music might be given away for free to attract a larger fan base to live concerts; these same fans go on to spend money on T-shirts, merchandise and memorabilia. This generosity can produce loyal, dedicated fans as the Grateful Dead will readily testify. By allowing their fans to tape their live shows and freely trade music amongst themselves, the band earned the gratitude of its fans and produced a body of devoted followers, willing to spend their hard-earned money on multiple concert attendances year in, year out, and on purchasing digitally re-mastered CDs issued by the band.

But what it does say about Test cricket that it requires subsidized attendance? Not very much that was not already known: televised cricket makes cricket solvent and subsidizing attendance to Test cricket makes it possible for the value of the televised product to be enhanced. If television is to be lord and master of cricket then why obsess over milking every last cent from the spectator in the stand? Why not make the television rights owner pay for the whole package—the game, and its spectators?

If Test attendance is not to be subsidized in India, Test cricket could be restricted to the most populous metropolitan centres—Delhi, Chennai, Bangalore, Mumbai, and Kolkata—each with a rich history of Test cricket at its historic grounds: the Feroz Shah Kotla, the M.A. Chidambaram, the Chinnaswamy, the Wankhede, Eden Gardens. In each of these cities, access to the grounds, whether via public transport or not, is relatively easier than it is in other smaller metropolitan venues, which, thanks to the pressure of real estate concerns, have built their stadiums away from established urban concentrations.

This remoteness is complicated by perverse logistical arrangements that make access to a Test match resemble an obstacle course devised by John Buchanan at a pre-series boot camp. For the BCCI has often scheduled Tests to start on a Monday, at venues located thirty kilometres away from the city, with little public transportation available. This presents an unattractive option to cabbies apprehensive about the lack of return fares. For the spectators, entrance is only possible via the exclusive sale of five-day passes rather than an à la carte selection of the desired day. It is small wonder then, that anyone shows up to watch at all.

When India has done well in Test cricket, like completing a historic run chase in Chennai in 2008 against England, or during Sehwag's epic 293 at Brabourne Stadium against Sri Lanka in 2009 and India's attempt to force a win at Eden Gardens against the South Africans in 2010 (with the top spot of the Test rankings on the line), crowds have flocked in. At these moments, Test cricket becomes everything it used to be in an Indian stadium, and worries about its demise are temporarily placed on hold. And here again, the wheel comes full circle to a conclusion that sounds familiar: the best thing for Test cricket worldwide would be a strong Indian Test team. The Indian sponsor wants nothing more than to ride on the back of national glory, no matter what the format. Subsidized attendance at home provides both vital crowd support and enhances the televised spectacle for both the distant spectator and the sponsor; the strength of the Indian cricket team will do the rest. In a country keen to assert the Shining India brand, this is all that is required. Who would dare speak of the death of Test cricket when confronted with the sight of an Indian stadium full of fans cheering on their men in white?

The applicability of the let-my-people-in-for-free solution in contexts other than the Indian one might seem dubious, but it need not be so if the game's administrators are honest enough to acknowledge that the primary source of revenue for cricket today is television and that gate receipts come second. And if the 'product' can be suitably polished for the rights holder by the provision of a subsidized stadium audience, then perhaps only greed holds back cricket administrators from taking this route.

Whither One-Day Internationals?

These days it is not just Test cricket that is said to be threatened by Twenty20. The one-day game, the harbinger of so much change to cricket worldwide, not least because it made the BCCI wildly rich, has had its viability questioned, its position deemed untenable. Its faults appear to be many: too long, too predictable, and too flaccid in its structure. This is largely because of the middle-overs period, where batsmen spend most of their time stabilizing innings after poor starts, or slowing down after fast ones in response to fielding restrictions being lifted. Twenty20 was born of the need to do away with the middle overs; just the first and the last ten overs will do, thanks very much.

But the format's biggest problem is not of its own making: too many one-day internationals are staged every year and fans have become saturated. There are only so many variations possible on a theme, and one-day cricket's possible twists and turns appear to have been exhaustively explored and repeated over the years. Most ODI series are easily forgotten. These pull in crowds for a day's entertainment—there is little not to like about spending a day in the sun, talking about cricket and drinking beer—but otherwise they are entirely forgettable and nondescript; the cricket becomes background muzak. A surfeit of short tournaments or excessively long ODI series in an era of plentiful televised coverage has left fans bloated, much like those unfortunate gustators stumbling out of a Brazilian rodizio, sick to their stomachs of the excesses indulged in. Goethe warned us of the dangers of a succession of good days. The cricket spectator, with his rejection of over-scheduled cricket, has seen fit to remind us of the wisdom of that adage.

The twists and turns possible in one hundred overs will become less commonplace if fewer games are played; so cricket's administrators need to take better care of this particular golden goose. Letting it out less often to play would be a good start. The one-day game could be salvaged by returning it to serving as a brief appetizer for Test cricket; three or five one-day internationals before a Test series is a perfect aperitif and would also partially ameliorate the problem of the missing tour game on a Test tour. The modern series of seven games and the numerous one-day cups that untidily litter the cricketing landscape are crashing bores that need speedy eviction from the cricketing calendar.

The charges levelled against Twenty20 cricket—too short, too compressed, destructive of batting skills, contemptuous of bowlers, not 'real cricket', 'merely festival cricket'—are precisely those levelled against one-day international cricket as it rose to prominence in the late 1970s and early '80s. The ODI fought for respect, and slowly but surely fans came to appreciate its particular offerings, to understand that it could, via increased revenues, subsidize the longer version of the game and bring in a new audience base for cricket.

One-day international cricket also has a place in the cricket calendar in offering a reasonable middle ground between Tests and Twenty20s. It offers fans the chance to see their heroes for longer, on a stage that lets them display their skills without premature termination of play, an important consideration in the fan's appreciation. Cricket, with its unique blend of the team and the individual, in its setting up of the batsman versus bowler drama, offers fans a uniquely extended contact with the display of individual skills. Consider football: even the world's most gifted players are allowed to dazzle only briefly on its stage. Johann Cruyff and Diego Maradona were able, on their best days, to perhaps rack up a few minutes of ball contact in a ninety-minute game; in cricket, Sachin Tendulkar can bat, and Shane Warne can bowl, all day long. The cricket world would be an immeasurably poorer place if the only contact we had with the genius of Tendulkar or Warne had been their brief sorties in Twenty20 cricket.

When Tendulkar did score a century in the 2011 IPL, one wondered whether he enjoyed that innings as much as he enjoyed his one-day international or Test hundreds, whether the shorter innings provided Tendulkar the physical pleasure associated with a longer innings. Tendulkar's IPL century took him 66 balls; would he have liked to bat some more, given the undeniable form he was in? For a batsman, part of the tactile, sensible pleasure of batting is the pure physicality of the ball making contact with the bat, the marvellous, transmitted sensation of the timing of the stroke. In this sense, even a well-timed defensive shot, which keeps out a good ball, can provide pleasure to a batsman. Thus, the more contact with the ball, the longer the batsman can spend in the 'zone', one marked by the pleasure of making contact with the ball through the bat, an extension of his body; when a batsman is given out, his disappointment is grounded in not just the denial of a bigger score, but also in the denial of the pleasurable physical sensation of the batting experience, taken away by the umpire's finger or the bowler's brilliance, or both. This constraint on the canvas available for the batsman's expression can, like in many other settings, act as a spur to creativity, as evidenced in the proliferation of unorthodox shots that are now commonplace—the reverse-sweep, the Dilscoop, the helicopter shot, the Misbah. But it can also lead to the termination of a feast all too soon.

These considerations prompt a rather delicious thought: might it be that the salvation of the longer forms of cricket lies in the preference expressed by batsmen for a format that, to put it bluntly, lets them bat longer? Those forms offer its players—batsman and bowlers alike—the other side of the extended viewing pleasure for the fan; it offers them the chance to preen their wares for longer periods, to extend their display of virtuosity and excellence, to engage in self-indulgence in a team contest. Part of the resolution of the crisis of competition amongst cricket formats might lie in the expressed preference of players for qualitatively and quantitatively varied modes of expression.

The birth of Twenty20 suggests that cricket administrators have a rather different strategy in mind when it comes to popularizing the game's different formats: by rule-change, by interventionist legislation.

Tiresome Tinkering

Cricket legislators' most beloved method of solving all of cricket's problems, and to popularize Test and one-day international cricket, is tinkering with their rules and playing conditions. Every form of cricket faces the constant interference of the cricket legislator.[30] For instance, among the proposals floated to make Test cricket more 'attractive' or 'viable' are day-night Tests using pink cricket balls. This suggestion received support from Cricket Australia and the MCC, who staged a match under these conditions in March 2011 in Abu Dhabi.[31] The experiment revealed that pink balls last up to nearly seventy overs, a reasonably close approximation to the requirements of a Test match and thus indicative of its successful deployment if the playing conditions for Test cricket were to be altered.

But the conservative sceptic might well ask why the cricket administrator remains stuck on a singular note of wanting to 'change' the game whenever there is talk of creating new spectators. Cricket administrators all too often employ the flawed premise that the 'product' whose management and care they have been entrusted with is one that needs desperate measures of resuscitation. This attitude, which treats the normal crests and troughs of a game's financial fortunes and its following by fans as a serious illnes, leads administrators to make the fatal mistake of thinking that the game requires radical surgery. In these circumstances one might dispute the diagnosis and rightfully worry about the prescribed medicine.

This is not just a matter of aesthetic discomfort at the idea of Test cricket played in coloured clothes at night. Rather, independent of the format in question, it is a rejection of the claim that tinkering with a game's laws and playing conditions is how it is 'made' more popular. Simplicity is seemingly a virtue unappreciated by cricket administrators, who delight in rendering the game ever more baroque and Rube Goldberg-device–like, festooned with rule changes and little doodads designed to go off at intervals to wake up the presumably somnambulist spectators. Inexplicably, the spectator's task has been rendered ever more intractable by the need to comprehend the special set of rules for different formats. And the further the game in the international stadium is from the game played on the maidan or the county oval, the further it inches away from the imagination of the fan.

The correct reaction to the existence of multiple formats should be more simplicity rather than more complication. Indeed, if cricket is supposed to survive in a brave new three-format world, then why not make format change—that of reducing overs and time—the only one? On their own, these two restrictions radically change the nature of the contest and the spectator experience; the moment an innings is restricted in length to make it complete, as opposed to its natural conclusion by the batting side's dismissal or by declaration, the game changes dramatically since the draw is eliminated. Would not Twenty20 and the fifty-over game offer precisely the same thrills of a guaranteed finish in compressed time even if there were no PowerPlays and no bowling or fielding restrictions? Limited-overs cricket is not inherently a more complicated form of the game; it is the format that most casual cricketers play the game in. This simplicity should be embraced rather than rejected. To take this conservative route is to expect the cricket spectator to have the intelligence to figure out the difference between the various formats, and that the game's administrators seem unwilling and unable to do.

Further rule change in cricket's multiple formats therefore seems gratuitous; some regression instead might be more desirable. For instance, a simple retreat in Test cricket would be to lift the ban on bouncers so that Test cricket provides something—the spectacle of the intimidation of the batsman by the fast bowler—that Twenty20 cricket and fifty-over cricket do not currently provide. With helmets, better protective gear, and arguably truer wickets available to batsmen, there is little to fear in this reversion to the playing conditions of yesteryear. The oft-made suggestion of returning to uncovered wickets surely merits reconsideration too.

Similarly, in limited-overs cricket, a return to basics, by hewing to sparseness rather than complexity, would be desirable. Consider the lame contrivance of the PowerPlay. It has added little excitement for the spectator, distracted the captain and increased his workload, but exciting one-day games continue to find it neither necessary nor sufficient. It does seem to have generated an employment scheme for commentators and journalists who delight in second-guessing the timing of a PowerPlay, or in praising a captain for its 'skilful' deployment.

Limited-overs cricket is also guilty of marginalizing the bowler in its rule changes, of labouring under the conceit that cricket is solely about one side scoring more runs than the other. Rolling back egregiously bowler-unfriendly legislation and restoring the bowler and the bowling captain to roles other than containment is crucial. One option would be to get rid of the ten-over bowling quota; this would allow the outstanding exponents of the art of bowling a larger space within which to exert control, and diminish the importance of the part-time bowler (there are no corresponding restrictions on batsmen, who are not restricted to facing a pre-set number of deliveries). But this change would not work without a reduction in the number of one-day games played in a year. Otherwise, captains and teams run the risk of injuring top-class bowlers because of over-bowling. Yet another regression would get rid of field restrictions on the number of players in catching positions and the use of fielding circles; this might be viewed as running the risk of games featuring all fielders blocking boundaries, but this possibility would be the same for both teams, and batsmen would simply be forced to be more inventive in their run-making, perhaps by scrambling more singles, always a crowd-pleasing sight.

ODIs should, however, retain a slightly stricter interpretation of wides; indeed, Test cricket would be better served by bringing its calling of wides partially into line with one-day standards; a calibration of the two extremes of wide-calling to a more sympathetic call in one-day internationals and a harsher call in Test matches would be an aspirational mean. This would prevent Test cricket from being hijacked by blatantly negative tactics of containment (much like the requirement of a minimum number of overs in a day has acted to prevent some of the appalling time-wasting tactics of the past).

These changes might also make one-day captains remember the old nugget of wisdom that nothing stops a batting offensive in its tracks like the fall of a wicket; scoring rates are best reduced by the introduction of a new batsman to the crease. The only modern team to take the approach of 'containment by wickets' in one-day internationals, including the setting of Test match fields, was, unsurprisingly enough, the Australians, who, during the 2001 limited-overs triangular series against England and Pakistan (in England), employed Test match slip fields for the new ball. It is almost established wisdom that such fields will be too expensive in the one-day game. But to take advantage of them, a batsman has to still try and bat aggressively against a new ball used by a quick bowler. It is scarcely credible that a captain and an opening bowler would not back themselves under these circumstances.

These changes will only partly address the problem of the over-scheduled one-day international. While the IPL season also features too many games, it does provide one lesson for both Test and one-day cricket that is worth imbibing. Each of its season's games contributes points towards a visible, tangible end: its championship. Perhaps devising a rational one-day World Cup and a Test championship could solve the problem of the 'meaningless' one-day international and invest bilateral Test encounters with greater significance.

Looking For Champions

The ICC, its member national boards, the world's fans and players, often seem to be in agreement that the future structure of international cricket should feature world championships for each format of the game. A desirable side-effect of this would be to introduce some coherence into the world's cricketing calendar which, as many have rightly complained, is over-scheduled and conveys the impression of pointlessness.[32] But motivating the current staple diet of bilateral encounters and finding worthy champions via rational formats for world championships might turn out to be an instance of doomed circle-squaring, for most proposals for restructuring world cricket run into the seemingly insuperable constraints of the ICC's Future Tours Programme, and the body's obsession with revenue generation.

THE HOLY GRAIL: A TEST CHAMPIONSHIP

A world championship for Tests is recognized as a worthwhile goal by just about everybody; how it is to be done is, as everyone also seems to agree, the hard part. In the absence of a championship, modern Test cricket has struggled to crown champions. One Test series after the other is deemed an unofficial 'world championship', but this seems a poor substitute for a definitive anointment. The great West Indians of the 1980s and the Australians of the late 1990s and early 2000s attained the status of 'world champions' through an extended period of consistently high performance and by beating all and sundry in a variety of conditions. There is no such undisputed 'world champion' now, and the ICC's rating system often seems a poor substitute.

However, even though Test cricket's existing rating system is frequently derided, teams still aspire to the number one ranking and might employ it as motivational incentive[33] (England's press, fans and team certainly thought so in the summer of 2011). Fans, of course, find it easy to claim bragging rights and invest particular series or games with importance because of their effect on the ranking's top slots. India's second Test against South Africa in Kolkata in 2010 was one whose outcome would have displaced a rankings leader. This had a noticeble effect on the attention paid to its result.

Interest and pride in the ICC's ranking system has grown slowly. When India moved to No.1 in the world rankings in 2009, its feat did not excite Indian fans excessively though sober-minded aficionados made note of the fact that it reflected recent Indian consistency. (The number one ranking also affected Indian scheduling of Test cricket as the BCCI, with great alacrity, and admittedly, by showing a keen sensitivity to the aspirations of the Indian cricket fan, scheduled more Tests, even if not always in the preferred three or five Tests format.) These rankings have started to become part of the cricketing conversation amongst players, journalists, and fans. When the top rankings stand to change as a result of an encounter between the top two teams—as in the India and England 2011 Test series—interest is particularly intense.

But a cup format for a world championship, understandably, remains the most natural, popular, and gratifying for spectators.[34] The reaction of Indian fans to winning the 2011 World Cup offered an interesting contrast to the emotions on display when the Indian Test team became No. 1 in the world Test ratings; the denouement of a cup facilitates such emotional response. But the challenges for a Test cricket championship are aplenty, for its time requirements are immense.

Most straightforwardly, a Test world championship appears best served by a format of short home-and-away series featuring at most three nations, similar to the Rugby Tri-Nations. If the tournament is restricted to two nations it would have the salutary effect of allowing a longer series between the two, perhaps consisting of three Tests each played at home and away. Such a tournament, staged every four years, would require qualification in the intervening period to eliminate the remaining Test-playing nations—a structure similar to that of the soccer World Cup.[35]

This four-year-long process of qualification—also involving short home-and-away test series between each pair of Test-playing nations—should hold the cricket world's attention as every series and every game would acquire importance by virtue of the points it stacked up for the championship series. This qualification period would obviously feature both mismatches and cliff-hangers. But just like the soccer World Cup, these would be put into perspective by the prospect of qualifying for the elusive championship series. Furthermore, the extended nature of this qualification would reward consistency while ensuring that current no-hopers, like Bangladesh and Zimbabwe, by drawing upon home advantage, or by pulling off upsets, might be able to keep their dream of a passage to the final alive.[36] The qualifying period would have to feature a fair point assignment system that rewarded results and not the cricketing equivalent of 'sitting on a lead'.

The championship series would provide an encounter between the two—or three—nations that had shown the most consistency in the intervening four years. Some ingenuity would be required to pick a champion in the case of a tied series, but this could be tackled by a system of points that favoured wins and recognized advantages acquired and held—especially via positive, attacking cricket—in drawn games. In the absence of a coherent system for breaking ties, a shared world championship would not be the end of the world; the two teams sharing the championship would still be the cricket world's two most consistent teams.

It is now perhaps time for a reality check. The current economic imperatives of the ICC and its Full Members, well reflected in the current Future Tours Programme, would never permit such an arrangement; the ICC plans for a Test championship, originally scheduled to be held in 2013 in England but now postponed till 2017, simply picks the top four countries from the existing rankings table and throws them into a playoff of sorts. It is hard to imagine India agreeing to play a series of home-and-away Tests against Bangladesh or Zimbabwe that would dent the value of its television rights deals. Furthermore, this qualification calendar would not address the revenue maximization demands of boards determined to cash in on money-spinners like the India–Australia encounters or the need to accommodate historic rivalries like the Ashes. The ECB and CA would not permit fiddling with the calendar for Ashes tours; more to the point, they would not allow any scheduling that would disrupt the notion of the Ashes being retained or regained. Some way should be found to preserve the Ashes, of course. A home-and-away combo of six Tests might satisfy some fans but would still run the risk of not satisfying the dedicated Ashes fan used to the idea of the 'overseas campaign' for the Ashes.

In this sense, the FTP is scant improvement over older, arbitrary bilateral arrangements that often resulted in long gaps between Test encounters between Full Members. While the qualification process could, if given time, start to generate its own aura and set of myths, it is hard to see how it could ever be bootstrapped and started up in the face of resistance from the ICC's richest Full Members. Some modifications to the qualification process could protect rivalries like the Ashes, but it is unclear if anything could address the concerns of boards that are not interested in playing economically unattractive Test series. Similar problems crop up when the seemingly settled situation of the one-day World Cup is confronted.

PLANNING A WORLD CUP AND GLOBAL EXPANSION

Though World Cups currently exist for both ODIs and Twenty20 cricket, all is not well. Historically, the ICC and its members have not been able to settle on a format that reconciles various and seemingly divergent imperatives: globalizing the game, maintaining viewer interest over the duration of the tournament, eliminating mismatches, rewarding consistency, and crowning a worthy champion. But the passion of cricket fans and the brilliance of the world's cricket players have ensured that Cup tournaments have been largely successful, with a couple of notable exceptions when fans and players alike felt that the desiderata above were not satisfied.

Most prominently, the 2007 World Cup was a long drawn-out failure, universally derided as the worst ever. This judgment was eminently fair, given the Cup's catastrophically bad, money-grubbing, nakedly greedy management by the ICC. Rather than fixing the manifold problems of organization—such as over-inflated ticket prices, onerous ground restrictions and too many mismatches—the ICC, transfixed by the format, which made it possible for India to crash out and for the tournament to suffer financially thanks to the loss of television audiences and sponsor monies, eliminated two Associate teams and rejigged the group stages of the 2011 World Cup.

The 2011 World Cup, held in India, Bangladesh and Sri Lanka, and featuring fourteen countries, was still too long at forty-five days.

Its format, set up to ensure that higher-ranked teams enjoyed almost certain passage to the quarter-finals, made the preliminary stages run the risk of utter irrelevance. But the World Cup was hailed as a success, and most of the cricketing world agreed that both the World Cup and the one-day international, previously hailed as dying species, had been resurrected. There was, of course, little chance that the World Cup would have failed in the subcontinent. (Scepticism about the fate of the one-day international would have been tempered by paying attention to the television ratings of the seven-game ODI series between India and Australia in 2009, though a few months after India's World Cup win, empty stands during the India–England ODI series prompted more worry.)[37]

But the 2011 World Cup raised again for the ICC, the perennial question of the place of Associate Members in the World Cup, especially given Ireland's giant-killing efforts against Bangladesh and England (a repeat of their 2007 efforts at beating Pakistan) and the patchy performance of the other Associates (Canada, the Netherlands and Kenya).

The ICC's next tweak of the World Cup, however, was to recommend a smaller one, in terms of participants, for 2015; the number of matches was reduced from forty-nine to forty-eight. The Associate Members bore the brunt of this change: their numbers were sharply reduced to the point of elimination. Predictably, the ICC initially went for the television-friendly option of arranging more games between Full Members and forgot about the Cup's ability to globalize the game by allowing Associate Members to play against the world's best and keep aspiring for eventual Test status. It had also diminished the Cup by turning it into something approximating an invitational tourney—rather than a true 'World' Cup—with admittance restricted to those who had already found favour as Full Members. The neglect of Associate Members was made more inexplicable by cricket's pressing need, in the face of ever greater competition from other sports and modes of entertainment, to find new fans in new demographics.

The ICC's decision provoked howls of protest from the Associates. These were loud enough to cause the ICC to reinstate the original number of fourteen countries for the 2015 World Cup and to gingerly approach a solution always considered unthinkable: qualification for the World Cup. Such a qualification system over the intervening years' one-day internationals would ideally require the construction of a four-year calendar featuring home-and-away series between Full Members. The bottom two Full Members at the end of this period could then play in a qualification tournament featuring the top-ranked Associates. This qualification process would make individual one-day internationals more meaningful as every game played anywhere in the world would contribute points for the World Cup. Given the uneven quality of the Associates in 2011—Ireland excelled, Kenya sank, Canada and the Netherlands promised but failed to deliver—and the weaknesses of Full Members like Bangladesh and Zimbabwe, a qualifying tournament that pitched the best Associates versus the worst Full Members would help select an appropriate roster for the World Cup and ensure that cricket's one-day championship had earned the right to be termed a genuine 'World' Cup.

As in Test cricket, a seemingly straightforward solution runs up against the financial and political realities of the ICC: its Full Members seem unlikely to agree to a structure that could result in any of them missing out on the Cup and its associated remunerations which, thus far, have come rather easily to them, given their one-way qualification for Full Member status. In a qualifying competition involving countries at the bottom of the qualification table, Full Members could be beaten by leading Associates and miss out on the World Cup: Ireland beat England in the 2011 World Cup, and could also have beaten Bangladesh, Zimbabwe and the West Indies. In particular, the prospect of a World Cup without India, however unlikely given the extended nature of the qualification process, is likely to send chills down the ICC's spine. The ICC would not accept any arrangement that might risk the commercial appeal of the World Cup in the massive Indian market. Furthermore, Full Members with established rivalries are likely to not want to be constrained by the requirements of a qualification process that might bite into precious time that could be more profitably utilized arranging one-day games against each other.

So the World Cup remains in limbo; Associates are welcome but seemingly on sufferance; Full Members at the bottom of the table see no incentive to improve as their place in the 'finals' is guaranteed every four years; and the length of the Cup and its mismatches continue to grate. The expansion of the game to include more countries playing the highest form of the game—Test matches—seems a rather forlorn hope in these circumstances. Meanwhile, the question of whether the current Cup format even rationally picks out a suitable champion has been pushed to the background.

By the ICC's recommendation that the 2012 Twenty20 World Cup be shrunk from sixteen teams to twelve, global expansion of the game has not been helped either. This move seems retrograde, given Twenty20 cricket's ability to make an impact on new markets amongst both fans and players. An outstanding, highly visible performance in the Twenty20 World Cup by an Associate Member could bring its players to not just the attention of Twenty20 leagues like the IPL and the BBL but also to fence-sitting fans back home. Indeed, given the greater potential for exciting upsets in Twenty20, the ICC's decision seemed especially mysterious. Surely a greater number of Associates in the Cup would entail a greater number of potential upset-causing banana skins for Full Members? But perhaps that's the problem; one the ICC seems reluctant to face up to.

The ICC is in danger of becoming an exclusive club, its World Cups invitational tournaments, thanks to cricket maintaining a caste system via the status difference between Full and Associate Members. This difference is also reflected in the ICC's annual conference where Full, Associate and Affiliate Members are assigned varying weights for their votes. Most problematically, the promotion of an Associate to Full status is irrevocable. But Zimbabwe achieved Test status in 1992, and peaked in the late 1990s; Bangladesh is still struggling to be competitive in Test cricket; Kenya were peaking when its Test status was rejected in 2001 and has since declined;[38] in recent times, every Full Member, in its own inimitable way, has suggested its utter incapacity to play Test cricket.

If cricket is to expand, it must either devise a tiered system that allows for movement between tiers—to incentivize national boards to maintain their cricketing standards and not complacently count on the income windfall of being a Full Member—or it should do away with distinctions between members, ease qualification for Test status, and organize a genuine four-year qualification tournament for its limited-overs formats. The current system is an uneasy compromise that works to no one's advantage. The artificial maintenance of the Full Member club with its 'pull up the ladder, I'm aboard' attitude hurts cricket

in a world offering ever more diversions and where the current Full
Members themselves do not treat cricket as more than a minor sport.
Arguments for Test cricket to be made more inclusive have never had
more resonance than they do now.[39]

Cricket's membership has changed slowly, and when it has, new
relationships have not been nurtured so that the average cricket fan has
not had his horizons expanded by dealing with a variety of players or
teams. Cricketing history continues to feature as highlights a familiar
list of teams, players and locales; rivalries between nations and teams
which could have been nurtured have not been taken care of. It would
help too, if cricket's journalists developed catholic tastes and paid more
attention to the margins of the cricketing world. This is an old problem;
the list of cricketing feats and great Test matches mysteriously always
come back to a familiar list of either England versus Australia games
or games involving one of these two, staged in England or Australia,
which the journalists of the two countries could have been bothered to
attend. Great Test feats that take place far away from the eyes of the
cricket world's information order slip rapidly into obscurity.

The ICC's imperatives for global expansion are more likely to be
met by a club system that by rewarding outstanding individual products
of fledgling systems is able to spark a concomitant growth in local
cricketing scenes. The expanding Twenty20 leagues, committed to
finding the best short-format players for their rosters, and equipped
perhaps with global scouts, could do a far better job of this than the
reluctant ICC has, trapped as it is in a situation where its members are
more interested in national board incomes than in the sporting health
of the game worldwide. Eager cricketers from Associate and Affiliate
ICC members will be the loudest applauders of the success of the global
Twenty20 franchise, for in its success lies their best chance of playing
top-class cricket against the best in the world, all the while making a
living by practising their most prominent skills.

Cricket in the US

Such optimism about the ability of Twenty20 leagues to globalize the
sport forces a reckoning with cricket's actual challenges in regions of

potential growth. If these are insurmountable then plans for expansion might be moot. Of the most promising candidates for the further growth of the game and possible subsequent promotion from Associate to Full Member status—Ireland, Scotland, Kenya, the Netherlands, Canada, Afghanistan, USA, Denmark, Bermuda, Namibia, Oman, Nepal, Uganda, UAE[40]—the most intriguing is the US and its money-spinning markets. Success there would do much to help cement cricket's place in the world of sports.

Cricket's ability to find a foothold in the US would justify the optimism about its prospects in countries where it is prima facie not so marginalized. The relationship of the US to cricket has some lessons to offer; ones that would be of value to members of the Anglo-Australian combine as they struggle to come to terms with the displacement of their erstwhile genteel cricketing culture by the brashness of the new Indian presence. And even if cricket were never to take root in the US, these lessons are instructive in understanding cricket's possible growth in other parts of the world.

The challenges faced by cricket in the US are exceptional. The slow, painful, emergence and flourishing of soccer in the US, its increasing popularity and its ability to captivate the US when the World Cup rolls around every four years, shows that cricket's growth in the US is not impossible. But while soccer has a huge following there, it remains little understood. Plenty of soccer artistry is unappreciated by a large segment of the population. Its example shows how far cricket has to go.

At the turn of the twentieth century, a Martian studying international cricket on Planet Earth could have been excused for thinking that it formed a triangle consisting of England, Australia and the United States. First-class cricket flourished in Philadelphia, and indeed, the 'Gentlemen from Philadelphia' beat the Australian Test team by an innings in 1893 and 1896. But by then, in the wake of the Civil War, cricket had already lost some of its American following to baseball, and this brief Golden Age served as its last and final hurrah. From that time to the deserved—and still current—status of cricketing wasteland was not to take too long.

Now, despite the presence of the US in the ICC and its team's participation in ICC tournaments, in its sheer, benighted, deliberate ignorance, its aversion to the game, its apparent refusal to consider and assign it any sort of respectable status, the US appears to be the world's ultimate disaster area for cricket. Other countries pay cricket benign inattention, but in seemingly deliberate hostility or indifference to cricket, the US remains Enemy No. 1. Most Americans' response to cricket remains stuck in a familiar groove, that of the strange, quaint game which takes five days to complete, is hard to understand, features bizarrely named fielding positions like deep fine-leg, and is played by posh Englishmen and slavish colonials.

When baseball commentators want to emphasize that an MLB game is dragging on interminably, comparisons are invariably made with cricket. Meanwhile, any print article in the US on cricket incessantly harps on the unique incomprehensibility of the game—a guffaw-inspiring judgment, given the Byzantine complexity of NFL penalty rules—or on the jaw-dropping durations of Test cricket. And then there are the inevitable snarky mentions of the quaint customs of 'tea', enough to make one wish this interval had been named differently, and of 'drinks'. (Americans might be forgiven for thinking that gin and tonics were consumed by players to help deal with the tedium of the game.) Much snickering too is directed at the gigantic amounts of protection worn by pusillanimous cricket players. And it would be too much to ask of Americans that attention be paid to the rich body of cricketing literature, possibly more varied and complex than that associated with any other sport except baseball. CLR James's classic *Beyond a Boundary* has made it to the reading lists of many American history departments, but his work stands out in splendid isolation in that position.

This classification of cricket confirms the game's marginalization in the American mainstream. Cricket has made some of the same inroads as soccer did many years ago, but despite the size of immigrant communities that play the sport, despite the growing presence of cricket leagues in the US, the introduction of cricket as a recognized game in New York schools, the presence of large expatriate populations from cricket playing countries and even an American cricket team that plays in ICC tournaments, cricket remains a profoundly misunderstood game in the US.

Thus, the US has not provided a friendly home for cricket. To play cricket in a cricketing country is to be surrounded by the game and its trappings: walking around in whites, carrying a cricket kit bag, playing games on city council grounds meant for cricket. In the US, as Joseph O'Neill noted in *Netherland*, cricket, despite being proudly played by immigrant communities, sticks out, and is played on sufferance. To play cricket in the US means participating in an oddity, something not fitting in its surroundings. Music fans will find the feeling familiar; the traveller, the immigrant, will not have failed to notice artistes and genres sounding discordant in alien settings. Ministry and Al Jourgensen sound jarring in a car parked in Delhi's Sabzi Mandi; Pandit Jasraj sounds odd on one's iPod, strapped to the hip, while walking down a Manhattan street. Cricket has a cadence and a rhythm of its own, demanding a location, a tuning with its setting. In the US, that correlation is missing.

Unfortunately, cricket's supposed popularizers in the US have not helped. Shashi Tharoor's 2007 *New York Times* op-ed on cricket, a rare opportunity that should have been seized to explain the game's attraction for its sundry admirers,[41] featured gratuitous reductive analyses about the US, its cultural inclinations, and pointless baseball bashing. Cricket's snobbery was reinforced and, unsurprisingly, Tharoor was taken to task in the 'Letters' section.[42] Tharoor is not alone in this regard. Most cricket fans talk down to baseball and its fans. But the assumption that baseball is a poor cousin of cricket is a hostile, superficial attitude, and Americans rightly bristle when confronting the cricket fan convinced of his game's superiority.

A full analysis of why cricket has never managed to take root in the United States would necessitate the recounting of a complex story involving economics, culture, and the unique brand of American nationalism. Most of the prima facie answers—cricket is too complex for Americans and too slow for the American psyche, cricket takes too long and does not fit in with the hectic American lifestyle, Americans are too insular—fail to do justice to the question. The visible passion of the baseball fan addresses some of these suggested answers, while others are genuinely problematic in indulging in too much essentializing and reveal far more about the person offering them.

Perhaps the answer to the American puzzle of cricket lies in the year 1776 when the US declared its independence from the British Empire, in the year 1812 when it fought a war against England. Perhaps the answer lies in the intellectual struggles of the American transcendentalists and pragmatists who fought hard to evolve a uniquely

American spirit and sensibility. These facile solutions to the puzzle of cricket's absence in the US might contain a kernel of truth: Americans have grown distant from their old country—if they ever entertained notions of one—quicker than other former colonies like Australia or even India; the establishment of an American identity, though always an issue for debate and contention, has enjoyed some security in the American context. For unlike other former colonies—like Australia, for instance—the US established a distinct identity very quickly. Australia is still debating whether it should lose the Union Jack and the Queen. These debates were settled a long time ago in the US, which has self-consciously grown out of the shadow of the Empire. There is little chance it will go back again.

Concomitantly, American sporting culture has set out on a distinctive, independent path. It is no coincidence the dominant sports on the American landscape feature local provenance and modification: basketball, devised by James Naismith in 1893, gridiron football, derived from variants of rugby, and baseball.

Unlike the countries of the Caribbean and the Indian subcontinent, there has been, for a very long time, no colonial master lording over the US, and no felt need for vindication in light of a superior's soft bigotry. Thus, as part of its national journey, America has not required competition on an international stage set up by its erstwhile colonial masters. It has had plenty of other arenas to display its sporting prowess, and local, well-organized, professional sporting franchises in its home-grown sports have made such a display moot. The US does not look to the Commonwealth for cultural and political community either; it is not part of any political bloc, it defines its own. Most fundamentally, cricket accomplishes no larger agenda in the US, and if it is to do any such thing, it must reconfigure its image in American eyes.

Cricket's association with all things English is perhaps the single biggest stumbling block in the local acceptance of the game, for one shadowy corner of the American psyche might still rebel against English imports (other than professional football players for Major League Soccer and perhaps a movie star or two). The knee-jerk mockery directed at cricket in the US media is not surprising then. For when such derision is on display, most notably in a television advertisement that features a cricket game, whether it be a tourism clip for the Caribbean or something else, it is inevitably in the setting most beloved of traditionalists: the pastoral village game in an English setting, invariably rather staid, featuring in the background, cucumber sandwiches- and parasol-holding landed ladies escorted by men in striped top hats, while portly men in creams amble up desultorily and deliver donkey drops which are clumsily hoicked past geriatric fielders in immaculate whites. In these settings, cricket does not so much resemble a game as it does a government-mandated exercise programme to replace drug prescription benefits for the rich and elderly. The game looks ugly, slow, ossified, and almost offensively archaic on American television.

The media picture of cricket in the US is that of an English game, not a world game, and this distinction is crucial in understanding American sympathies. For instance, the perception of cricket in the US does not feature the 'black power' of the West Indies, an interesting and fertile connection between cricket history and broader American cultural themes. I was especially reminded of this by a pair of African-American security guards at my US graduate school, looking on appreciatively at a telecast of the West Indian team playing in the 1987 World Cup. The context of the game had changed for them; it was not a white Englishman's pastime anymore; it was about an arena for the display of black skills and power. Those security guards might have had an interesting reaction to the successive blackwashes handed out to England by the West Indies in 1984 and 1986, and the power and glory of the fearsome West Indian pacers. The success of the West Indies in the 1980s and 1990s was a non-story in the US, but it could have tapped into a rich reservoir of black pride and sparked interest in cricket in a new dimension. Stevan Riley's documentary, *Fire in Babylon*, which opened at various venues in the US in 2011, including the Tribeca Film Festival in New York City, emphasized both Caribbean history and politics, and the non-genteel nature of the fast–bowler–batsman relationship. In doing so—and despite its often dubious history-telling—it might have done more to promote cricket in the US than any ICC tournament.

If cricket is to make inroads into the American scene, it must convey itself as a harbinger of a greater cosmopolitanism to the American landscape, one that taps into a multiculturalism present in the US. Until now, cricket has seemed retrograde in promising to return the US to a time of greater provincialism and insularity. Where cricket has made its greatest strides in the US, it has emphasized its modern, multicultural leanings as opposed to the old 'white men in whites' image. The presence of cricket's historic Anglo-Australian culture is of little interest to the groups interested in playing cricket in the US. That culture, so prized by cricket's older masters, is perceived as archaic and a holdover, a museum curiosity at best in a society that prides itself on looking forward.

Thus, for cricket to become popular in the US, it must present itself as an American sport, even if the Americans in question are not Anglo-Saxon Protestants but the members of its rainbow nations. Soccer has dutifully followed this path. As immigrant communities have grown in size, the game has become more visible, and a new set of images has replaced the older ones. While the 'soccer mom' and her brood remain resolutely white and suburban, and while American fans of soccer faithfully follow the EPL, they associate soccer too, with South America, Africa and Asia, and notice its importance in its immigrant enclaves.

Perhaps it is only ironically appropriate that the US be reintroduced to cricket by Indians. Not the unhappy natives confined to alcoholism-stricken reservations but the rich and increasingly politically powerful Indian-American community. In this context, it is not surprising that the IPL should have been noticed in the US; it was a visibly Americanized version of cricket with nothing English or staid about it. It is not completely impossible to find second-generation Indian Americans interested in the IPL. Indeed, a noisy gaggle of boisterous second-generation Indian American teenagers clustered to watch the IPL's cricket is, if not a common, then at least a not-unknown sight in American suburbs. The television subscription for the game might have been purchased by their parents or relatives, but no matter, the IPL had suddenly made real the strange game those same family members often spoke about. Based on that much evidence, the IPL could make significant inroads into a potentially lucrative market in the US.

These speculations are not as guilty of castle-in-the-sky-building as might be thought. The global availability of international cricket on television and the presence of immigrant television networks have meant that youngsters from South Asian backgrounds, struggling to find acceptance in their local settings, have an easy fall-back in a game that connects them to their families, cultures and histories in a way that local offerings might not. The presence of the game is much larger in their lives thanks to its visibility.

Cricket might still find a home in the US. But the 'old country' with whom allegiances will be built when this happens will not be England, but a rather more diverse set of nations, one more reflective of the changing demographics of the American landscape.

CHAPTER 5

Cricket and Media

One-day cricket turned India into a cricketing superpower. This oft-made statement needs slight qualification. First, India became an economic force to reckon with in cricket before it became a genuinely sporting one. Second, it was the media that really did it; more specifically, satellite television, whose twenty-four hour sports channels thrived on a steady diet of limited-overs cricket—first of the fifty-over variety and lately Twenty20—and helped create the world's biggest market for cricket (Test cricket took a back seat—a five-Test series is now virtually unknown in India). Lastly, if the success of ESPN and the NBA is plausibly analysed as driven by Michael Jordan's career, then Sachin Tendulkar, the Star Network and modern Indian cricket have had a similar symbiotic relationship, worthy of commemoration in the annals of media studies, and fully deserving of the gallons of ink that might be spilled on it by scholars of cricket.

Satellite television also made possible telecasts of overseas games, and not just those that featured India. Indian youngsters playing cricket in the streets and gallis so beloved of photographers and Coke commercial-makers, now suddenly found a species of game not seen before. This had many far-reaching effects: some sacred idols were carefully dismantled as Indian fans, used to lionizing international players, were exposed to extensive coverage of their actions and words, thus displaying imperfections and foibles in those previously imagined perfect; it also built other ones, for it enhanced the celebrity status of cricketers and turned them into entertainers and pitchmen. Indian youngsters aped the mannerisms and modes of behaviour of their heroes and sometimes villains. They began to internalize the aspirations linked with the achievements now visible, day and night, in their living rooms. At least some of the change of the demeanour of the Indian cricketer and the Indian fan, much commented on by opponents, whether on cricket teams or in Internet-argument forums, finds its origin in their exposure to a world of cricket made available by satellite television's plentiful offerings.

But most importantly, the satellite and one-day international era reinforced a role long played by television in the modern age of cricket: the financial puppeteer.

The Modern Master

Cricket has flirted with insolvency in the past; when Jagmohan Dalmiya took over as ICC President in 1997, its coffers could only cough up some $30,000,[1] but his rapid wheeling and dealing, entrepreneurial acumen, and cricket's television audience, the majority of which is resident in India, assures its present flirting-with-the-billions prosperity. This economic revolution, kicked off by Dalmiya and continued by Lalit Modi, ensures that the story of modern cricket is punctuated by media dollar signs as much as playing statistics. The litany of high-value deals, especially those made by the BCCI, is never-ending. The influence of the massive amounts paid for television rights ensures that a primary concern is the engineering of the spectacle to keep the money flowing in. Every single instance of Golden Goose Homicide alluded to this book—the over-scheduled one-day international, the length of the IPL season, and the cultivation of benign pitches to assure five-day Tests being just three prominent examples—can be traced back to the influence of the combined baleful eye of the media rights holder and the greedy board director.

The influence of television is thus deep and fundamental on both the present and the future of the game: Test cricket is threatened by more telegenic forms; the World Cup's membership and format depends on rights deals; Twenty20 excess is linked inexorably to its made-for-television nature. Television writes the checks; how much should cricket dance in response? The main challenge for cricket's future is to forge an economically sound relationship with television that is sensitive to the game's ethos and the relationships that players and fans have with it.

These constraints are not easy to satisfy, for television's function is largely entertainment,[2] notwithstanding the presence of the twenty-four hour news channel, situated amongst an assortment of talk shows, situation comedies, movies, and increasingly tacky 'reality TV' contests. Cricket takes its place amongst this cornucopia uneasily, jostling for space and demanding attention, largely by promising to deliver the same goods. Worries about the maintenance of the gap between sports and entertainment are particularly accentuated when cricket becomes not just any old 'product' but a 'television product' first and foremost, to be sold to the highest bidder without regard for its further care, perhaps to be dressed up, prettified, its blemishes artfully disguised. This makeover can result in obscuring its essential features, like the struggle between bat and ball, pushed to the margins in Twenty20 cricket's made-for-television short boundary fences. Sometimes the action on the field itself gets overshadowed; for example in telecasts which incorporate adornments such as the IPL's 'strategic timeouts' and commercials after every over.

The presence of the product commercial in cricket telecasts in India, in particular, seems to indicate that sponsor and advertiser priorities have completely trumped those of the game's community. NEO, Zee, Ten Cricket and indeed, whoever else happens to be broadcasting cricket in India, have desecrated the sport not just by the number of commercials shown but by allowing the commercial to intrude on the game itself. Cricket viewers were first forced to adjust to an abrupt break at the end of an over, the prime advertising space for commercials, and then, to one at the fall of a wicket, thus depriving the viewer of crowd and player reactions and instant, high-quality replays from several angles. The leisurely return to the game after commercials means missing out on the first ball of the over to follow.

Not content, television stations have moved into the over itself; the smallest lull in play is now aggressively utilized for a commercial. This is being taken to its logical conclusion: the commercial has moved from the billboard on the boundary to the painted signs on the field and the ghastly imposed banners on slips, visible during a bowler's run-up. Meanwhile the game is literally forced to occupy a smaller space, reconciling itself to a shrinking television screen whose borders may display print advertisements between deliveries. Thankfully, Ten Cricket, one of the worst offenders in this regard, was served a show-cause notice by the Indian Ministry of Broadcasting and Information for violating its advertisement codes during its coverage of India's 2010–2011 tour of South Africa.[3] Perhaps similar reckonings with justice await other offenders.

These butcheries of the televised 'product' are all blots on the game. Any self-respecting manager of such a lucrative 'property' would not tolerate such slipshod treatment. But the BCCI shows no inclination to impose a set of quality controls on those broadcasters into whose care it has thrust the game. Its utter lack of respect for the game, its cynicism in its willingness to disregard the concerns of the fan, stands exposed by this indifference.

In general, cricket's relationship with television is marked by excessive deference to its demands. This is in sharp contrast with other professional, commercialized sports, which are just as dependent on sponsors and television rights. For a sport that prides itself on its traditions and history, this difference is unflattering. As Mukul Kesavan points out, television channels have long wanted to 'divide football into four quarters instead of two halves to make more time for commercials. But football's administrators have consistently refused on the ground that this would change the nature of the contest'.[4] But in cricket, it seems that every scheduling decision, every rule change, every tweak to playing conditions, is done with the television rights deal in mind. The demands of the long-term future of the game, perhaps taken care of by less crowded cricket calendars, perhaps by ensuring cricketing balance on the field, perhaps by removing distinctions between members of the ICC, speak to a wisdom that needs to dawn, and soon, on cricket's administrators. They would do well to remember that television rights deals will get better if the game can show a devoted following, which cricket appears to be in danger of losing if it cannot retain its self-respect.

Complaints about televised coverage are especially poignant for the modern cricketing fan to make because modern television makes available access to the game hitherto undreamed of, in a manner that sparks genuine aesthetic pleasure. Where the 'ancients' delighted in the photograph, the 'moderns' can draw on the high-definition television spectacle, exposing, clarifying, highlighting and making possible catharsis and yes, entertainment. As a result, the relationship between the fan and the player has the potential to be a much richer one, exposing the fan to a greater appreciation of players' skills, while making evident their many limitations. Cricket fans are currently confronted with an embarrassment of visual riches, not via the gimmickry of the spider-cam but by the appropriate utilization of technology to bring about a mature realization of what is truly beautiful about the game.

The Cricketing Spectacle

A cricket fan, accustomed though he may be to thinking of himself as peering into the very heart of his beloved game, is dealing with an experience derived via the pronouncements of those who write on the game, comment on it, and those who, most importantly, televise it. Where cricket might once have provided a spectacle of its own to be portrayed on television, it is now increasingly the case that television demands and manufactures a particular spectacle.

Cricket's central stage, the pitch, pushes the spectator to the periphery. The location of the pitch—some sixty to ninety yards away from the boundary ropes—as the centre of the game, as its 'middle', the actual venue of action, ensures distance from the spectator. At the fall of a wicket, the incoming batsman, walking out to replace his unfortunate predecessor, is aware, with each step, of approaching a locale, a setting, where the rubber, so to speak, meets the road. Part of the tension associated with the fall of a wicket is the batsman's awareness that the action has not begun by his setting foot on the field, not till the pitch is arrived at. This central location of action makes cricket more remote than other games; the cricket spectator with the radio glued to his ear while watching the game at the stadium is still a common sight, as is the cricket spectator with binoculars. Cricket fans are more intrigued than the fans of other sports to find hitherto hidden dimensions to the action taking place on the field, sometimes revealed by players' autobiographies, sometimes by umpires, sometimes by the media. This distance of the spectator breeds a greater myth-making process and perhaps contributes to the richness of literature associated with cricket.

It is unsurprising then, that televised cricket should have had a revolutionary effect, for its magnification offered a glimpse of something hitherto unseen and unheard. The lens of the television camera revealed a world with its own dynamics, and much like the microscope changed man's relationship to the world of the miniscule, the television camera changed fans' relationship with the game. The spectator is now subject to the manipulation of the image and its accompanying voices, to the combination of narrative and moving image. Sometimes the most significant changes are induced by the voice of the commentator that imposes itself between us and the action, and subtly and not-so-subtly guides our interpretation of it.

The televised spectacle changes the nature of the game played. It affects its participants and their interactions on the field, and drives the responses of those who watch, react, and dissect it. The players, aware of the dissecting eye, the magnifying lens, the amplifying microphone, and the close-up, respond, conform and manipulate; they both resent and revel in the spectacle. As media and cultural theorists, and perhaps particle physicists, never tire of pointing out, our observations rapidly turn into participation: the players are ever more conscious of the television coverage of games as giant screens and nightly highlight reels remind them of their mannerisms, sometimes in close-up. The sensation of living in the parallel world of the television production can take hold quite quickly. On its razzle-dazzle stage, there is no prize for sedateness and plenty of temptation to turn up the demonstrativeness a notch.

The televised spectacle bears a relation to the game akin to that which a motion picture bears to the real world; it draws on it, but its grammar is different and the meaning it conveys especially so. The cricket fan at the stadium realizes that a cricket game is a television show and he just happens to be at its studio performance. He might experience the same dissonance that occasionally afflicts visitors to the recording of popular late-night talk shows. On screen, the genial, wisecracking David Letterman looks right at you; in the studio, his gaze is directed at the camera. In the studio, the applause-generating sidekick runs out with jokes to get the crowd warmed up; on screen, the laughter appears as an organic component of the entertainment. In cricket, the telecast producer, by dint of expert editing and camera changes, slices, chops and dices the action into chunks laid out for the spectator. The movement and cutting between shots, the change in focus to different aspects of the action, all create a product related to but distinct from the game in the 'middle'. It is this product that fans respond to, that players are sensitive about, that commentators of the game comment on.

A NEW MORNING

Most Indian commentators trace the beginning of a particular kind of national cricket mania to 25 June 1983. But for some, the preferred date is 3 March 1985, when India played Australia at the Melbourne Cricket Ground in the final Group A match of the Benson & Hedges World Championship of Cricket, held to commemorate the centenary of the Victorian Cricket Association. That was the day Indian viewers first watched the live telecast of a cricket game by Channel 9. Cricket was presented as a perfectly packaged assemblage of glitter and gloss, a hundred overs long, with a definite result at the end of it.

Those settling down on that rather chilly Delhi morning had little inkling of what was in store. It began innocently enough as Kapil Dev sprinted in to bowl the first delivery of the game to Graeme Wood. As he did so, a scraping, knocking sound, that of the bowler's boots making contact with the crease, issued from our television sets, followed by the unmistakable sound of bat on ball; the stump microphone had suddenly and dramatically made its appearance. A few minutes later, Robbie Kerr was gone, bowled by Kapil Dev, and the rattling sound of his dishevelled stumps was a sweet one. Cricket had gone from being a remote encounter of sporting heroes to a game with a sudden, dynamic, physical immediacy. The fan was at the ground, in the midst of the action.

Accustomed to Doordarshan's pathetic late-for-the-action telecasts, Indian fans were stunned by the quality of the television coverage on the Channel 9 network. It was made especially sweet by the fall of Australian wickets at a pace likely to induce the thought that the screen images were from a highlight film; the reaction of the Indian fan to a slaughter of their hopes might have induced a different reaction. On Channel 9, the visual quality of the Indian team was enhanced; Indian fans could feel a resurgence of the feeling awakened in 1983 as the multiple camera angles and high-resolution slow-motion replays enabled a new appreciation of their heroes.

Illustrated histories of cricket are revered for their depiction of the game and for the opportunity they provide to inspect the beauty of the players at closer range: the power of the fast bowlers, the skill of the batsmen, the ingenuity of the spinners. What the television camera has done, with spectacular success, is to make this beauty ever more finely perceptible, dramatically and instantly. In so doing, it delivers on an aesthetic promise and makes the game visible in a way that enhances its appreciation, one that need not just be that of the awe-struck spectator, but possibly that of the player, privy to a dimension of the game that reveals a tactical space the spectator had not dreamt of before.

None of this had been projected by Indian television. The game's many varied qualities had been obscured by substandard coverage. It had kept many Indian fans from appreciating Indian achievements over the years. But in those heady days of March 1985, in full glory, they burst forth from the television screen and demanded recognition. The arc of the spinner's flighted delivery, the perfect leg-break Sivaramakrishnan bowled to Miandad in the final, the yorker by Kapil Dev that dismissed Qasim Omar first ball, the wristy grace of Mohammed Azharuddin, the perfect side-on action of Kapil Dev, all these came across in a manner hitherto unknown.

Indian fans watched the endless replays, the clarity of the images, the varied and multiple angles that covered the dismissals, and the clever graphics. We had not realized that all this could possibly be associated with a cricket game. The Australian telecast turned cricket into a form of entertainment that could be enjoyed by a much wider demographic. It made the far-away spectacle of a game played by men in whites into a living-room tamasha of brightly attired athletic performers displaying a perfectly tuned entertainer's sensibility. All of this on the magnificent stages of cavernous Australian stadiums.

As India's opening bowlers smashed through the Australian top-order, leaving it tottering at 4-17, it was not just that they had pulled off a feat for which Indians had seemed perpetually destined to be on the receiving end, they had done so in brilliant clarity. When, with a mixture of Srikkanth-freneticism and Shastri-phlegm, India strolled to the victory target, it had not only beaten Australia in Australia, it had done so on Australian television, its players' athletic abilities magnified by the telecast. Indian cricketers, in slow motion, in close-up, praised to the high heavens by all those seemingly knowledgeable international cricketers whose names we had only read about, turned into demigods. A week later, India beat Pakistan by the same comfortable margin in the final. The hype of the awards ceremony, the victory lap on the Audi, these put the final touches to the pictures drawn for us that week. From now on, the game would be linked with the televised spectacle, and Indian fans knew what they wanted to see on the tube.

Channel 9 had pulled off the most amazing trick of all, one it continues to do to this day in high-definition. It successfully creates an eight-hour movie, which uses as its raw material a cricket game. It chooses a particular focus, a viewpoint, a perspective, and amplifies and enhances it; its production can indulge in the magnification of the minor, and elevate the mundane to next day's news.

With today's elaborate televised spectacle available for inspection, it is instructive to see a cricket match in the flesh and to compare that with the television coverage of a game. The sense of surprise that these minor scramblings of men in white on a field are the subject of all that drama on the television is genuine. Sometimes the query 'Is that all there is?' springs readily to our lips, for we become aware of the creation of illusion. And sometimes we choose to return to the television because we realize that an essential aspect of our relationship with the game is one engendered by visual media; it is that which will sustain our relationship to the sport. Indeed, that feeling might come as a relief, to know that our elaborate imaginations of the game still persist and can find their freest expression thanks to the stimulus of the televised spectacle, by its enhancement and magnification.

SLOW IT DOWN, TURN IT UP

The first slow-motion replays of televised cricket served two purposes. The primary, and obvious one was to show the action again, to 'replay', to help the spectator who had missed it because things went by 'too quickly' or because one's attention had been diverted. But the secondary was ever-present: to show the action as it actually unfolded, in finer detail. In almost every case, the cricket spectator noticed a previously ignored aspect of the game: perhaps the various components of a fast-bowler's action or the batsman's execution of a stroke. The slow-motion replay, as it improved, became a feast for the eyes, because it assured us that the beauty we saw in cricket photographs was actually present, that it was not just a creation of the photographer. The replay became a bridge between the frozen, almost artificial staging of the still cricket photograph and the blurry quickness of an old-fashioned television replay. We came to see that the cricket photograph arose from the action, that television images were thousands of photographs stuck together, that the photographer had reached in and plucked one out of the ether.

Viewing the highlights reel of Kim Hughes's 214 against India at Adelaide in the 1980–81 series is an awe-inspiring experience for Channel 9's telecast showcases the most attractive and dynamic strokeplayer of the modern era in full flight. What makes the experience complete are the slow-motion replays of Hughes's shots. Again and again, a perfect cricket photograph springs up and passes away. That momentary glimpse is enough. Hughes strikes us speechless; the power and beauty of his shots in slow motion come through as never before; the rewind button does double duty.

Slow-motion replay has made possible a finer appreciation of the art of catching as well. Indians first viewing Channel 9's 'classic catches' were stunned to see that it was possible for catches of such agility, skill and dynamism to be held. The television camera had taken a bundle of legs and arms and broken it down into a sequence of motions that captured the leap, the reach, the grasp, the tumble, the holding of the ball to the bosom. And then amazingly, the fielder stood, ball still grasped in his hand. A dedicated cricket fan can now spend hours watching classic catches on YouTube.

With super slow-motion now available at 1000 frames a second, with 4000 frames just around the corner, another dimension has come to the fore. The discerning cricket fan is able to inspect the physical endeavours of the players ever more closely. There is a new beauty on display: the wrist action of the leg-spinner, the flexing forearm muscles of a batsman as he launches into a square-drive or the athleticism of the wicketkeeper diving down the leg side. The stress of a fast bowler's action is now visible: the awesome power of his stride; the painful, wrenching twist placed on his body's core; the jarring impact on his ankles and knees; the powerful, dynamic propulsion of his body through the bowling crease. It is hard not to wince, even as one's eyes remain resolutely fixed on the screen. Sympathy for the fast bowler, for his desire to rest his aching bones, is a natural result as Freddie Trueman's remark on the tiredness that awaited the man who would break his aggregate wickets record becomes comprehensible. The modern fan will remain ever-thankful that he was able to see Waqar Younis in action. But he is even more grateful that he saw Younis in a time when his action could be captured in all its glory and power. Even one not normally enamoured of cricket's attractions, when confronted with such visual evidence of its splendid beauties, is likely to be awestruck.

Slow-motion replay has also enabled the oft-noted but not fully appreciated role of video in coaching and training. This has served to make sure that mystery bowlers do not remain mysteries for too long, that batsmen are subjected to a relentless examination by an array of analysts off the ground, as their actions are stored away to be dismembered, frame by frame, for future reference and tactic development.

Like the slow-motion replay, the stump microphone has moved the spectator closer to the action and made possible access previously denied. The most obvious effect is that it has made real sounds that are part of cricketing lore and literature but which, before its advent, were not clearly heard by those at the ground. It also introduced the different sounds that bowlers make at the moment of delivery: the heavy thud of the fast bowler's steps, the scraping and grinding of the spinner's pivot. Most famously, it has let us become voyeurs as we listen to players sledging, chatting and complaining during a game. The modern fan often wishes that the television commentator would stop talking relentlessly over the stump microphone.

In giving us access to these conversations, the stump microphone also performs one salutary function. It demystifies cricket by reminding us that it's just a game played by a bunch of men in all their glorious imperfection. And it often does so by reminding us of the informality that lies behind the sometimes ponderous cricket analysis that accompanies each Test match.

During the 2008 Mohali Test between India and Australia, Amit Mishra, India's tyro leg-spinner, after a brief conversation with his captain M.S. Dhoni, trapped Michael Clarke leg-before with a googly on the penultimate ball of the second day's play. What made the last over distinctive was picking up on the stump microphone just how informally the two cricketers communicated. For Dhoni did not walk up to Mishra and on entering into a long conference gravely decide to implement his desired tactic. Instead, Dhoni simply shouted down the pitch, 'Try it from the other side,' and not, 'Amit, I think you should bowl around the wicket.' Mishra did not comply the first time; he shrugged off the directive and continued bowling over the wicket. Dhoni persisted, calling out the same line again. Mishra finally complied and dismissed Clarke.

This little moment was hugely entertaining. The entire conversation took place in Hindi, which provided a flashback to the games I had played as a youngster back in Delhi, with their particular slang and inflections; it was a reminder that the action, even in an important Test match, is made up of little moments in which cricket players, informally, and on the spur of the moment, try out a cricketing trick or two. The informality of it all was like a breath of fresh air for one subjected to several hours of television commentary.

Not all television innovations have been pleasurable. Spider-cam has achieved the remarkable feat of making the game less realistic, because bizarrely enough, it has reduced the dimensions of the cricket field and changed the visual perspective so that a live cricket match looks exactly like a video game. And players are often not happy about the intrusions of the telecast, most notably the stump microphone, for too much of their unvarnished language might leak into living rooms and spark retribution from sanctimonious cricket administrators. Here the innovation brings a focus to the game that might be undesirable and distorting, and reminds us that the spectacle can manipulate by providing too much access to the middle.

THE ARSONIST AND FIREMAN

In this regard, a little story told by Eknath Solkar about the time he made Geoffrey Boycott his bunny is instructive:

> In the second innings of the first Test at Old Trafford [during the 1971 Indian tour of England], I was fielding at forward short leg when he tried to flick Abid Ali away. I stopped the ball instinctively and challenged him to run, wagging my finger at him as I spoke. He was taken aback. In the very next over, I got him to edge one and Farokh Engineer took a wonderful diving catch, almost at first slip.[5]

It was certainly the first time anyone had read of any such interaction between Solkar and Boycott, even though Boycott's difficulties against Solkar's amiable seamers were legendary.

Equally interesting was the reaction of the readers to Solkar's confessions. To a man, no one seemed to pick up on the import of Solkar's story, that he had sledged Boycott, dismissing him by using as part of his repertoire of tricks, the very same strategy some would find offensive today. Wagging fingers at a batsman, chatting with him, challenging him to run: all of these certainly sound like 'mental disintegration'. An Indian doing this in the Golden Age of Gentlemanly Cricket—for this is how most Indian fans regard their cricketers and that period—should be shocking. But it is not, and it should not be.

For to read stories of cricket matches of yesteryears is to be reminded again and again that they have always featured chatter in the middle, that grown men, when thrown into close competitive proximity, will often behave and interact in a fashion that would not meet the approval of Miss Manners. Ray Robinson's *On Top Down Under* features dozens of reports of banter and edgy verbal interactions, all taking place out in the middle on the hallowed twenty-two yards, right from the moment Test cricket began back in 1877. Those are Australians we are talking about. But Solkar's story reminds us that even our pure-as-driven-snow Indians were not above a little roguery when it suited them.

But imagine for a second that a modern television production team, perhaps Channel 9 or Sky, featuring eagle-eyed commentators, had covered the Test at Old Trafford. Then the Solkar–Boycott interaction would not have gone unnoticed. Had it not been directly visible, we would have been directed to it by a replay, perhaps in slow motion, with ample opportunity to try and read lips:

> Things are getting a little testy out there. During the last over, Solkar and Boycott had a little run-in. Here's Solkar, running up to Boycott, and oh boy, he's sure got a lot to say. And Boycott's not looking too happy. These Indians are never short of a word out in the middle. And, let's look at it again, here comes Solkar, running up, and he's making a gesture, and Boycott's giving him a bit of a look too. Pretty tense stuff, the battle is definitely heating up.

Yes, indeed, things are a little testy out there. But there are very few encounters between adults that, if even slightly competitive—university faculty meetings, for instance—do not get a bit testy. But they are not telecast live, with every single run-in replayed endlessly in slow motion, all the while accompanied by inane commentary, as part of an entertainment package. Our daily encounters could also be similarly entertaining if packaged in the same way.

Not coincidentally, concerns about player behaviour have grown as their actions are relentlessly highlighted. Lip-reading is possible, and every bodily gesture, every stare, glare and mutter is replayed and focused on; television commentators gleefully thrive on the resultant visible conflict. Therefore, complaints from players that the game has been sanitized, and that a supposed instance of player misdemeanour on the field has been blown out of proportion, are worth taking seriously, and worthy of not simply being dismissed as the complaints of a pampered lot. The disproportion between the actual time an incident of 'player misbehaviour' took on the field and the time spent replaying it or talking about it, mostly by providing amateurish psychobabble about player motivation, is grotesque.

This excessive spotlight on player behaviour has meant that cricket often comes across as precious, outmoded and irrelevant in a world whose denizens are used to brusque interactions and seem quite capable of distinguishing between obnoxiousness and edginess. This interaction of televised coverage with behaviour control on the field is akin to herding people for a photograph and then, on realizing they are capable of mugging for a shot, to commence a bombardment of mutually contradictory and ultimately hypocritical instructions for behaviour: be an entertainer, but a circumspect, serious, moderate one. The cognitive dissonance this creates can only be imagined. Administrators of the game must love the passionate celebrations of the players on the field; they need to reconcile themselves to the fact that that wonderfully exuberant whooping and hollering is also capable of being diverted to scowls and screams.

A deadly combination of replay, overanalysis and the freely dispensed platitude can thus lead to a counterproductive sanitization of cricket, rendering it distant from fans' lived experiences and moving it ever closer to being a package wrapped up neatly in management consultancy jargon, a fate one would not wish on a corporation, let alone a cultural passion like cricket. The dual blessings of the camera and microphone thus bring with them a responsibility to utilize them in a way that is sensitive to the game's offerings, one always thankful to the access they provide while alert to the possibility of their co-optation for less-benign ends.

Cricket on the Internet

Talk of cricket and the media is incomplete without mention of the Internet, for nothing has quite driven the nationalist passion that infects modern debates on cricket like the presence of this still-nascent medium. Cricket, like modern politics, heeds the demands of the twenty-four–hour news cycle: events are processed, critiqued, and subjected to the various flavours of nationalist sentiment, quickly, extensively, and their news promulgated far and wide. Here, television and the Internet provide a tightly coupled feedback loop to each other: a cricket game is telecast; it is responded to by fans online; this reaction becomes known to television; commentators, cricketers and fans all converse on Twitter and Facebook about the televised coverage; cricketers, by virtue of being bloggers and tweeters alike, supply additional detail, fuel controversy, leak material which might have remained confined to dressing rooms, and sometimes even settle disputes online. This feedback cycle, like most, often amplifies and distorts.

On the credit side of the ledger, cricket writing and journalism's best hope remains the voluble, energetic, and still-growing community of cricket bloggers. The quality and depth of the analysis provided by the best cricket bloggers often puts established journalists to shame. A quality cricket blogger brings a passion and honesty to his analysis that makes for a pleasant change from the jaded perspective of the professional journalist; it is his most important aesthetic contribution to the world of cricket writing. The blogger is also crucial in keeping the professional journalist honest, in calling out factual errors, and in highlighting the overstated and hastily-arrived-at conclusion. Rare is the cricket journalist who does not hesitate before putting a 'fact-laden' article online, knowing his work is likely to be examined and checked for facts by the blogging community.

The community of bloggers has also enabled the creation of a new world information order in cricket as previously unheard voices finally find a forum. It has moved cricketing conversations away from the usual syllabi and enabled a change in perspective and focus not previously possible when the same old journalists wrote on the same old topics. Cricket bloggers write about playing cricket in remote locations. They detail their personal relationships with the game, their struggles to understand its recent changes, and provide access to quirky bits of cricket history. They are sometimes fans, sometimes players, sometimes analysts; they come from every part of the cricketing globe, and the range and diversity of their insights have made cricket a richer game. Indeed, the quality and quantity of historical, statistical, and economic analysis of cricket provided by bloggers is so staggering that one can say, without exaggeration, that a new, virtual, cricket library has emerged online. In 2011, when the ICC asked for feedback from the world's cricket community to aid it in the game's governance, the best feedback came from bloggers who, more often than not, cited other bloggers as having provided prescriptions for the future guidance of cricket.[6] If the ICC could bring itself to pay attention to these recommendations, it might find that a blueprint for the future of the game has been delivered to it.

But while the Net enables a form of virtual travel to distant cultures, it also facilitates a dispiritingly xenophobic conversation. For while the desirability of looking beyond national boundaries in one's cricket appreciation is acknowledged, it is not easy to internalize, and a medium that permits anonymous, shoot-from-the-hip discourse is simply begging to be swamped by the nationalist frenzy so visibly manifest in cricket fans.

This is not all the medium's fault. The average modern cricket fan has only met a few cricket fans from other countries, if at all; he can see players and grounds on television, but is still limited by the poverty or the richness of his imagination in constructing a fully-fleshed out image of the opposing fan and the culture he represents; the modern fan is also, often, less interested in the cricketing histories of the countries that play cricket. The expatriate fan is able to meet cricket fans from other countries in person, talk to them, ask them about their favourite players and grounds, and trade the odd 'favourite cricket moment' story. But so long as the fan stays online, his cricketing conversations remain susceptible to hijackings of a very particular sort.

For here, cricket fans do converse, at great length and often with great depth, but the anonymity of the Net, the speed of the distribution of messages, and the twenty-four–hour asynchronous link too often lead to a conversation that, while rich with a diversity of insights, factual detail and analysis, is also unfortunately infected by a great deal of rudeness, misunderstanding and invective. The 'flame war' was, as far as electronic conversations on cricket are concerned, an early, persistent, and tiresome companion. And the content of the flame wars was not just passionate disagreement. It quickly degenerated into chauvinism and deliberate ignorance; these electronic conflicts can exhaust and dishearten even the most steadfast cricket fan.

The mixed blessings of the Internet are scarcely news. As a medium for building an international community of fellow cricket lovers, it remains unparalleled. For many cricket fans, when the desire to engage in a conversation and express thoughts about the game grows too strong, blogging, chatting on Twitter, writing on newsgroups, Facebook walls and blog comments sections seems like a natural alternative. For the expatriate cricket lover, it is the only way to maintain one's sanity. But that does not mean communication on the Internet cannot exacerbate misunderstandings, shade subtlety and often lead to more corroded discourse.

CLOSE ENCOUNTERS OF THE NET KIND

A full socio-historical account of cricket on the Internet can ill-afford to ignore the nationalistic battles fought between cricket fans on the now-almost-archaic networking fora of Usenet newsgroups and the chat channels of the Internet Relay Chat (IRC). This 'disappeared frontline' is indispensable in understanding the history and future evolution of cricketing nationalism online, for the passion and the disputes remain the same even as the battlefields have shifted.

Cricket on the Internet might have begun in 1988. By then, most Indian fans had found Usenet newsgroups, and began to read and post on soc.culture.indian, the Indian news, culture, and politics newsgroups. By 1988, cricket scores were being posted on three Usenet newsgroups: rec.sport.misc, soc.culture.indian and soc.culture.british. The posting of Indian cricket scores on soc.culture.british was made under the innocent assumption that members of the Commonwealth possessed a neutral interest in cricket; after all, Indians were interested in scores of matches that did not feature India. The denizens of soc.culture.british did not, however, appreciate the posting of these seemingly irrelevant scores and suggested that Indians keep to their own newsgroups. This suggestion, made not too politely, led to an epic flame war. The English suggested that Indians acquire appropriate manners and gentility, perhaps by being recolonized; Indians suggested the English needed to recover from their colonial hangover; the English, in turn, retorted that Indians needed to get over their post-colonial angst. If this sounds familiar, it should be. Much the same 'debate' continues today.

The flame war had one positive effect: the need for a newsgroup dedicated to cricket was acutely felt. Finally, in 1990, the cricket newsgroup, rec.sport.cricket, was born. Fans quickly discovered that it could be a place to post 'almost-live' updates of scores. For the Indian expatriate, taking refuge in the Indian cricket team's activities, in this virtual space, assuaged an acute homesickness; reading scores on the Internet at work with a cup of coffee brought one closer, just a bit, to the left-at-home morning newspaper and cup of tea.

There was a great deal of quality cricket writing on rec.sport.cricket. The quality and range of this corpus was such that the material made available by the print media paled in comparison. But cricket fans on the newsgroup were often deeply disappointing. There was no mistaking the hostility that swamped fan interactions on the Internet, no mistaking the strange vision that many fans had of each other's countries.

Usenet newsgroups had the unfortunate habit of, all too soon, being used for the playing out of an aggression expressible in a form only possible in their confines. Flame wars were common and the 'signal-to-noise ratio' was sometimes low. To the online cricketing community's credit, it produced more meaningful discussion than most groups. (The Middle East politics newsgroups, one need hardly point out, were wrecked from the very beginning.) But rec.sport.cricket still suffered from the most common afflictions of newsgroups: there was a cyclical nature to most of the discussions; readers would troll i.e., make outrageous remarks to provoke flame wars; remarks that you would not dream of making to someone face-to-face were glibly made to faceless strangers, sitting far away on their own terminals.

Into this space stepped the India vs Pakistan and Anglo-Australian Axis vs The Subcontinent rivalries with their mutual suspicion and disregard. On the Internet, you can write anything, you can read everything. Indian fans suggested all Pakistani cricket performances at home be discounted; Pakistani fans offered physical and mental weakness as an explanation for the non-production of Indian fast bowlers; English fans preened and strutted in their self-proclaimed status as guardians of the game; Australians loudly proclaimed their cricketers' right to sledge anyone, anywhere, anytime, anyhow. The cricket newsgroup enabled staggering displays of both erudition and ignorance.

The Internet Relay Chat (IRC) brought a new dimension to cricket coverage on the Internet; it made it possible for cricket fans to chat with each other in real-time and, soon enough, to follow cricket 'commentary', text versions of (hitherto inaccessible) ball-by-ball commentary typed in by a diligent fan with live access to a game. The channel members would read the streams of text scrolling on their screens and chat on another channel.

The progenitor of this commentary was Robert Elz and his first line-by-line transcription of each ball's action came during India's tour of Australia in 1991–92. Later, as IRC cricket chatter became more established, it grew in sophistication. Cricketers gave interviews on IRC; a member of the IRC cricket channel community sat them down at a terminal, solicited questions from channel members and then typed the answers in. (I once 'moderated' an interview with Aamir Sohail in this fashion.)[7]

It was a strange and intriguing mode of interaction; like Usenet newsgroups, its promise was ambivalent. I discovered some community on IRC as I 'met' cricket fans from all over the world. I would often log on just to chat, to assuage loneliness. Nothing made my seclusion worse than finding that none of my 'friends' were 'on', and the only people on the channel were strangers. There were plenty of long rambling conversations on IRC, plenty of nostalgia exchange and the standard 'where-are-you-right-now' conversation. The need to put faces to names grew so strong that websites with photographs of the denizens of IRC's cricket channel were put up. I became part of a small band of Indian fans that set up a private channel to chat amongst ourselves when commentary on India's matches was on.

The need for that private channel hints at what was problematic about IRC: it was a great medium for tracking live scores and for simple one-liners as comments on a match, but a horrendously bad one for reasoned discussion or argument. IRC was never anything more than a slightly organized anarchy. On the cricket channel, a great deal of abuse was thrown around, the worst culprits being Pakistanis and Indians. There was little self-policing and the flame wars between Indians and Pakistanis grew tiresome. It was a live version of the flame wars on rec.sport.cricket. These happened in real time and quickly clogged up the channel. There was no way of stopping them other than via the operators, those privileged human users of the IRC channel, the people 'in-charge', who were not appointed by a formal process but slowly grew into those positions through a rough, loosely organized, quasi-meritocratic system.

But human operators have nationalities and very soon, battle lines were drawn. The bickering between IRC residents and the heavy handed, inconsistent application of rules by operators became increasingly problematic. Too soon, any slightly edgy conversation between an Indian and Pakistani or worse, between any subcontinental resident of the cricket channel and an Anglo-Australian operator ended with the operator exercising his authority and banishing the user from the channel. While the flame wars on the channel were despicable, the patronizing attitude of the IRC operators seemed worse. If an Indian fan ever came close to experiencing solidarity with a Pakistani one, it was when a sanctimonious operator urged subcontinental fans to learn some manners.

In those years of online cricket fandom, starting from the posted scores on rec.sport.misc in 1988–89 and continuing on to rec.sport. cricket and IRC during the 1990s, I, like other cricketing fans, made a few friends from other countries and learned about other cricketing cultures. But it was all too easy to get caught up in a pointless, angry dispute, to let feelings be hijacked by falling for transparent flamebait. I was no angel; my greatest embarrassment is to find online traces of my intemperate pronouncements.

Fan interaction on the Net continues most visibly, spectacularly, and sometimes usefully, via the growing number of cricket bloggers and the many online cricket discussion forums. But sometimes the blogging world shows the shape and form of the world left behind on rec.sport. cricket and IRC. Bloggers do engage in extended debate with each other, sometimes heatedly, but the true action occurs in the comments sections. For here, the blog commenter can drive even the most sanguine of cricket commentators batty. The eloquent Mukul Kesavan was happy to retreat from his work as a blogger with ESPNcricinfo, worn out by the endless vituperation sent his way. The lofty Gideon Haigh had started to reveal, by the time of the John Howard ICC-president fiasco, an increasing impatience with the Indian fans who swamped his comments space with insulting speculation about his true paymasters. No one, it seems, is quite as angry, ignorant, or bloody-minded on a blog as the commenter, regardless of nationality.

THE INDIAN FAN

The nationalist impulse runs especially strong in Indian fans online as the modern BCCI versus the Rest of the World debate heats up. Every website, every blog, be it Indian, Australian, Pakistani or English, feels the ire of the irate Indian patriot. Thus, a large percentage of comments on a cricket blog 'protest' the bias of the author against all things Indian, or the BCCI, the IPL, or the refusal to acknowledge Indian players as the best. Conversely, many blog posts and comments are dedicated to a review of the cricket world's ills and how they may safely be blamed on the BCCI and its 'overpaid' team of 'stars'. The India–Pakistan flame war is a relatively minor occurrence now; as Pakistan's fortunes declined, and India–Pakistan encounters lost their lustre, so did the passion behind the once-fierce spats between the two groups of fans. More often than not, in a modern flamefest, the Indian fan is responding to an Anglo-Australian take on the game. But if the Anglo-Australian media or fan feels singed by the heat of the Indian patriot, he should spare a thought for the Indian team, which is the real target of Indian fans' wrath most of the time.

Some of the passion and sometimes unbalanced adulation visible in Indian fans' interactions online may be traced to the fact that for many, cricket is entertainment, a tamasha. This conflation places unique demands on Indian players, nowhere better revealed than in the adulation that renders Sachin Tendulkar a God and makes M.S. Dhoni's haircut a media event. Furthermore, the Indian fan is often a consumer of the game, rather than a player; many fans often seem content to passively lap up the game, less as a sport than as a repository for a great deal of wishful thinking, day-dreaming, endless taxonomizing and statistical pyrotechnics. For this kind of fan, impatience and overwrought expectations are natural accompaniments to the game, and sometimes result in the flipside of his devotion: the ugliness of the brawl with Indian players in a Caribbean bar after the 2010 Twenty20 World Cup or the attacks on players' homes after the 2007 World Cup debacle.

The Indian fan thus offers a broad spectrum of reactions, from flirting with misautogeny to hyper-prickly defensiveness. Meanwhile, the Indian cricketer has come to subconsciously internalize worries about the fans' reactions, perhaps most visibly manifest in the excessive caution displayed by Indian Test captains over the years. Who would dare risk an unconventional gambit, one that might lead to defeat, with the fear of a media-inspired fan explosion lurking around the bend?

Perhaps the saddest aspect of Indian fans' immense expectations, in the demand for nothing less than victory all the time, is the failure to applaud visiting players' performances at Indian stadiums. Indian fans, an ever-more socially and economically variegated group, are no longer neutral fans of the game; they do not seem obligated to follow the old public school code that demanded the opponent be appreciated; they are just as unlikely as any other group to turn up to watch neutrals play, and in recent years, their appreciation for the opponent has fallen to negligible levels. The churlishness of the current generation of Indian fans—who are less-than-generous in their acknowledgement of the opposition, and engage in seemingly unbalanced vitriolic attacks on virtual opponents on the Internet—appears to be a function of the whole-hearted adoption of a narrowly nationalistic conception of fanhood and an enlarged membership. This new audience has its own behavioural codes, often in clash with the more gentlemanly notions of the cricket watcher of yore. Sometimes the newer audience imbibes the hoary traditions of the old; sometimes the influence goes the other way.[8]

So just as Indian crowds provided some of cricket's most thrilling spectacles thanks to the sight of colourful packed stands alive with the sound of vociferous, passionate fans, they have also provided the stunning, sepulchral silence that greets the cracking of a boundary by an opposing batsman. Aravinda Da Silva's memorable innings in the 1996 World Cup semi-final was characterized by both dazzling strokeplay and the deathly quietness of the capacity Eden Gardens crowd. It was an odd framing of the scene. While it would be too much to expect a home crowd to cheer the fall of an Indian wicket, it did not seem unreasonable to hope members of an Indian audience would put their hands together once in a while for the opposition's batsmen.

It is some cause for wonderment that the Indian fan has developed overwrought expectations of the Indian team over the years. Till recently, the Indian team had never approached the consistency of champion teams. The local maxima of a good performance in one tournament or Test series was, and often still is, succeeded by the minima of a catastrophically bad performance (as the 2011 and 2012 tours of England and Australia demonstrated most graphically). What is consistent about Indian teams is their inconsistency. Perhaps this roller coaster induces the exaggerated, fierce and imbalanced reactions so characteristic of the Indian fan, grounded as they might be in a deep-rooted insecurity engendered by a lack of trust in the Indian team.

The purpose of therapy, Freud reminded us, was to get the patient from misery to common unhappiness. Indian fans, like neurotics the world over, would make themselves, and possibly others, especially those online, less miserable if they could adjust the settings on their expectation meters and come to grips with the 'reality principle'[9] in their domain of interest.

A partial explanation for Indian fans' reactions might be found in the overenthusiastic hyping of Indian cricket, to the exclusion of all other sports, by the numerous cricket channels on satellite television, whose din only seems to have grown in recent years. This hyping might have led to some Indian fans confusing economic power with genuine cricketing power.

By 1999, Indian television channels, having practised their art during the 1996 World Cup, had raised the hype machine to a new level of operational efficiency. The cricket coverage on multiple channels was relentless, naive and bizarrely optimistic that India would win in England. But there were stronger teams in the tourney, South Africa, Pakistan and the mighty Australians being three of them. Besides, English pitches were not friendly to Indian batsmen. An early exit seemed eminently reasonable, and India's eventual failure to win the 1999 World Cup was unsurprising for anyone who found the disconnect of the hype from cricketing realities disconcerting.

The coverage of the 1999 World Cup reminds us, as modern coverage of the Indian team often does, that nowhere else in the world does the attention and time spent on cricket by a group of fans seem so disproportionate to the actual achievements of their favourite team. The attention paid to the Indian team by politicians, the hype of the Bollywood–cricket team connection, the endless television coverage, the cricket tragics like me—the Indian fan seems caught up in the fortunes of a team whose overall record was, and in some respects still is, what might be termed a bit spotty. For all the hype associated with it, one might think the Indian cricket team was the Brazilian soccer team: multiple world champions, consistently ranked amongst the world's best. The gap between the hype and the actual accomplishments of the team often raise uncomfortable thoughts about the paucity of national achievement in sport, about the need for the fig leaf provided by the national cricket team.

Many Indian fans, of course, do not live in India. They are no less important for that as far as the evolution of world cricket is concerned, for they contribute both to a greater television audience for the BCCI and promise new avenues for the growth of cricket overseas as well. These are cricket fans separated from home and from a cricketing community. Every Indian loss in a country with a local Indian community is a lost opportunity to give these 'boys overseas'—the large, vocal, Indian diaspora—something to cheer about. It's yet another burden for the Indian team to bear, but it is one it should be familiar with.

When the Indian team first toured the West Indies in 1953 the Indo-Caribbean spectators who came out in throngs to see them play saw it as a chance to affirm their own masculinity and pride against the constant pinpricks of the white and the black West Indian. When India won the World Cup in 1983, Indians resident in England were happy to affirm that 'World Cup jeetne ke baad hum mahinon tak chati nikaal ke chalte the London mein'. [For months after India won the World Cup, we walked around in London with our chests stuck out.] After Kolkata 2001, the best place in the world to be an Indian fan was Australia. Nothing will quite match the feeling of walking out on Cleveland Street in Sydney's Surry Hills, hearing the exultations of the 'locals' who had turned out at the Crown Hotel to watch the dramatic final moments of that game, or the pleasure of the conversations over coffee the next day at work.

When the Indian team plays overseas, its members do duty of a sort very different from the one they do when playing at home. When they play at home, they provide entertainment and a display of sporting skills. When they play overseas, they provide ammunition for bragging rights, comeback lines and a cushion of respect. Part of the frustration of the diasporic fans, sometimes expressed online, sometimes off, comes from the team's perceived failure at backing them up in the edgy conversations they seem to be perpetually engaged in about cricket. By far the most vocal is the Indian expatriate who has to listen to his English, Aussie, South African or Kiwi 'friend' ask him (on or offline), 'Say, Vijay, what about your boys last night?' The Indian, used to endless jokes about his accent, his country's poverty (a barb still available despite the recent astronomic growth rates), the weird movies with the actors who sing songs while performing choreographed dance numbers in exotic locales, seethes within and curses himself for having been born in a country whose cricket players do not provide him sufficient rhetorical ammunition for these encounters. The Indian expatriate and immigrant, used to having his masculinity questioned by the cultures that surround him—sometimes those who think the badminton of Prakash Padukone, Pullela Gopichand and Liem Swie King is merely a lawn game, who think 'field hockey' is just a 'girls' game'—wants his team to stand up for him, to take up cudgels on his behalf on distant fields. The bristling, defensive, irate online persona seems a natural consequence of these interactions. I should know; I have exemplified this type myself at times.

The diaspora is still, slowly, settling into societies not fully adjusted to their differences with this particular 'other'. The Indian cricket team gives these uprooted people one point of contact, sporting, with the local culture, even if it is in a country that does not play cricket. The diasporic Indian desperately needs that point of contact to be one of pride, to be highlighted and bragged about, not to be hidden away or disowned. His expectations, even more heightened than when he lived back in India (if he ever did), add to the Indian team's already heavy baggage.

The diasporic fan can be more sensitive than the Indian fan in detecting slights and the lack of a proper acknowledgement of India's cricketing status. The diasporic fan, for instance, watching the IPL, is often able to pick up on matters left unsaid by fans back home. After the IPL's first season, more than one Indian expatriate blogger was to note that too much credit went to Shane Warne rather than to the Indian Rajasthan Royals players for their fight for the title, that IPL team management— along with the battery of coaches and physiotherapists—was almost always not-Indian and almost always praised effusively for guiding and helping bring to maturity, young, callow, Indians.[10] The post-colonial sensitivity of the diaspora fan can be just a little more acute.

WHY SO SERIOUS?

One common reaction to the diasporic fan and the home-based Indian fan in online debates is disbelief that Indian fans could be so unbelievably over-the-top in their sensitivities, so relentlessly paranoid in their assessment of the cricketing world's conspiracies. But a quick highlight of a part of the subtext to the sensitivities of Indian fans might offer a glimpse into the accumulated feelings that lead to this state of affairs.

Consider umpiring and India's vexed relations with umpires over the years. Why Indians would ever think particular umpires, such as the unfortunate Steve Bucknor, were prejudiced might be made clearer when considering that while there might be no overt prejudice in umpiring decisions against Indian teams, the alert fan has not been ignorant of internalized attitudes, often revealed in subtle fashion on the field.

Here are two small, anecdotal vignettes. During the epic 2001 India–Australia Kolkata Test, the Indian twelfth man ran onto the ground with either gloves or a bottle of water or a message or all three for the batsmen at the crease. Peter Willey, then umpiring, waved him off the ground imperiously, much like a district collector might have waved his khansama off the gymkhana polo grounds. It is not idle to wonder whether he would have employed that body language for an English or Australian player, or whether he would have walked over to have a quiet word with him. During the Delhi Test against Australia in 2008, Billy Bowden called a dead ball on V.V.S. Laxman, cancelling the runs made by the batsmen for running on the pitch. When Laxman, a gentlemanly and courteous cricketer, seemed to inquire of Bowden why the runs had been cancelled, Bowden put a finger on his lips, much as a schoolmaster might chastise a schoolboy. Would Bowden have used such a patronizing gesture to an English or Australian player?

Umpires are professionals, always quasi-avuncular figures on the cricket field, but they are human beings prone to the foibles of our species. So are Indian fans, in believing that prejudice subconsciously underwrites patronizing behaviour. This is not exculpation for any seemingly irrational expressions of paranoia or insecurity, but a small glimpse into what might be the basis of the expressions of this very large, very vocal and very passionate group of cricket lovers.

THE DADA FACTOR

The Indian fan's seemingly hyper-prickly nationalism has been catalyzed by many other factors, of course. Consider the oft-written–

about Saurav Ganguly, the poster-child for the claim that the modern Indian cricketer has left behind the defensive, timid persona of the past. Most Indian fans were not prepared for Ganguly's on-field and off-field demeanour, all the more so as it rapidly became more visible on his assuming captaincy. Their personal reactions were often of unease, for Ganguly seemed an embarrassment for India as a captain: he squabbled with umpires about no-balls, gesticulated loudly and angrily at ground staff and batting partners, and handed out pouts and sulks aplenty.

But for most Indian fans, everything changed after the 2001 Australian tour of India. The familiar orchestrated campaign in the travelling Australian press contingent to denigrate the opposing captain, wildly successful in making sure that every Australian cricket fan perceived Ganguly as the Antichrist, and also available for Indian fans to read online, raised the hackles of most Indians. Ganguly was not keen to dispel these assertions; a part of him revelled in being described thus. Steve Waugh's patented 'mental disintegration' might have been deemed borderline unsportsmanlike and not in keeping with the game's traditions, but it was deemed copasetic compared to Ganguly's alleged shenanigans. The ascription to Ganguly of appellations such as 'rude' and 'unsporting' seemed particularly precious, given the great Aussie tradition of sledging. But used they were for Ganguly, all for giving Waugh a send-off or for making him wait at the toss. The latter event, in particular, suddenly became the locus of all worth preserving in cricket. Being punctual for the toss became the acid test for a cricketer; a test made up, administered, and graded by the Australian media, fan and player community. Ganguly flunked; Indians cheered him for it.

Indians noticed too, that while Ganguly was sledged by the Australians, he was not registering complaints about it to anyone; he seemed to exemplify the Australian ideal of 'leave it out on the paddock, mate'. Those Indian fans that learned that Ganguly was sledged about his wife and his alleged female friend during the 2001 series were quick to notice the contrast his reactions presented with those of Glenn McGrath during his slanging match with Ramnaresh Sarwan in 2003.

The Australian media's treatment of Ganguly was part of one thread of current critique directed by the world media at Indian players, seemingly as accessory to the critique directed at the BCCI: that of the powerful arrogant board, represented by arrogant lazy cricketers, gutless poor players of the short ball, exhibitors of 'cowering pusillanimity'.[11] The relentless depiction of Indian cricketers as spoilt, effete layabouts, lacking in moral fibre, struck most Indian fans as wildly discordant with their knowledge of the conditions under which most Indian cricketers had grown up and played their cricket. The Indian players were not just millionaires; they were also young men who had overcome many struggles—including an opaque selection policy and a heavy-handed, arbitrary board—to succeed in cricket. The constant sneering at Indian players as slothful, indolent types especially infuriated Indians who could easily consult writings of the colonial era to confirm that, indeed, the natives are still lethargic, still lounging about in the shade, still reluctant to put in an honest day's work when called by bwana. (Yuvraj Singh must be the only cricketer in the world to be pilloried for yawning on a cricket field, the difference between a physiological reaction and a psychological one apparently unknown to those that seized upon his body language as evidence of a lack of commitment.)

This aspect of the online conflict of the Indian fan with the rest of the world was in fact revelatory of a conversational frame persistent in cricket, one that complicates cricket's future considerably.

A COMPLICATING FACTOR

The journalistic vigilance required to keep an eye on those in power is not to be underestimated. The most indispensable entity in any power arrangement remains the muckraker, the gadfly, nipping at the flanks of the lumbering heavyweight. But the form of the content of the journalistic broadside is crucial and in this regard, the world's cricket media, in its critical takes on the latest debates roiling world cricket, has stumbled and often badly. Too often, critique of the BCCI, or commentary on the Indian cricket scene, seems incapable of rising above the reliance on overused, old, reductive tropes, ones Indians, even those inclined to be severe critics of the BCCI themselves, are weary of.

The standard perceptions of the BCCI are not without basis in reality: the BCCI often displays the clumsy, bumbling, cynical manipulation of power by those not accustomed to wielding it. But in journalistic appraisal too, the Goldilocks principle holds: honey and ginger are both required, but in judicious proportion. A journalist who failed to do justice to African-American sensibilities while writing about Barack Obama would be justly accused of poor deployment of his rhetorical arsenal. And for most Indian fans, the Anglo-Australian perspective all too often still sees itself as the centre of the cricketing world, all too often identifies its views, exclusively, as those good for the game, and more depressingly, reveals traces of archaic, unexamined prejudices.

The cries of 'hypocrite' that rise from the Indian ranks when a representative of the Anglo-Australian combine, whether media, player or administrator, deigns to dispense advice to the BCCI or the Indian team are thus indicative of a particularly crucial division in the world of cricket, one whose continuance is likely to be damaging to the game's future. These accusations of hypocrisy often serve to obscure the bits of valid critique provided by the Anglo-Australian axis and are rightly pointed out as ad-hominem attacks. But while such a formal critique's logic is impeccable—after all, even heroin addicts make a good argument when they ask us to stay away from their deadly mistress—only part of the evaluative apparatus for an argument is based on such formal notions; the rest of it is sensitivity to the rhetorical form of the argument.

Thus it is not likely that a hypocrite will be listened to, and hypocrisy is an easy accusation to make against an entity that wallowed in power's privileges when it suited it the most. Indians are even more unlikely to listen to any argument, any critique, which while perspicuous in content, is packaged in a form revelatory of prejudices and retrograde world views. The advice to Indian fans that they evaluate the argument, not the arguer, is unlikely to fall on sympathetic ears in such circumstances. The future course of the game then runs the risk of derailment if the cricket world is unable to find a balance between the smarmy, smug, patronizing, dismissive attitude of the erstwhile masters of cricket—Anglo-Australian administrators, players, fans and the media—and the overly sensitive, chauvinistic response of the BCCI, its post-colonial allies, and the Indian fan.

Many Indian writers, present company included, are happy enough to seriously examine the ways of the BCCI; there is no lack of concern for cricket or reluctance to call a spade a spade. What many Indians will reject, however, is the constant treatment of the Indian presence in cricket as a noveau riche embarrassment at a garden party hosted by the genteel Anglo-Australians. For they are not slow to point out that the party continues because Indians pick up the tab: if the commentator wished to snigger about the Indians in private, he was free to do so, but the days they could do this publicly and not get hauled up for it are over.

The BCCI has made matters worse by an opaque communications policy and poor public relations management. Most BCCI pronouncements on the game are abrupt, inadequately articulated and poorly defended. It issues very few informative press releases, its website is not updated frequently, and its spokespersons could do with a seminar or two in media management. The poorly handled DRS crisis of 2011, when the BCCI could have articulated its stance in far greater detail and clarity, and shown its resonance with other such perfectly reasonable doubts—often expressed by umpires themselves—about the system's possible inaccuracies, was but the latest example of the body's inability to control discourse in a manner that would pre-empt some of the inevitable BCCI versus the World bickering. The BCCI could do worse than hire a couple of good cricket bloggers to write regular columns, provide news on BCCI cricket initiatives, and explain the policies of the organization.

But in general, all one had to do when questioning why so many seemingly level-headed Indians cheered the BCCI even when it was on the wrong side of a cricketing dispute, or being pig-headed and opaque, or became embroiled in the centre of yet another dispute that began with accusations of its dominance over world cricket was to realize that a language, replete with admonishments, finger-wagging, tsk-tsking, conjuring up visions of schoolmasters sonorously lecturing recalcitrant schoolboys or feisty natives was unlikely to resonate with the Indian fan. (Matters are more complicated than this, of course, for while the pronouncements of the English press can provoke the genuine ire of the Indian patriot, part of the Indian psyche apparently still craves the approval of the English journalistic phalanx and will not rest content till they approve of the BCCI and praise all things Indian in cricketing contexts. It might be worth asking too, why the offended Indian patriot does not stem the tide of journalistic offense with positive counter-discourse rather than merely reacting to perceived slights.)

The Ashes-obsession of the Anglo-Australian media has not helped.

There are very few Indian fans who are not irritated by the relentless harping on the Ashes, the constant, disrespectful looking beyond current opponents to talk about future prospects in the Ashes, or the persistent dismissal of all other Test encounters and locations in the world as being of no import in Anglo-Australian reckonings of cricketing quality. And the familiar dismissal of losses in the subcontinent as due to poorly prepared pitches, or the identification of 'pacy green-top' with cricketing quality and 'spinners' wicket' with cricketing perversion, is a weary trope that ensures that all subcontinental performances are marked with a figurative asterisk as far the English or Australian journalist is concerned.

Some journalistic takes on the BCCI feature the usual mix of awe at the dollar amounts of its television deals with the standard caveat about its contrast with other aspects of Indian reality. Thus, Michael Atherton was moved to write in a piece ostensibly about the rise of the economic power of the BCCI on the back of television rights deals, 'Television did for Indian cricket what it did for English football: even in a country where running water can be hard to come by, where four-fifths of the population lives below the poverty line, 86 per cent list watching television as their main hobby.'[12]

Unfortunately for the points that Atherton wanted to make, he chose to gratuitously remind his readers of facts Indians are conversant with but do not necessarily like to be reminded of. Indian readers who stand by the BCCI—even while feeling little affinity with, or sympathy for it—will continue to do so as long as they are united in joint outrage at such perceived insensitivity. An Indian journalist writing an article about an English corporate acquisition while prefacing it with a sharp, brief, tangential comment about English poverty in the north might help English readers realize the sensibilities of the Indian cricket fan. Or perhaps if Indian journalists wrote how the Sydney Cricket Ground provided a pleasant contrast to nearby Redfern's infamous 'Block', the former Aboriginal ghetto and scene of race riots in this century, Australians might be equally irked. More realistically, if Indian cricket writers, in every article about Australian cricket, noted that there were few to no Aboriginal cricketers in the Australian XI, then even Australian readers who dislike the corporate pronouncements of 'stakeholders' and the like that are periodically issued by CA, and who abhor its confusing, unprincipled lurch towards the BBL, might find themselves supporting Cricket Australia (CA) more than they would like. (Indian fans have not been slow to notice that for all the castigation of the IPL and the BCCI by the supposed saviours of Test cricket, a Twenty20 league was their most straightforward solution to cricketing crisis.)

The response to critiques of the BCCI's operations or the influence of Indian cricket on world cricket is usually fury, a pique at the constant complaints about Indian influence. The thin-skinned Indian patriot, especially one resident online or abroad, is now ubiquitous. But in the modern, nationalist-bickering–infested cricket world, it is not just Indians who are likely to feel outraged. The Australian fan, enraged at Cricket Australia's apparent subservience to the BCCI in all matters cricketing and financial, and irritated and vexed by the Indian team's refusal—before the 2011–12 tour—to obligingly roll over and provide the Australians gallant opponents who ultimately lose in the 'spirit of 1977–78', is perhaps the only one to match the Indian fan in his online indignation, an attitude that reflects the internal conflict generated by Australia's changing place in the modern world, from US-dependent to Asia-dependent, from cricket-supremo to IPL-dependent.

Even cricket's magisterial historian, Gideon Haigh, was moved to fury during the John Howard case, calling the rejection of his candidacy for ICC president 'a calculated insult both to the individual and to the nation that elected him', and a decision designed to 'rub Australia's noses in it'.[13] This is not to accuse Haigh of overreaction; it is to note that it is not easy to separate the team or the board from the nation, and that a feedback loop of offense, outrage, and defensive counter-offense now seems destined to dominate all cricketing conversation.

ANTIPODEAN AGONISTES

To truly get up an Indian patriot's nose today, you must be Australian. India's cricketing relationship with Australia is particularly intriguing. One would imagine them to be natural allies, given their common antipathy to the English and Australia's support for India in its early cricketing days. But later, things went sour. Australia's 1969–70 tour was marred by riots and ill-will, and the Australians did not return till 1979–80 when Kim Hughes's Packer-depleted side reluctantly toured. Then, in 1984, after yet another extended gap, Australia agreed to play a series of ODIs in India. After India's three-Test tour in 1985–86, Australia played a solitary Test against India in 1996, before kicking off the now-familiar arrangement of frequent tours in 1998 (India had not been invited to tour Australia between 1985–86 and 1999–2000). Not coincidentally, India's cricketing riches were on the rise in the late 1990s. Since then, the two countries have recognized the other's ability to facilitate its own revenues while their plentiful misunderstandings, both on and off the field, continue merrily apace.

But Australia's dependency on Indian largesse in cricketing monies riles Australians, perhaps still sensitive to the fact that a nation as powerful as theirs in cricketing terms, which has done far more to cherish and preserve Test cricket than any other, should find itself so tightly bound with a bunch of hit-and-giggle promoters whose team seems strangely prickly on the field, and which seems to have internalized Australian cricketing lessons about on-field behaviour in its own idiosyncratic fashion.

A focal point of India–Australia cricket relations in recent times is the Harbhajan Singh–Andrew Symonds Monkeygate affair which, despite endless analysis, is still instructive. It does not need an Indian commentator to point out that the Aussies 'dobbed' Harbhajan in, that the old Aussie adage of 'leave it out on the paddock' was ignored, and that not for the first time, the Australians had seen fit to draw a line of acceptable on-field aggression, the discovery of which presumably meant becoming either Australian or a mind-reader, neither of which seemed particularly likely for an Indian cricketer.

What followed after the Australian complaint was truly astonishing. In a he said-she said scenario, the match referee Mike Procter simply took Symonds's side. The Indians protested. To those familiar with Indian run-ins with match referees over the years, this reaction should not have been surprising. From the time that Brian Jarman told Venkatapathy Raju that rather than complaining about Brian McMillan's threat of physical assault he should have retaliated, to Venkatesh Prasad being pulled up for excessive celebration during India's tour of Australia in 1999–2000, to Virender Sehwag being fined for aggressive appealing during India's tour of South Africa in 2001, the litany of Indian complaints about match referees has grown. The inconsistent application of the rules of cricket conduct and the nonsensical definition of 'dissent'—nowhere more visible than in Stuart 'Teflon' Broad's invulnerability—has been unmistakable over the years, and most Indian fans remain unmoved by the quoting of statistics showing Indians guilty of the most offences.

When the smoke cleared and Harbhajan had been acquitted, the positions of the two sides had become well-entrenched. Australians despised the whingeing Indians; they despised their own board just as much for having rolled over; the Indians thought the Australians to be the real racists. Ludicrous rumours of chartered planes readied for a quick getaway, of plans for the Indians to take their bats and go home, ran amok. Australia, always convinced of its blue-collar credentials, was quick to label the Indians the new English; bizarrely enough, so did the Indians thus regard the Australians.

No resolution of the crisis appears to have taken place in the minds of Indian and Australian fans alike when it comes to online disputes; the battle lines are still clearly drawn. Perhaps that is only to be expected in the clashes that take place between two cricketing nations engaged in a busy makeover. Australia, keen to assert its new-found role as guardian of cricket's oldest traditions and the scourge of racism on the cricket field, and India, the eager usurpant of the cricketing throne, and successful internalizer of the unbridled brashness that it perhaps sees as the reason for Australia's success.

But the two countries are drawn together now, ever more than before. India–Australia series are amongst the cricket world's biggest money-spinners and their boards easily the world's most dedicated when it comes to maximizing cricket revenue. There might have been a time when the former ACB was a fuddy-duddy compared to the TCCB—this was certainly true during the Packer crisis[14]—but CA is now eager to take Twenty20 to new heights and to boldly go where few national boards have gone, even if this means doing severe damage to its internal domestic cricket structures. Its partner in this enterprise is more likely to be the BCCI than anyone else. The Big Bash League is the most prominent competitor for the IPL, and Australian cricketers are the IPL's best imports. Indian cricketers, if granted permission by the BCCI, could also be lucrative purchases for BBL franchises if BBL games are telecast back in India. Co-operation off the cricket field will take newer forms; perhaps Australian franchises will buy stakes in the IPL, perhaps Indian ones in the BBL. The shape and form of this relationship, underwritten by the passionate followings of two groups of fans who seem doomed to talk past each other, promises to be the most intriguing of the new alliances in the Twenty20-reconfigured world.

The Harbhajan–Symonds fiasco did not just highlight race relations, nationalist divides and the changing guard in cricket. It also shone a spotlight on the game's regulation by the cyborgian combination of umpires, match referees and technology, a recurrent and persistent fault line in modern cricket.

CHAPTER 6

Technology and the Regulatory Regime

The debates over the role of technology in cricket's umpiring, most visibly about the role of the Decision Review System (DRS), are persistent, enduring, and likely to take on several different shades before they are satisfactorily resolved. They are incorrectly framed via the impoverished dichotomies of Luddite versus technology enthusiast, bold reformer versus conservative stick-in-the-mud, and predictably and drearily, as BCCI intransigence versus Rest-of-the-World flexibility. There are, instead, several entangled issues at hand, worth teasing out individually, especially when it comes to determining technology's role as umpiring aid or umpiring regulator.

First, an enthusiast about technological interventions in some domains of cricket—say the introduction of stump microphones to enhance cricket telecasts—might not be reconciled to them in umpiring. In some parts of the game, technology might be felt to induce a distortion rather than an enhancement. Second, technological aid to the umpire to enable better decision-making is an issue best kept distinct from whether the same umpire is to have his decision-making vetted by technology not available to him. Third, it is not inconceivable that a vigorous proponent of a—not 'the'—DRS might be disinclined to introduce it pending satisfactory evidence that the technology meets benchmarks of accuracy. Such resistance is incorrectly viewed as opposition to the concept of a DRS; someone unwilling to cross the oceans in a leaky boat would be unjustly accused of superstition. Fourth, worries about damage done to the essentials of the game are to be taken seriously. Much of what we term our relationship to the game is built on such intangible factors and we tamper with them at our peril. But for this, the essentials are to be carefully isolated. Umpiring error is not an essential, indispensable aspect of the game,[1] but the finality of the umpire's decision ought to be. Lastly, keeping the umpire technologically non-enhanced is sharply at odds with the projected evolution and current development of the game. Umpires are judged and viewed in the light of a certain technological framing of the game. Their absence from a similar evaluative apparatus is an imbalance that needs to be corrected.

When Regulation Gets it Right

Before addressing any of these issues, it is worth paying attention to a technological intervention which is now commonplace in cricket and which cricket fans have come to accept as an integral part of the game. That intervention's fate should tell us a great deal about what is possible in cricket's relationship with technology.

Many theories have been put forward to explain the modern increase in the number of Test matches that do not end in a draw. The usual suspects are better fielding, the dominance of Australia, faster scoring, better catching, more aggressive batting habits inherited from one-day cricket, poorer batting techniques, and so on.

A small contribution has been made by the use of side-on cameras to help decide line decisions such as stumpings and run-outs. It would be surprising to find that the number and frequency of these dismissals has not increased since the introduction of the side-on line camera. The run-out decision is a notoriously hard one, and always has been for umpires. Two events must be tracked simultaneously: the advance of the batsman and his bat towards the crease, and the dislodging of the bails, sometimes confused by the possible loss of the ball by the fielder. As any amateur cricketer finds out when pressed into umpiring duty at the local park, the judgment of the temporal priority of these events is difficult. It is even more so in higher-level cricket in the face of the fielders' appeal and the sounds of the crowd. Umpires need to quickly move into position to make an effective call, and while this is not challenging when the batsmen are running two or three, it can take some nimble stepping when a quick single is on. Batsmen have been given out when they were in, and not out when they were out; the latter has been a more common occurrence in the history of the game.

The adjudication of stumpings is a little easier when the batsman is dancing down the track to a spinner, but stumpings attempted when the batsman overbalances on a forward defensive stroke, or when the batsman is dragged forward and then tries to slide his feet back into the crease, create harder decision-making scenarios for the umpire. Dismissals of the latter kind are now more common in cricket, thanks again to the side-on camera and the third umpire.

The reliance of the on-field umpire on the side-on camera is almost complete. Very few umpires now raise their finger as an immediate response to a run-out or a stumping appeal. The turn to the third umpire and the gesture signalling the request for replay is now ubiquitous. Many a viewer is stunned to see just how far batsmen were out of the crease on a requested replay. Even the archetypal no-brainer run-out is now referred, and justifiably so. Few humans are inclined to take chances, or perhaps trust their own judgment, when a 'quick' check is at hand. Indeed, when umpires do give batsmen out without referrals, fans are prone to falling out of their chairs in surprise. The non-replayed decision has become so rare.

Of all the technological additions to cricket over the years, this must be the most satisfactory. The referrals do not take excessive amounts of time and the overwhelming majority, if not all, of the decisions are correct. Viewers of the game do not mind this particular intrusion too much. It has taken away some of the pleasure of watching an umpire's finger go up shortly after the stumps are sent flying by a direct hit and an appeal shakes the remaining timber, but that has correctly been perceived as a small price to pay for knowing the decision came out correctly, and that the game is one wicket closer to a result. For a new-generation umpire, accustomed to the use of side-on cameras for line decisions, the absence of one in a match would be perceived not so much as an opportunity for him to develop or show off his run-out adjudication skills, but rather one in which the possibility of his making a crucial error in the conduct of the game has been enhanced.

Regulation and the Nature of the Game

Early worries about the use of technology in umpiring often centred on the inadequacy of the technology. Some of those worries have been displaced, partially because HawkEye, Hot Spot and Snickometer have become relentlessly ubiquitous and thus increasingly inclined to be the recipients of trust, partially because each has been explained and clarified with some of the degrees of error of each understood and accepted.

Of these technological aids, the most familiar, HawkEye, remains the most controversial. While HawkEye's pedigree in high-technology applications such as missile-guidance systems, and its use in other sporting domains such as tennis, ensures a reasoned foundation for the claims of accuracy made on its behalf, its limitations are not unknown either, especially when it comes to the contentious issue of path prediction, as opposed to path tracking. HawkEye's limitations in factoring in the effects of late swing are not unknown. But perhaps even if it does not induce perfection, it might still enhance the accurate location of the point of pitching and the point of contact with the batsman's pads. Whether umpires themselves are capable of being similarly competent in all these dimensions is, of course, pertinent to determining HawkEye's role in cricketing adjudication.

Given the persistent scepticism directed at HawkEye, the ICC and HawkEye's designers should co-operate to subject the technology to more intense scrutiny via a series of tests with published results, where the predicted trajectory could be compared with the actual path of the ball or with umpires' decisions. Funnily enough, the best analyses of HawkEye have been carried out by bloggers, not by the ICC.[2] Some progress on this front would have brought some clarity to the often-ignorant debates about the supposed infallibility (or flaws) of HawkEye during the 2011 DRS disputes. The quoting of the percentage accuracy of HawkEye in these debates, frequently used as a cudgel to be used on the BCCI, was particularly meaningless as it was never clear what sets of numbers were being used as a baseline for comparison.

A more aesthetically tinged worry about technology-aided decision-making is that it would break cricket's flows and rhythms. But as in the case of third umpire run-out decisions, technology can simply introduce a new rhythm to on-field proceedings. It is now an accepted part of the game to wait for the third umpire to make up his mind, for the roar of the crowd and the hugging of the players to be prompted not by the umpire's raised finger, but by the replay flashed on the screen, followed by the third-umpire's decision. The delay following the appeal by the fielding side is now part of the game's rhythms. (But as the 2011 New Zealand–Australia Hobart Test 2011 shows, it can interrupt what might be an especially dramatic denouement of the Test.)

Part of the resistance to technology in umpiring is grounded in an apparent epistemic claim: that umpires are best placed to gather evidence and adjudicate, that the technology is ill-placed to carry out the task assigned. This viewpoint does not deem the technology inadequate, but rather views it as being fatally handicapped by its location vis-à-vis the game. The umpire's placement for leg-before decisions is close to perfect in terms of his frontal placement, but for a host of other decisions this is not so clear. As the sight of nimbly skipping umpires during run-outs indicates, sometimes they need to move. Even in the case of leg-before decisions, the crucial judgment of the bounce of the ball is best achieved in a sitting position, eyes level with the bails, a position rarely possible, attempted or achieved by umpires. Instead, the current standing position is susceptible to errors in giving batsmen out to deliveries sailing comfortably over the bails. And late swing can also be problematic for umpires, especially in causing a perception of an edge-induced deviation in cases where the bat strikes the pad at the exact moment when the ball passes the bat.[3]

In general, worries about technological intervention dehumanizing the game bear a strong resemblance to those expressed over the possibility of new technologies displacing and destroying essential, human components of their domains of application. The history of technological absorptions in this regard shows a mixed intermingling. For instance, email did severe damage to the written or even printed letter, but epistolary relationships still flourish, writing has not died out, and while a stamped envelope in my mailbox from my friend in the UK has been replaced by an email in my Gmail inbox, the pleasure of anticipating and receiving a reply to a communication remains the same. It is perhaps unlikely that collections of email correspondence, as opposed to the revelatory collections of written correspondence of yore, will be published. But amidst all the dross of tweets and one-liners online, of misspelled, curt and rude emails, good writing is still found in electronic form. The well-written email is not unknown and neither was the poorly written letter in the past.

Thus, even if a substantial charm of the game is displaced by a technology, it might bring in its wake its own 'invented tradition', its own particular generation of pleasures, hitherto unknown, like, say, the satisfying and convenient asynchronicity of email, and the ability to draft and redraft at will. If technology were to make it easier for the game's laws to be upheld while continuing to highlight the excellence of the game's players, and not, say, the alleged incompetence of the umpires,[4] then one might hail this as a good bargain.

Worries about the loss of unpredictability in cricket and its role in the building of the character of players are, in this context, misplaced. The unpredictability of the game lies in the player's exercise of his skills, not in the ability of the umpire to get a decision right. The imperfections and inconsistencies of players are to be glorified and exalted, but not those of the adjudicators. Maradona's inconsistent protection by referees worldwide in the face of brutal man-to-man marking did not make the games he played in more charming; it was an extreme turn-off for the football fan.

If players lose a chance to build character because their opportunity to deal with a bad umpiring decision has been taken away from them, cricket still leaves them plenty of chances to develop such courage. They can show the ability to recover from a dropped catch, a loss of form, or an injury. Cricket does not lose its character-building capacity merely because one of its character-building exercises has been taken away. The cry of 'Get on with it' will still resonate, especially for that most dreaded of all cricketing occurrences, the loss of a game.

Technology's most pernicious effect would not be to slow down the game as much as it would be to obscure the game, to muddy its previously clear outline. That is a sin of which it cannot be absolved, and indeed, should not be. The classic example of this was the situation that prevailed before the formalization of referrals, when batsmen stood their ground on fielders taking catches, and umpires, rather than taking a decision on the field, referred it upstairs. Given the inadequacy of the technology for the task placed before it, the absence of a review structure built into the rules and the invariable overturning of the appeal, the situation that resulted was intolerable. Thanks to the presence of technology, not only had the game been slowed down, but a galling ambiguity had been introduced into the game. The spectacle that resulted was unedifying: umpires abdicated their responsibility to take a decision on the ground and took refuge in a non-existent review or referral system. This situation was underwritten by the confusion caused by the mysterious reliance on a system that promised no clarity.

Unfortunately, this situation persists in referred catches. Very rarely is the technology able to answer the question put to it. Whether batsmen always took a fielder's word in the past when they claimed a catch may only be determined by accurate historical research, but what is unquestionable about the referral for catches is that a part of the game that had been relatively unambiguous before has been considerably muddied. Technology has not dispensed justice; it has not clarified matters; if there ever was a poster child for the pernicious effect of technology on a game, this is it.

In soccer, the introduction of technology is feared for its potential creation of a tiered system in which the game played in the favelas and barrios is not the same as that played at Wembley.[5] International soccer might thus come to resemble an entity sharply and unattractively distinct from that familiar to its street- and park-level exponents. But in cricket, this particular genie is already out of the bottle. The use of side-on cameras for line decisions has ensured for a long time that there is a crucial difference in the adjudication of the international and first-class game from that of the club, park, school, or street. Here, as run-outs show, there is a difference in the ensuing results; some errors might escape umpires' eyes at lower levels of cricket—imprecise decisions that would not go undetected at higher ones. A player at a higher level is likely to be aware of the different standards—not different rules—at play; such awareness is likely to become part of his perception of the game. But there is no evidence to suggest that a player at lower levels of cricket runs slower towards the safety of the crease because he knows a side-on camera will not catch him in the act of being a few inches short. The cricketing instinct to head for the safety of the crease is unlikely to be affected. Thus, it is unlikely that the playing of cricket will change significantly because of the introduction of technology aided umpiring at higher levels.

What Do The Umpires Want?

The community most directly affected by technology, that of umpires, has had, at best, an ambivalent reaction to technology. For every umpire, like Aleem Dar, enthusiastic about its introduction, there has been another one, like Simon Taufel, who has expressed worries about the technology in use and the deskilling and eventual irrelevance of umpires.[6] Yet others have spoken of the influence that the presence of technological aids has had on their umpiring. The most famous example of this, of course, has been the citing of HawkEye in their judgment of leg-before decisions, such as those given for balls straightened by the leg- or off-spinner, which strike the batsman playing defensively forward. Correspondingly, HawkEye has influenced batting techniques as batsmen have come to realize that the bat-behind-pad defence which had worked against leg-befores is unlikely to work any more.

The desirability of umpiring as a profession, though, is subject to a host of other factors. The benefits for the umpire in his job are interestingly intangible; as Simon Taufel has famously pointed out, the umpire is still guaranteed the best seat in the house. And the current hostility directed towards, and embroilment of, umpires in disputes over non-technologically aided decisions might be a worse disincentive than the introduction of technological review. Certainly, not for the last time, Indian and Australian fans, and Steve Bucknor and Mark Benson, would have fervently wished the DRS had been available during the 2008 Sydney Test where fans and media were able to inspect the quality of a decision while the umpire was not. In the presence of real-time technological inquisitions conducted by television commentators, technological aids for the umpires might be viewed as an essential part of their arsenal, a provisioning of the very same tools used to examine the quality of their decisions.

Most importantly, given the current technologically-enhanced display and inspection of the game by two of its most significant modern constituencies, the spectator and the television commentator, it is unlikely that adjudication can operate at a level removed from the scrutiny that is placed on it. That is, if the television spectator, arguably more numerous and important now, and the television commentator, ever more powerful, are watching one version of the game, then the umpire is increasingly hard-pressed to remain distinct. To introduce technology aided umpiring is to do no more than to merge the televised version of the game with the live game, with the umpire brought into line with the image of the game that is likely to drive its future. The paying spectator at the ground is not watching the 'authentic', the 'real', or 'genuine', version of the game, but is merely watching that which serves as the raw material for the version broadcast, marketed, sliced-up into highlights, and consumed. The umpire is merely being brought into line to play the part he must play in this continued marketing and production of the spectacle.

The DRS Debate

Ironically, the introduction of the DRS has not lessened many of the controversies associated with umpiring. Too often, it is misused: batsmen appeal against a decision hoping to be reprieved, as opposed to calling out a glaring error; at these moments, there is something comical about using the heavy-handed arsenal of infrared imagery and ball-tracking to try and overturn an umpire's honestly made decision. And neither is the current system insusceptible to the errors of the off-field umpire's interpretation either. Indeed, as of 2012, the most prominent umpiring controversies were those involving it: the not-outs given against Sachin Tendulkar and Ian Bell in the 2011 World Cup, the sundry glitches that arose during the 2011 India–England and 2012 Pakistan–England Test series, the debates over its worldwide adoption, and the uneasy compromise worked out by the ICC at its annual conference in 2011.

Some blame for this messy state of affairs can be traced to the DRS' provenance: in 2008–2009 it was introduced in Test cricket without being trialed adequately at lower levels. A simple one-year dry run conducted in first-class tournaments all over the world would have generated a wealth of evaluative data and enabled far more perspicuous decision-making by the ICC and its member boards.

The initial introduction of the DRS was instead utterly incoherent. Had some clarity been on display then, the unseemly BCCI versus the Rest-of-the-World dispute in 2011 could have been avoided; that particular conversation should have taken place much earlier. Because the DRS altered the conditions pertaining to a batsman's dismissal, its implementation in Test cricket demanded uniformity. All Test-playing teams should have proceeded with a uniform understanding of the system's rules and usage, with the system's glitches and built-in human idiosyncrasies everyone's cross to bear. It should have been, at the very outset, implemented with a uniform set of conditions in place, in every single Test played in the world, or not at all. Its piece-meal implementation, subject to the whims of individual boards and the local availability of technology, was a state of affairs that was bound to lead to the messy tangle in place for the 2011 India–England Test series.

So for too long, the cricket world has been treated to the spectacle of the highest form of the game being played according to different sets of rules depending on the location of the game and the identity of the participants. It was bad enough formats of the game had proliferated. Two versions of Test cricket were positively horrendous. The uneasy and inefficient compromise of 2011 that allowed games involving India to proceed under a different set of rules had only partially ameliorated this situation.

Aid or Review[7]

But the DRS, even if successfully implemented, raises its own questions. An umpire forced to overturn his own decision is an 'unedifying spectacle'.[8] A different process might achieve the same results without a referral at all. It is now time to confront an issue raised earlier: should technological intervention in umpiring aid the umpire or review him?

As a reminder, given the entrenchment of side-on cameras for line decisions, the debate about technological intervention in cricket has long since moved away from the question of its desirability and possibility to one exclusively about umpire review. But the issues of technological intervention and umpire review are not identical, for technological intervention or technology-aided umpiring is possible without the overruling of the umpires on the ground. Rather, when an appeal is to be made, the umpire could simply consult the best technology available and make the decision on his own. Here the umpire remains the final authority, his decision-making merely supplemented by technology.

Fans, players, umpires and administrators seem willing to tolerate the delays that result from a technological review system. If that is the case, why not provide the technical power of the review system to the umpires on the ground? Some technological components would be available on the ground to the umpire himself; others would be available off the ground and their data could be made available to the field umpire to facilitate his on-field decision-making.

Umpires could carry lightweight tablet PCs or smartphones capable of displaying Hot Spot, HawkEye and Snickometer output.[9] This technological intrusion into the game would be no more time-consuming than those made today. Television replays could be shown in real-time to the viewer at home while the umpire uses them to make his decision, one to be accepted as final by players just as they accept DRS decisions as final. Hot Spot, Snickometer and the stump microphone could be used to adjudicate those aspects of dismissals that demand forensic examination, such as the presence of an inside-edge for LBWs or deflections for bat-pads and caught-behinds. Thus, the current off-the-ground information assessment would instead be carried out by the field umpire. For instance, in the case of LBWs, the on-field umpire could use HawkEye output to determine that the ball did not pitch outside leg-stump, hit the batsman in line and would have gone on to hit the stumps. With a quick glance to confirm—or overturn—his original impression, the umpire could make his decision with the same level of accuracy as the existing DRS process, but on the field. Umpires could retain complete control over the decision. There would be no need for overrules because technological aids would be available to him at the very outset. That this possibility has not been considered thus far is indicative both of a poverty of imagination and the premature locking-in of the debate into a frame that does not permit a happy compromise with cricketing traditions.

CHAPTER 7

Oh Say, Can You See? Final Words on Cricket

There are enough spoils at the rendezvous of victory for everyone
– Aimé Césaire

Cricket's future need not be a zero-sum game, where every gain for the world's growing Twenty20 leagues can only be paid for by a loss to Test cricket. And grow these leagues will, for given the presence of the IPL and the BBL—whose members are likely to form international partnerships once Indian investors begin to participate, and where the BBL might even conceivably consider inviting an IPL franchise to participate—it will not be too long before England and South Africa consider leagues similar in structure, organization and possibly pay scales. These Twenty20 franchise-based leagues will offer many more cricketers a chance to make a living from playing the game and could even point the way to a possible judicious reconciliation of the now-competing—and possibly cannibalizing—situation of multiple formats and club–country conflict.

One possible trajectory of cricket's future path could see cricket emulating football's current arrangements. Professional cricketers could play franchise cricket in Twenty20 and one-day formats all year long, in domestic, quasi-international leagues, with non-overlapping windows to maximize movements between labour markets, and then be called on at specific times of the year for a small number of international Twenty20 and one-day encounters, which serve as qualifying matches for quadrennial World Cups. Hopefully, clearly specified union-and-labour lawyer-vetted contracts signed by franchises and national boards will safeguard interests all around. Test cricket's place within this scenario will be a function of player and fan interest alike. It might be that only some countries will show the desire and the wherewithal to field Test teams. In this scenario, arbitrarily arranged bilateral encounters would be sharply limited, as will triangular one-day tournaments.

Cricket should be prepared for some seminal legal disputes if clubs and countries are unable to resolve their disputes via co-operation. In particular, player–board conflicts like those of Shahid Afridi and the PCB in 2011 will bear close scrutiny. Much like *Grieg vs Insole* did, future club–country–player clashes in court will clarify many power relationships and establish important legal precedents. Much lucrative employment awaits sports and employment lawyers as cricketers in India and elsewhere seek professional representation in dealing with franchises and in clarifying the nature of their contracts so that they can artfully juggle club–country commitments. And if the power of the franchise grows, players will need legal representation in dealing with their new paymasters and in evolving a wholly new set of labour relations. The need for a players' union will not diminish; it will only grow as the game moves on to the next level of professionalization.

Given the importance and continued growth of Twenty20 leagues, franchises might come to be entrusted with domestic scenes in each of the cricket-playing countries. Co-operation between national boards and the new franchises could be enhanced in a manner similar to that suggested for the domestic scene in India, where franchises could revitalize domestic cricket by demanding the availability of international players for their competitions, and seek representation on joint administrative councils with national boards.

The most extravagant possibility of the franchise-based world, that national boards will be replaced by franchises who might go on to stage Super Tests similar to those of the WSC, played between either multinational collections or even national outfits, needs to be seriously entertained, especially if fans make clear that they are only interested in watching the highest quality Test cricket. From the current ten Test sides playing today, it would be possible to put together fewer high-quality sides that could play at a higher skill and competence level. Some Test sides might have more players in their ranks than can be accommodated into their national teams; they could find employment in the new franchise system when not confined by national boundaries. Some countries might not have eleven genuine Test-class players to field a national eleven but they might be able to offer at least a couple of quality players to one of the Test-playing franchises. These players could serve as an inspiration for others in their local systems and thus boost its development. If plans for a Test championship—staged amongst franchises' or nations' teams—come to fruition, cricket would offer three world championships of interest to two non-disjoint fan demographics.

The primary worry for Test cricket will remain the interest of players in the longer forms of the game. If the desertion by players of Tests turns from a trickle into a flood, the game might well and truly be over. But if cricketers still find the legend of Test cricket an inspiration and consider their performances in it a true test of themselves, especially against top-class opposition, then Test cricket will prosper. But it will still need careful stewarding: the possibility of subsidizing attendance at Tests and the willingness to incur losses subsidized by other formats should be seriously considered. The primacy of the television rights deal makes these loss-leader solutions possible, and it would be a shame to ignore them.

Nothing will improve cricket's lot more than the professionalization of its management, whether by changing the personnel of national boards, or by introducing new administrative bodies.[1] If franchises are able to both provide better remuneration and more professional management to cricketers, the contrast with national boards will be a pleasant one, lessening any desire a cricketer might have for dealing with their vagaries.

New Modes of Consumption and Distribution

Cricket's future growth and popularity will be enhanced if it can embrace and judiciously utilize the opportunities provided by new network media. Such adoption affords it an opportunity to address the changing patterns of consumption of its fans. This claim may be illustrated by the salutary example of the movies, which were once exhibited in large buildings, in time slots compatible with the work schedules of its viewers. But mobile phones, changing work patterns, and the presence of digital streaming services have now changed this rather simple and inflexible picture. Given all the hand-wringing about the death of the movie theatre—and sometimes even the movie—thanks to the VCR, the DVD or the thirty-minute sitcom, the cinema hall and the movie still show remarkable resilience. But movies are watched differently now: on mobile devices, or home theatres with surround sound, away from chattering crowds eating popcorn and talking on cellphones. The example of book-reading is instructive too. Considering the entertainment available today, readers are not reading less; they are, however, consuming books differently, using hand-held readers. If the 'product' is good enough, the consumer is happy to pay and consume.

Cricket similarly faces an embarrassment of riches in the ways it could make itself available for the faithful. ESPNcricinfo's cricket app is but a tiny indication of this potential. Consider the advantage that broadband video streams have now made available to the dedicated cricket fan. When they first became available, these were a way of bringing cricket to those viewers who were denied access to regular telecasts. The classic example of this was in the US, where Willow TV started live streaming services in 2003. Initially, the quality of the telecasts was mediocre and its availability was too closely tied to a particular technical platform: the Windows/Media Player combination. By 2011, Willow TV was broadcasting high-definition streams using Flash Players which made it possible to broadcast live cricket on all platforms—Windows, Mac, Linux—and on smartphones, tablet computers, and the like.

The cricket fan is no longer tied to the living-room television when it comes to watching the game; it is available on the road and at work (thus facilitating endless hooky-playing). Broadband video streaming has demonstrated its distinct advantages over a satellite television subscription. A broadband video subscription is portable; a satellite television subscription is not. A cricket fan armed with a laptop, a smartphone or a tablet PC, and a wireless connection can watch a live telecast anywhere: I watched India's dismissal of England for 198 in the 2007 Trent Bridge Test not at home but at a university cafeteria in Chicago—while travelling for a conference—discreetly, with a pair of headphones, on a public computer. I watched the opening Test of the 2010 Ashes at my in-laws' home in Cincinnati, on a laptop laid out on the dining table in the kitchen, even as my mother-in-law served me heaping plates of biryani. Broadband video has also made available the interactive video scoreboard: by clicking on its various components, replays are made available. Clicking on a batsman's fours column replays all his boundaries; clicking on a bowler's wickets column replays wickets; clicking on the 'fall of wickets' column replays all wickets. Most streaming services make available full replays and highlights of each game for viewers unable to watch the live telecast.

The IPL has already drawn upon some of the new media's potential by utilizing YouTube for streaming the second season's finale. YouTube carried the IPL's sixty matches live to fifty million viewers worldwide—40 per cent of the viewers were outside India—except the US where games were shown fifteen minutes after completion,[2] a constraint that was repeated in the fourth season.

Given the importance of Internet streaming in the game's future consumption, the BCCI and ICC should act aggressively to ensure that all future television rights deals include provisions for live telecasts and highlights packages to be simultaneously made available worldwide on the Internet. The national boards and the ICC will need to work with media partners to cut through the thicket of rights, permissions and 'territories', for this messy tangle can severely restrict access to a game. More often than not, territorial rights constraints do not permit viewers in particular geographic regions to view games. In 2011, US viewers were unable to watch the India–West Indies Test series, which was available only in Canada. Given the importance of the US diaspora—the largest number of hits on ESPNcricinfo issue from the US—it seemed strange that the BCCI had not ensured that significant fan populations were not denied access to the games.

Such imperatives are crucial, for the greater the availability of the game, the greater the chance that new fans will be attracted to its offerings. Here again, the example of the music industry is worth emulating. The presence of on-demand, free music sites such as Grooveshark and Spotify has enabled music fans to come into contact with the music of new artistes on whose concerts and merchandise they are willing to spend their hard-earned money.

But aspects of cricket's relationship with innovation and the new media are still mired in primitivism. In 2009, when Adam Voges took a spectacular catch in a one-day game, its video became a hit on YouTube till it was taken down in response to a copyright claim by Cricket Australia.[3] As far as self-goals went, this was a particularly painful one. Cease-and-desist letters are still sent to fans who put up cricket videos on YouTube. Cricket's administrators do not seem to realize that their work of popularizing the game is being done for them by such fans.

Cricket should learn from the troubles of the music industry and break out of the mental logjam created by importing the language of 'intellectual property' discourse into the game's administration. If Giles Clarke's silly pronouncements about 'piracy' being the 'biggest danger to cricket' are any indication, cricket administrators have a long way to go.[4] The BCCI had shown signs of wanting to jump on the 'intellectual property' bandwagon a few years ago when it threatened to crack down on Indian mobile phone operators who were making cricket scores available via SMS for a small fee. The mystery inherent in treating a cricket score as 'intellectual property' when it could not fall under copyright, patent, trademark or trade secret law did not seem to have occurred to anyone in the BCCI. Fortunately, the body has shown remarkable initiative, even if forced on it by the loss of its television rights deal holder, by providing live streams of cricket in India on its website.

The greed of cricket administrators in such matters is not new; David Halberstam reminds us in *October 1964* that the Yankees' owner in the 1950s, George Weiss, rejected live broadcasts of their games on the grounds that it would be 'giving the product away for free'. Attitudes like these are retrograde. Cricket administrators need to ensure that their attitude towards the Internet's possibilities is not similarly dinosaurish.

The ICC and the BCCI could make a simple start by making available all highlights of all international games on their own YouTube channels. Every ICC event should demand as part of its rights deal that high-quality highlights packages be made freely available. These have a significant part to play in the popularization of the game. Their presence on the Internet will not significantly affect the value of the live televised product. Instead, as with free or subsidized attendance for Test matches, they will enhance the value of the live product. In this, as in many other ways, the possibilities for bringing fans into closer contact with their game via the Internet have scarcely been explored.

Copyright restrictions have also served to restrict the making of cricket documentaries which could showcase cricket history and introduce new demographics to the game's rich traditions. Permissions for archival footage remain the single biggest stumbling block in a documentary-maker's work. Most film-makers are frustrated by the time spent on negotiating for permissions and rights, time that could be better spent on editing and writing. This is an occupational hazard in documentary film-making, but with 'intellectual property' talk having run amok, and copyright terms extended beyond all reasonable measure, this situation has become worse. There are gigantic video and film archives of cricket games available with the BBC, the ABC, Doordarshan, Channel 9, and Pakistan Television (amongst others). If permission to use these can be granted, those granted access should digitize and remaster the material available to enable them to make high-class documentaries. Comprehensive highlights packages of these archived Test series could be made available on DVD for the fan inclined to keep a personal record of a particularly fond cricketing memory. If Test cricket is to be preserved and shepherded through the storm at hand, it needs its unique and manifold offerings to be highlighted in the most visually friendly fashion possible.

Cricket also needs to build more museums. Lord's and the Melbourne Cricket Ground house the two most famous cricket museums and libraries in the world; the BCCI could and should invest in something similar, akin perhaps to a Cricket Hall of Fame, based in India. The new Indian cricket fan, exposed to the IPL, and only dimly aware of the feats of yesteryear, could be helped in his history lessons by the BCCI.

Fans are Friends Too

Cricket's managers would do well to co-operate with the fans in their running of the game. The national boards of the world need to find a way to make their administration of the game more interactive. They must listen closely to fans, not just by noting stadium attendance, but by asking for their feedback and paying attention. As an example cited earlier, consider Russell Degnan's comprehensive blueprint for restructuring world cricket. The time and effort put into this labour of love is staggering and demands adequate recognition and attention. Or consider that the best video archive of cricket action clips on the Internet is one put together by an Australian fan on YouTube. Again, one's mind boggles at the effort put in to curate this collection.

Franchises and clubs talk a great deal about cultivating fan relationships; cricket's national boards could learn from this. The game needs to move away from its current masters—politicians and honorary appointees—and into the hands of fans and players; they are its sustainers and true romantics. They can be trusted to keep the game's best interests at heart even when confronted with the impeccable logic of the modern-day master, the market.

As the history of Cricinfo makes abundantly clear,[5] dedicated fans can do a great deal to make access to the game possible. The devotion, dedication and labour of the Internet pioneers who set up the services that have turned that fledgling enterprise into the world's largest single-sport website is truly awe-inspiring. Cricinfo is now ESPNcricinfo, but before its commercialization—and its starting to provide employment to many cricket fans—it was entirely fan- and volunteer-run. But such fans are not in charge of the game and neither are they treated as partners. Instead, the BCCI has a hostile relationship with the current ESPNcricinfo, viewing it as a pesky gadfly rather than as a lifeline and resource for cricket fans the world over, often doing more to popularize and market the 'product' than the BCCI or the ICC. The prestigious media partners of the national boards and the ICC often do not bother to cover the remote corners of the cricketing world. But Cricinfo does so diligently. Ball-by-ball text commentary is available, as I write, for Test cricket, English county cricket (both divisions), the ICC Intercontinental Cup, the Sri Lanka A tour of England, the ICC U-19 World Cup qualifying tournament and the Sri Lanka Inter-Provincial Twenty20 tournament. These unglamorous corners of the cricket world need the spotlight shone on them as well if cricket is to flourish.

The unpleasant spat between the BCCI and Cricinfo in the IPL's opening season, when Cricinfo was denied media access to all games, was a reminder of the skewed, ahistorical, fan-unfriendly approach of the IPL council. If the game, as opposed to the balance sheet and the desire to maximize revenues, was paramount, then a friendly relationship with Cricinfo might have been deemed important by the IPL. But that would have required some knowledge of the game's history, and that, sadly, has been lacking in many levels of management of the game.

Trust the Game

Cricket's future flourishing is almost certain if those placed in charge of it find a way to rediscover their love for the game and stop being apologetic about it. Sometimes a simple fact about cricket is worth remembering: it is a wonderful game to play. Over and above the sociological and historical analyses that explain why a game flourished and took root in a particular social setting, it is the simplest of answers that might be the most illustrative: the game survives because people want to play it. Sometimes soccer's simplicity is pointed out as a reason for its popularity; one ball can keep twenty-two young men or women occupied. Well, in cricket, one piece of wood and any roughly spherical object can accomplish the same trick. Shots of the maidan, the beach and the county oval are part of cricket's iconic images. The experiences recorded in them should be remembered and promoted.

Cricket provides pleasures for its players and fans in quite a unique fashion. These differences from the rest of the sporting world should not be apologized for; instead, they should be praised and preserved. The oddity of the LBW should be exalted; the eccentricity of the Test match should not be disowned. Other games have shoehorned themselves into the straightjackets of the industrialized, hyper-corporatized world; why join the rat race? A cricket administrator should reconcile himself to the notion that his 'property' is an oddity, but a lovable, valuable one, one to be cherished and treasured. There is no need to be apologetic about the game, no need to constantly tinker with its rules in order to pretty it up for the modern age. There will always be competing diversions; cricket cannot hope to convert everyone. But even a small slice of the modern world's entertainment pie should be enough.

Whither, Cricket?

Cricket's uniqueness as a game and its loyal following will ensure that the game will survive and flourish. Its eventual form and content, of course, remains to be determined. But many international teams cannot pay their best or even marginal players wages that can compete with the new Twenty20 leagues that seem to promise the best way to spread cricketing wealth more broadly and fairly. So India's monies and worldwide community will still drive the game, and ambitious tycoons like Mukesh Ambani or Vijay Mallya could still play the role of a new Packer or Chandra. The global growth of the game in the Twenty20 format seems assured. Whether Test cricket will find a way to survive remains to be seen, especially if the most money is made in Twenty20, if the best players of the next generation are diverted to it, and if it offers the largest and most representative international competitions and gets the most air-time on television.[6]

The brave new world confronting the cricket fan today declines its older role of propping up archaic colonial presumptions and dreams. The dismay engendered by current changes is due to the fear that the brave new world will be committed to propping up in turn a new set of puppeteers, ones inclined towards wallet-filling, even at the cost of the loss of some of the game's most cherished offerings. The most important imperative for cricket's administrators is to realize that the game's modern financial health has come about because of a rich storehouse of imagination created by cricket's Test history, which underwrote the passion and fervour of the limited-overs revolution. One-day internationals and Test cricket enjoyed a symbiotic relationship for a long time; the two peacefully coexisted even as players moved between forms, made themselves specialists and appointed new captains. But the greed for the one-day international threatened its very existence and that same greed threatens Test cricket as well. The temperance of this greed could ameliorate the challenging problem of preventing a rift between the haves and the have-nots. The poet whom I have chosen to quote at the beginning of this chapter expresses my sentiments more eloquently; the false dichotomies of poverty and wealth that frequently derail cricketing conversations and lead to myopic decisions need to be exposed.

The ugly, racially tinged conflict between the fans of cricket and sometimes between ICC members, presents a far more intractable problem. Its members and communities will have to find a way to both get over the past and acknowledge their internalized prejudices. I must confess that I am not sure how the gap between the two conflicting communities—BCCI/India versus the Rest of the World—can be bridged. But exposing more fans to the history of the sport, to its rich and varied past, can only help. The more educated the fan about the game's history, the less likely he is to fall prey to facile generalizations and ignorant discourse. Nothing can be done about the patronizing, prejudiced, lazy journalist or the narrowly chauvinistic fan, determined to resolve nationalist insecurities on a field; cricket fans are doomed, as are fans of every other sport, to be exposed to their puerile ramblings. But cricket blogging continues to give great hope; the modern fan is lucky to have so much high-quality incisive writing on the game made available to him. Perhaps cricket fans, by writing honestly, by finding means of communication other than those available through conventional media channels like newspapers and the television, by making themselves more knowledgeable by listening to others like them, can evolve a mode of discourse that is not as coarsened as the one today. Hope springs eternal and all that.

Cricket is still an oddity in the sporting world but it has been given a new lease of life, the chance to expand and make available its offerings via the new kinds of media and the enthusiasm of a large, mobile and moneyed audience. This is a moment when the game can expand and entrench itself more solidly in the sporting world's imagination, thanks to that brash new entrant, Twenty20. Just like one-day internationals introduced new fans to the game, exposed them to cricketing skills and even roped some of them into Test matches, Twenty20 could do a lot of good to the game.

But cricket must find a way to connect its future with its past. To introduce a discontinuity at this point is to amputate and reject. The world of cricket needs to ask itself whether that is the correct expression of gratitude for a form of the game whose engendered fantasies have made today's riches possible.

Notes

Chapter 1

1. AFP, 'Tired Dhoni Opts Out of Sri Lanka Tests', http://www.breitbart.com/article.php?id=080708074415.3vrykihi&show_article=1, 8 July 2008

2. Bharath Chandrashekharan, 'It's The process, Stupid', http://www.desi-living.com/2011/04/it%E2%80%99s-the-process-stupid/, 7 April 2011; PTI, 'Dhoni Admits Being Swayed By Emotions After Win', http://indiatoday.intoday.in/story/Dhoni+admits+being+swayed+by+emotions+after+thrilling+win/1/93502.html, 18 April 2010

3. Mukul Kesavan, 'Pigs Don't Fly–Why the IPL Won't Reform Itself', http://www.telegraphindia.com/1100429/jsp/opinion/story_12386595.jsp, *The Telegraph*, 29 April 2010

4. I thank John Sutton for this turn of phrase.

5. Mukul Kesavan, 'Cricket as Spectacle–Test Cricket Will Survive the IPL Only As Sporting Curiosity', http://www.telegraphindia.com/1080424/jsp/opinion/story_9177848.jsp, *The Telegraph*, 24 April 2008

6. Ibid.

7. Cricinfo, 'The IPL Mess', http://www.espncricinfo.com/infocus/content/story/infocus.html?subject=41

8. Sharda Ugra, Interview with Yuvraj Singh, http://www.espncricinfo.com/magazine/content/story/478169.html, 22 September 2010

9. Michael Novak, *The Joy of Sports*, Madison Books, Lanham, MD, 1994, p. 21

10. I have borrowed these descriptions from: Michael Novak, *The Joy of Sports*, Madison Books, Lanham, MD, 1994, pp. 22

11. Michael Novak, *The Joy of Sports*, Madison Books, Lanham, MD, 1994, Chapter 2

Chapter 2

1. 'Indians Not as Large-Hearted as Pakistanis', http://www.indianexpress.com/news/indians-not-as-largehearted-as-pakistanis-afridi/771281/, 7 April 2011, *Indian Express*

2. ESPNcricinfo staff, 'Shahrukh Khan Lashes Back at Gavaskar', http://www.cricinfo.com/ipl2009/content/current/story/398454.html, 5 April 2009

3. To be entirely fair, some similarly-tinged scepticism was later directed at teams in Australia's BBL.

4. Ashok Malik, 'IPL Has Added to MEA Options', http://www.dailypioneer.com/231173/IPL-has-added-to-MEA-options.html, 22 June 2011

5. A proper American-style draft has been recommended for the IPL on more than one occasion; its introduction will bring the IPL closer to modern international league standards (Desh Gaurav Sekhri, 'Never Mind the Auction, Here's the Draft', http://www.espncricinfo.com/magazine/content/story/517103.html, 5 June 2011).

6. Boria Majumdar, 'BCCI Should Be More Magnanimous', http://www.dreamcricket.com/dreamcricket/news.hspl?nid=7263&ntid=3, 28 August, 2007. This account is over-simplified; the BCCI based its *overt* case against the Pentangular on the grounds that it encouraged 'communalism' because of its religion-based teams like the Hindus, Parsees, or Muslims. Such highlighting of religious divisions seemed incompatible with the new political environment in pre-Independence, post World-War India. I thank Satadru Sen for this clarification.

7. Gideon Haigh, *Sphere of Influence*, Melbourne University Publishing, 2010, p. 126

8. Matthew 25:29: 'For unto every one that hath shall be given, and he shall have abundance: but from him that hath not shall be taken away even that which he hath.' In the political economy of the modern academy, the Matthew Principle means that professors and students of elite institutions will continue

to prosper while those of comparable quality but handicapped by a less-than-elite educational pedigree find their careers languishing.

9. Mukul Kesavan, 'V for Vendetta', http://www.cricinfo.com/magazine/content/story/354491.html, 13 June 2008

10. Ajay S. Shankar, 'ICL Players Claim BCCI Owes Payments of Rs. 1.27 Crores', http://www.cricinfo.com/india/content/story/367352.html, 2 September 2008

11. Ajay S. Shankar, 'Australia Spells Out Tough Stand on The ICL', http://www.cricinfo.com/ci-icc/content/story/359749.html, 4 July 2008

12. ESPNcricinfo staff, 'ICL Policy Could Cost England-BCCI', http://www.espncricinfo.com/ci/content/story/355733.html, 22 June 2008

13. Mukul Kesavan, 'V for Vendetta', http://www.cricinfo.com/magazine/content/story/354491.html, 13 June 2008

14. Sky Sports, 'BCCI Block Laxman Move', http://www.skysports.com/story/0,19528,12162_3866218,00.html, 25 July 2008

15. ESPNcricinfo staff, 'Tendulkar and Karthik Withdrawn from Twenty20 Game', http://www.espncricinfo.com/nzvind2009/content/story/392501.html, 27 February 2009

16. Nagraj Gollapudi, 'Nights at the Circus', http://www.cricinfo.com/icl/content/story/326124.html, 17 December 2007

17. G.S. Vivek, 'New Player Takes Guard for ICL Against BCCI: Lalu Prasad Yadav', http://www.indianexpress.com/news/newplayertakesguardforiclagainstbccilaluprasadyadav/209605/0, 10 August 2007

18. Reuters, 'Delhi HC Orders Companies to Let Players Join ICL', http://in.reuters.com/article/2007/08/27/idINIndia-29170020070827, 27 August 2007

19. Samir Gandhi and Rahul Rai, 'Cricket and the Competition Law', *Economic Times*, 28 April 2009; PTI, 'MRTPC Orders Inquiry Against BCCI For Banning ICL', http://articles.timesofindia.indiatimes.com/2007-09-06/top-stories/27972730_1_icl-reetinder-sodhi-indian-cricket-league, 6 September 2007

20. Anilesh S. Mahajan, 'Curtains Down on MRTPC', http://www.businessworld.in/bw/2009_09_12_Curtains_Down_On_MRTPC.html, 12 September 2009

21. ESPNcricinfo staff, 'BCCI Offers Amnesty for ICL Players', http://www.espncricinfo.com/icl2008/content/story/402028.html, 29 April 2009

22. Samir Chopra, 'How Many Ways Do I Dislike Thee, Lalit Modi?', http://eye-on-cricket.blogspot.com/2009/04/how-many-ways-do-i-dislike-thee-lalit.html, 20 April 2009

23. Mukul Kesavan, 'V for Vendetta', http://www.cricinfo.com/magazine/content/story/354491.html, 13 June 2008

24. PTI, 'BCCI Hikes Domestic Match Fees', http://www.rediff.com/cms/print.jsp?docpath=/cricket/2007/aug/21hike.htm, 21 August 2007

25. Gideon Haigh, *Sphere of Influence*, Melbourne University Publishing, 2010, p. 97

26. Michael J. Cozillo, Mark S. Levinstein, Michael R. Dimino, Sr., Gabe Feldman, *Sports Law*, 2nd edition, Carolina Academic Press, Durham, 2007, Chapter 14 passim.

27. ESPNcricinfo staff, 'BCCI Firm on Limitation of Player Endorsements', http://content-usa.cricinfo.com/india/content/current/story/289696.html, 9 April 2007

28. The Professional Cricketer's Association Mission Statement, http://www.thepca.co.uk/mission_statement.html

29. Michael J. Cozillo, Mark S. Levinstein, Michael R. Dimino, Sr., Gabe Feldman, *Sports Law*, 2nd edition, Carolina Academic Press, Durham, 2007, Chapter 14 passim.

30. ESPNcricinfo staff, 'Cook Eases Strike Fears', http://www.espncricinfo.com/england/content/story/512547.html, 25 April 2011

31. ESPNcricinfo staff, 'No Indians in SLPL Says BCCI', http://www.espncricinfo.com/srilanka/content/story/519526.html, 18 June 2011

32. Michael J. Cozillo, Mark S. Levinstein, Michael R. Dimino, Sr., Gabe Feldman, *Sports Law*, 2nd edition, Carolina Academic Press, Durham, 2007 , p. 702

33. Ibid., Introduction passim.

34. Ibid., pp. 706–708; http://en.wikipedia.org/wiki/Salary_cap

35. Cricket World, Gayle, 'Bravo, Pollard Turn Down WICB Contracts', http://www.cricketworld.com/gayle-bravo-and-pollard-turn-down-contracts/25651.htm, 29 September 2010; Firdoose Monda, 'Financial Losses Mar Zimbabwe's Test Return', http://www.espncricinfo.com/zimbabwe-v-bangladesh-2011/content/current/story/526773.html, 9 August 2011

36. Amrit Mathur, private communication

37. Tariq Engineer and Mohammed Isam, 'Associate Players Eyeing BPL Platform', http://www.espncricinfo.com/bangladesh-premier-league-2012/content/story/551798.html, 1 February 2012

38. Martin Williamson, 'Kolpak for Dummies', http://www.espncricinfo.com/england/content/story/299952.html, 28 May 2007

39. ESPNcricinfo staff, 'NZ Players' Association Chief Warns of Player

Drain', http://www.cricinfo.com/newzealand/content/story/439222.html, 13 December 2009

40. PTI, 'Hampshire Drop Afridi after PCB Withdraws NOC', http://www.deccanherald.com/content/165609/hampshire-drops-afridi-pcbs-withdrawal.html, 1 Jun 2011

41. I owe these thoughts to Russell Degnan, expressed via private communication.

42. ESPNcricinfo staff, 'West Indies Board Confirms $20M WIPA Lawsuit', http://www.espncricinfo.com/westindies/content/current/story/530103.html, 30 August 2011

Chapter 3

1. Sharda Ugra, 'Modi Kills His Own Dream', http://www.espncricinfo.com/indian-premier-league-2012/content/current/story/552470.html#quickcomment, 7 February 2012

2. Tariq Engineer, 'Is the IPL Still a Summer Blockbuster?', http://www.espncricinfo.com/magazine/content/story/522118.html, 7 July 2011

3. Tariq Engineer, 'Shifting Goalposts', http://www.espncricinfo.com/indian-premier-league-2012/content/story/552584.html, 8 February 2012

4. Chloe Saltau, 'Hodge Fears for The Traditional Game in the World of the Big Bash', http://www.theage.com.au/sport/cricket/hodge-fears-for-the-traditional-game-in-world-of-big-bash-20110728-1i2bc.html, 29 July 2011; Greg Baum, 'Money Talks and Hayden Joins Chorus', http://www.theage.com.au/sport/cricket/money-talks-and-hayden-joins-chorus-20110725-1hx3b.html, 26 July 2011

5. Peter J. Schwartz, 'The World's Hottest Sports League', http://www.forbes.com/2009/08/27/cricket-india-ipl-business-sports-ipl.html, 27 August 2009

6. Antony Chettupuzha, 'Pune and Kochi Win New IPL Franchise Teams', http://shortofalength.wordpress.com/2010/03/21/pune-and-kochi-win-new-ipl-franchise-sahara-and-rendezvous-sports-make-outrageous-bids/, 21 March 2010

7. Tariq Engineer, 'is The IPL Still a Summer Blockbuster?', http://www.espncricinfo.com/magazine/content/story/522118.html, 7 July 2011

8. In 2010, after the Modi–Tharoor scandal, the IPL council, abruptly, clumsily and heavy-handedly, in a spectacular twofer of alienation directed against sponsors and fans, terminated its agreements with Kings XI Punjab and the Rajasthan Royals. The franchises and the BCCI are in arbitration; this legal

battle rumbles on, providing a contentious and possibly reputation-eroding backdrop of public dirty-linen washing to the league's normal tales of sporting and financial success.

9. Especially clause 6.2.4, which states, 'No member shall have direct or indirect commercial interests in the matches or events conducted by the board.'

10. Sharda Ugra, 'The IPL Needs Independent Watchdogs', http://www.espncricinfo.com/indian-premier-league-2011/content/current/story/516834.html, 27 May 2011

11. Gideon Haigh, *Sphere of Influence*, Melbourne University Publishing, 2010, p. 191

12. Ashish Magotra, 'No County Cricket, No SL League: Players Need Their Union Back', http://www.firstpost.com/sports/no-county-cricket-no-slc-cricket-needs-the-icpa-back-28323.html, 20 June 2011

13. Gautam Bhattacharya, 'BCCI out to Malign ICPA: Arun Lal', http://articles.timesofindia.indiatimes.com/2003-05-14/interviews/27281875_1_aic-icpa-indian-cricket-players-association, 14 May 2003

14. Rajshekhar Malaviya, http://bleacherreport.com/articles/770736-lords-tons-have-no-muscle-vengsarkar-loses-to-don-deshmukh-politics-rules, 18 July 2011

15. R. Krishna, 'Wanted: A Board of Control to Control the BCCI', http://www.dnaindia.com/sport/interview_wanted-a-board-of-control-to-control-the-bcci_1375246-all, 25 April 2010

16. Ashok Malik, '"Cricket PIL" Takes Fresh Guard over BCCI Identity', http://www.indianexpress.com/oldStory/45593/, 23 April 2004

17. http://www.sci.brooklyn.cuny.edu/~schopra/MehraSuggestions.html

18. Press Information Bureau, Government of India, 'Salient Features of the SportsDevelopmentBill',http://pib.nic.in/newsite/erelease.aspx?relid=70001, 22 February 2011

19. ESPNcricinfo staff, 'Indian Bill Fails to Clear Cabinet Hurdle', http://www.espncricinfo.com/india/content/current/story/530491.html, 30 August 2011

20. Gideon Haigh, *Sphere of Influence*, Melbourne University Publishing, 2010, p. 190

21. Venkat Ananth, 'A Case for Franchise Cricket in India', http://cricket.yahoo.com/cricket/blog/venkatananth/9/venkatananth9, 27 September 2010

22. Ibid.

23. Ibid.

24. Ibid.

25. Ibid.

Chapter 4

1. This chapter owes a great deal to Gideon Haigh's various writings on the ICC; I have drawn freely, in particular, from 'Crisis, What Crisis', in *Sphere of Influence*.

2. David Post, *Jefferson's Moose: Notes on the States of Cyberspace*, Oxford University Press, 2009

3. Osman Samiuddin, 'ICC Gives Boards Two Years to Fall in Line', http://www.espncricinfo.com/ci-icc/content/story/521351.html, 30 June 2011; ESPNcricinfo staff, 'Sangakkara Slams Corrupt Administration', http://www.espncricinfo.com/srilanka/content/current/story/521971.html, 4 July 2011

4. Gideon Haigh, *Sphere of Influence*, Melbourne University Publishing, 2010, pp. 100–107

5. Ibid., p. 108

6. Samir Chopra, 'An Open Letter to Giles Clarke', http://blogs.espncricinfo.com/thepitch/archives/2012/01/an_open_letter_to_giles_clarke.php, 26 January 2012

7. Gideon Haigh, 'A Crisis Too Good to Waste', http://www.cricinfo.com/decadereview2009/content/story/440354.html, 22 December 2009

8. Ibid.

9. Shrikant Subramanian, 'The Case for Isolation', http://dopaisekatamasha.blogspot.com/2009/08/case-for-isolation.html, 10 August 2009

10. Mohan, 'Be Patriotic, Support IPL!', http://aralikatte.blogspot.com/2008/02/be-patriotic-support-ipl.html, 27 February 2008

11. Ibid.

12. Jonathan Dixon, 'Comments on The Case for Isolation', http://dopaisekatamasha.blogspot.com/2009/08/case-for-isolation.html, 10 August 2009

13. Shrikant Subramanian, 'The Case for Isolation', http://dopaisekatamasha.blogspot.com/2009/08/case-for-isolation.html, 10 August 2009

14. 'Comments on The Case for Isolation', http://dopaisekatamasha.blogspot.com/2009/08/case-for-isolation.html, 10 August 2009

15. Mohan, 'Be Patriotic, Support IPL!', http://aralikatte.blogspot.com/2008/02/be-patriotic-support-ipl.html, 27 February 2008

16. Shrikant Subramanian, 'The Case for Isolation', http://dopaisekatamasha.blogspot.com/2009/08/case-for-isolation.html, 10 August 2009

17. Ashok Malik, 'Pass the Gravy', http://www.cricinfo.com/magazine/content/story/453945.html, 30 March 2010

18. Tariq Engineer, 'Under the Shadow of the IPL', http://www.cricinfo.com/magazine/content/current/story/475758.html, 5 September 2010

19. Tariq Engineer, 'Big Jump in CL20 Television Ratings', http://www.espncricinfo.com/t20champions2010/content/story/480411.html, 7 October 2010

20. Chloe Saltau, 'Cricket Keen on a Starring Role', http://www.smh.com.au/sport/cricket/cricket-keen-on-a-starring-role-20110730-1i5jt.html, 31 July 2011

21. http://en.wikipedia.org/wiki/Cricket_test

22. Gideon Haigh, *Sphere of Influence*, Melbourne University Publishing, 2010

23. Ibid., p.179

24. Mukul Kesavan, 'Fear and Loathing', http://www.telegraphindia.com/1080515/jsp/opinion/story_9270679.jsp, 15 May 2008

25. Ibid.

26. I owe this thought to John Sutton, expressed via private communication.

27. Bill O'Reilly, 'A Cry from the Heart', *World Cricket Digest*, November 1982, Vol. 2, No. 1

28. Meenakshi Verma Ambwani, 'India–Sri Lanka Clashes Score High on TRP Test', http://articles.economictimes.indiatimes.com/2009-12-02/news/28404970_1_test-cricket-trps-television-rating, 2 December 2009

29. Gideon Haigh, *Sphere of Influence*, Melbourne University Publishing, 2010, p. 176

30. ESPNcricinfo staff, 'Runners Abolished, ODI and Run-Out Laws Tweaked', http://www.espncricinfo.com/ci-icc/content/current/story/520924.html, 27 June 2011

31. ESPNcricinfo staff, 'Dravid Backs Day/Night Test Cricket', http://www.espncricinfo.com/mcc/content/story/508873.html, 31 March 2011

32. The Australian blogger Russell Degnan has designed a comprehensive blueprint for the restructuring of the cricket calendar. This was submitted to the ICC for consideration and was, unsurprisingly, ignored. Degnan's design is available at http://www.deggles.csoft.net.

33. Russell Degnan, 'World Championships', http://deggles.csoft.net/post.php?postid=1423, 16 December 2009

34. Ibid.

35. Ibid.

36. Ibid.

37. Judhajit Basu and Siddarth Monga, 'TV Ratings Bring Good News for 50-Over Cricket', http://www.espncricinfo.com/india/content/story/434629.html, 15 November 2009

38. Russell Degnan, 'International Expansion', http://deggles.csoft.net/post. php?postid=1414, 11 November 2009

39. Andrew Nixon, 'Time to Open Up Test Cricket?', http://www.cricketeurope4. net/DATABASE/ARTICLES5/articles/000002/000218.shtml

40. Russell Degnan, 'International Expansion', http://deggles.csoft.net/post. php?postid=1414, 11 November 2009

41. Shashi Tharoor, 'Our Cricket Problem', http://www.nytimes.com/2007/ 03/23/opinion/23tharoor.html, 23 March 2007

42. Letters to the editor, 'Not Very Cricket, Is It?' http://www.nytimes.com/2007/ 03/24/opinion/l24cricket.html, 24 March 2007

Chapter 5

1. Gideon Haigh, *Sphere of Influence*, Melbourne University Publishing, 2010, p. 105

2. Ibid., p. 347

3. ESPNcricinfo staff, 'Show Cause Notice for Ten Cricket Channel', http:// www.espncricinfo.com/south-africa-v-india-2010/content/story/498445. html, 27 January 2011

4. Mukul Kesavan, 'Pigs Don't Fly–Why the IPL Won't Reform Itself', http://www.telegraphindia.com/1100429/jsp/opinion/story_12386595.jsp, *The Telegraph*, 29 April 2010

5. Eknath Solkar, 'Boycs Was Good but I Was Lager', http://www.espncricinfo. com/page2/content/story/425163.html, 14 November 2010

6. Russell Degnan. 'The Vexed Question of ICC Governance', http:// idlesummers.com/post.php?postid=1613

7. Interview with Aamir Sohail, http://static.cricinfo.com/db/INTERACTIVE/ INTERVIEWS/IRC/1998/AAMER_SOHAIL_03JUN1998.html, 3 June 1998

8. I owe these thoughts to Satadru Sen, expressed via private communication. Sen points out that the Indian fan experience highlights 'the emergence of a competing ethos on the cricket ground (and the Internet forum), made possible by…expanded affluence, easy communication…and the weakening of…cultural gatekeepers'. Sen goes on to say, '[T]wo major cultural shifts have taken place in India. One is that the old middle class is no longer automatically hegemonic; it has to share its cultural space and political–economic clout with the people who vote for Lalu, Mayawati and the Shiv Sena. The other is within the middle class, where the new consumer culture has replaced the emphasis on restraint with an emphasis on narcissism and instant and constant self-indulgence.'

9. http://en.wikipedia.org/wiki/Reality_principle

10. Rohan Mascarenhas, 'Post-Colonial Issues with the Rajasthan Royals', http://duckingbeamers.wordpress.com/2009/05/06/should-indians-like-the-rajasthan-royals/, 6 May 2009

11. Steve James, 'Virender Sehwag's Arrival Must Breathe Life into the Ailing Indians', http://www.telegraph.co.uk/sport/cricket/international/india/8677987/England-v-India-Virender-Sehwags-arrival-in-England-must-breathe-life-into-the-ailing-Indians.html, 2 August 2011

12. Michael Atherton, 'Modi Masterminds India's Billion Dollar Bonanza', http://www.telegraph.co.uk/sport/cricket/2335008/Modi-masterminds-Indias-billion-dollar-bonanza.html, 9 April 2006

13. Gideon Haigh, *Sphere of Influence*, Melbourne University Publishing, 2010, pp. 235–237

14. Gideon Haigh, *The Cricket War: The Inside Story of Kerry Packer's World Series of Cricket*, Text Publishing Company, Melbourne 1993

Chapter 6

1. Amit Varma, 'More Luddites Answered, but No Early Adopters', http://www.espncricinfo.com/ci/content/story/142120.html, 2 October 2004

2. Some progress appears to have been made on this front: Siddartha Talya, 'ICC Could Monitor Ball-Tracking Technologies', http://www.espncricinfo.com/ci/content/current/story/530564.html, 1 September 2011

3. Amit Varma, 'More Luddites Answered, but No Early Adopters', http://www.espncricinfo.com/ci/content/story/142120.html, 2 October 2004

4. Ibid.

5. Ibid.

6. Daniel Brettig, 'Umpires Ask ICC to Look into Hughes Dismissal', http://www.espncricinfo.com/sri-lanka-v-australia-2011/content/story/530864.html, 2 September 2011

7. This section owes its provenance to Russell Degnan's article, 'Umpiring In The 21st Century', http://deggles.csoft.net/post.php?postid=1511, 8 October 2011

8. Russell Degnan, 'Umpiring in the 21st Century', http://deggles.csoft.net/post.php?postid=1511, 8 October 2011

9. Ibid.

Chapter 7

1. The recently released Woolf report (http://static.espncricinfo.com/db/DOWNLOAD/0000/0093/woolfe_report.pdf) makes some important and sweeping criticisms and recommendations. It remains to be seen how seriously the ICC and its members will take it. It has already attracted some criticism for not saying more about the financial realities and imbalances of the modern game as opposed to its current focus on ICC governance (Sambit Bal, 'The Woolf Report is Well-Meaning but Naïve', http://www.espncricinfo.com/magazine/content/story/552288.html , 6 February 2012).

2. Heather Timmons, 'Google Sees A New Role For YouTube: an Outlet for Live Sports', http://www.nytimes.com/2010/05/03/business/media/03cricket.html, 2 May 2010

3. Gideon Haigh, *Sphere of Influence*, Melbourne University Publishing, 2010, pp. 235–237

4. Samir Chopra, 'An Open Letter to Giles Clarke', http://blogs.espncricinfo.com/thepitch/archives/2012/01/an_open_letter_to_giles_clarke.php, 26 January 2012

5. 'Cricinfo History', http://bluwiki.com/go/CricInfo_History, 3 July 2010. Full disclosure: since late 2011, I have received remuneration for my blogging efforts on Cricinfo.

6. I owe these thoughts to Russell Degnan, expressed to me via private communication.

Index

Acknowledgements

My editor, V.K. Karthika, offered encouragement and support throughout my work on this book; I am grateful to her for suggesting that I write a book on modern cricket; Ramachandra Guha and Mukul Kesavan helped this project get off the ground; Prema Govindan at HarperCollins helped bring this book over the finish line; Noor Alam, Russell Degnan, Sankaran Krishna, Rohan Mascarenhas, Satadru Sen, and John Sutton took the time to read my draft manuscript and offer comments; their generosity of spirit is much appreciated; Scott Dexter read an early introduction, reassured me I was on the right track and always talked to me about cricket whenever I wanted to; Rahul Dravid, Amrit Mathur and Rahul Mehra were patient, helpful and informative during their interviews; Mukul Kesavan, Gideon Haigh and Sharda Ugra did not just inspire with their writing, they were kind and generous with their support for mine; Sambit Bal and ESPNcricinfo provided me with a platform to think out loud about cricket; Tariq Engineer helped me with many pointers to information; Valmik Kumar read parts of a draft and offered useful comments. I owe special thanks to John Sutton, who has talked and watched more cricket with me in the past decade than anyone else; his love and passion for the game have helped ensure that cricket has retained a romantic hue in my mind's eye. David Coady spent many long hours talking to me about cricket; I thank him for humouring my obsession with it and for being so generous in his cricket appreciation.

Many have helped clarify my thoughts about this book and my relationship with the game: Ajaz Ashraf, Murali Agastya, Sumbul Alam, Caroline Arnold, Joseph Biehl, Arina Britz, Robert Bursill, Daniel Campos, Daniel Chaldi, Sanjay 'Tony' Chawla, Jill Cirasella, Tony Coady, Tom Connell, Wendy Fairey, Jason Florence, Mobina Hashmi, James 'JD' Howell, Amy Hughes, Jason Hughes, Scott Jackson, Victor Jauregui, Subash Jayaraman, Rex Kwok, Alison Kinney, Sree Krishna Kumar, Rakesh Kushwaha, Rohit Mahajan, Eric Martin, Doris McIlwain, Tommie Meyer, Anupam Mukherji, David Mutton, Maurice Pagnucco, Peter De La Penna, Nick Peterson, Teresa Poor, Christian Ryan, Karl Steel, Megha Sabharwal, Amit Sadana, Sumit Sadana, Gaurav Sethi, Mark Sheehan, Matthew Smith, Shrikant Subramanian, Tony Taylor, Joseph Thurbon, Rosemary Thurbon, Atul Tuli, Siddhartha Vaidyanathan, Mahek Vyas, and Vincent White. My sincere apologies to anyone whom I might have inadvertently left out of this list.

Crossfit South Brooklyn ensured I stayed sane during the summer of 2011; my mates at Centrals Cricket Club in Sydney helped me enjoy the pleasures of playing cricket (and even let me captain once!); Willow TV brought cricket into my home.

Thanks to Ashu, Ritu and Akul for tolerating my cricket addiction and my hogging the television whenever I visited India.

My deepest debt is, as always, to my wife and best friend, Noor Alam. Without her, this would all be drudgery.